# British Sci[illegible]n and Fantasy

*Twenty Years and Two Surveys*

# British Science Fiction and Fantasy

## *Twenty Years and Two Surveys*


The 1989 Mexicon Survey
compiled and edited by Paul Kincaid

The 2009 BSFA Survey
compiled and edited by Niall Harrison

First published by Odd Two Out on
behalf of the BSFA 2010

A catalogue record of this book is available from the British Library.

ISBN: 978-0-9558662-1-0

Cover image courtesy of http://www.wordle.net/.

Design and layout Martin McGrath
martin@martinmcgrath.net

Printed in Great Britain by the MPG Books Group, Bodmin and King's Lynn

Odd Two Out
48 Spooners Drive
Park Street, St Albans
Herts, AL2 2HL

British Science Fiction Association
61 Ivycroft Road, Warton,
Tamworth,
Staffordshire, B79 0JJ

www.oddtwoout.co.uk

www.bsfa.co.uk

# Contents

# Introduction

## *Niall Harrison*

Who writes sf and fantasy? How do they perceive their work? How do others – publishers, readers – perceive it? How do those perceptions change over time, or from place to place?

Such questions are at the heart of the two surveys of writers of sf and fantasy collated and analyzed in this book, which attempt to take a snapshot of the state of the British sf and fantasy field. The first survey was carried out and analyzed by Paul Kincaid, for the Mexicon III convention, in 1989. The second has been carried out and analzyed this year, by me, on behalf of the British Science Fiction Association.

So far as is practical, the 2009 survey has been designed to be comparable with the 1989 survey. The same ten questions have been used – along with one new question – the same style has been used to collate the answers, and in both cases the inclusion criteria were drawn as widely as possible, with both British-born and British-resident writers eligible to participate.

For the 1989 survey, 44 writers responded, with a spread that Paul considered to be representative. This year, there were 84 responses, from 148 invitations and an open call for participants advertised in Locus Online, David Langford's *Ansible* newsletter, and elsewhere. As in the 1989 survey, they run the gamut from famous to unknown, hard sf to fantasy, long established to new, and include writers published as "mainstream", by sf/f genre publishers, and as Young Adult. (In both cases, approximately a quarter of respondents are women. For the 2009 survey, at least, this means women are slightly under-represented; they accounted for approximately a third of invitations.) Inevitably, there were many writers whose perspective I might have wished for who could not, or chose not to, respond; most commonly this was because they were busy with other projects. But broadly speaking, I consider the 2009 survey, like the 1989 survey, representative of the sf and fantasy field in the UK.

The greater number of responses this year has enabled slightly more numeric analysis, although all coding of opinionated responses into neat little boxes should be taken as suggestive, rather than conclusive. Similarly, although I, like Paul, have attempted to provide a framework for what writers said, any analysis should be taken as tentative. Throughout the survey I have erred on the side of quoting writers at length, allowed them to speak for themselves to encourage readers to form their own conclusions as to any trends, and compare them with mine.

Because I do think there have been changes. The BSFA survey is a showcase of a field that is, in many ways, in rude health: its practitioners often confident, ambitious, and enthusiastic, its products diverse and, in many cases, challenging notions of what "British science fiction and fantasy" is and can be. The responses contain many insights and provocations, but if the survey as a whole says one thing, I think it says this: 2009 is an exciting time to be reading these genres.

On behalf of the BSFA, my thanks go to all those who responded to the survey; and my apologies to any writers I did not manage to contact in time. And to everyone: I hope you enjoy what follows. Any comments or queries can be sent to me at <niall.harrison@gmail.com>.

Niall Harrison
Oxford, November 2009

# Introduction to the Mexicon Survey

## *Paul Kincaid*

In an obscure way, this survey was inspired by Algis Budrys, our guest at Mexicon III. While Greg Pickersgill and I were discussing Budrys' critical work, Greg referred to a review, in *Benchmarks*, of something called the *Double: Bill Symposium*. This had been built around a survey of science fiction writers some twenty years ago, and the same thought occurred to us both: why not repeat the project, update it, tie it in to British science fiction. Hence the document you hold in your hands.

The questions asked are simple, obvious, some would say too obvious. But in attempting to find, and define, common ground, one has to start from a very broad base. The survey was intended to produce a broad view of British science fiction, to provide at least a first step towards identifying what, if anything, are its distinguishing features. I must leave it to the reader to decide how successful it has been in that venture.

Many British and British-based writers were approached. Some wrote back to apologise for not responding – Alan Garner, for instance, said that it would take a book to attempt an adequate response, and since he was deep into work on his next novel he wasn't able to attempt a reply within the timeframe involve. Others spoke to me along the same lines. In the end, however, 44 writers replied, and the spectrum, from famous to unknown, from long-established to new, from hard sf to fantasy, was covered so well that I think this does provide a representative survey of the scene.

On behalf of everyone involved in Mexicon, I want to thank all those who replied, and whose work provides the bulk of what follows.

Paul Kincaid

# List of respondents

## *1989 Mexicon Survey*

Brian Aldiss; Iain Banks; Paul Barnett (John Grant); David V Barrett; Barrington Bayley; John Brosnan; Eric Brown; John Brunner; Kenneth Bulmer; John Christopher; John Clute; James Corley; Robert Farago; Neil Gaiman; Stephen Gallagher; Mary Gentle; Alasdair Gray; Colin Greenland; Douglas Hill; Robert Irwin; Diana Wynne Jones; Gwyneth Jones; Leigh Kennedy; Garry Kilworth; Christina Lake; David Langford; Samantha Lee; Paul J McAuley; Ian McDonald; Graham Dunstan Martin; Lee Montgomerie; Kim Newman; Simon Ounsley; Jane Palmer; Christopher Priest; David Redd; Keith Roberts; Josephine Saxton; Elizabeth Sourbut; Brian Stableford; Alex Stewart; EC Tubb; Lisa Tuttle; James White

## *2009 BSFA Survey*

Joe Abercrombie; Nina Allan; Sarah Ash; Will Ashon; Steve Aylett; Tony Ballantyne; Iain Banks; Paul Barnett (John Grant); Chris Beckett; Chaz Brenchley; Keith Brooke; Eric Brown; NM Browne; Chris Butler; Alan Campbell; Ramsey Campbell; Mike Carey; Mark Chadbourn; Susanna Clarke; Paul Cornell; Elizabeth Counihan; Andrew Crumey; Colin Davies; Peter Dickinson; Jaine Fenn; Stephen Gallagher; Stephen Gaskell; Gary Gibson; Jon Courtenay Grimwood; Frances Hardinge; Nick Harkaway; M John Harrison; Colin Harvey; Mary Hoffman; Ben Jeapes; Liz Jensen; Graham Joyce; David Langford; Katherine Langrish; Rhiannon Lassiter; Tim Lebbon; Tanith Lee; Tim Lees; Roger Levy; Toby Litt; Bob Lock; James Lovegrove; Ian R MacLeod; Ken MacLeod; Paul McAuley; Juliet E McKenna; Suzanne McLeod; John Meaney; Paul Meloy; China Mieville; Deborah J Miller; Michael Moorcock; Richard Morgan; Patrick Ness; Mark Charan Newton; Stan Nicholls; Peadar O'Guilin; Ricardo Pinto; Gareth Lyn Powell; Christopher Priest; Alastair Reynolds; Adam Roberts; Katherine Roberts; Al Robertson; Justina Robson; Martin Sketchley; Kari Sperring; Brian Stableford; Vaughan Stanger; Charles Stross; Tricia Sullivan; Adrian Tchaikovsky; Lisa Tuttle; Ian Watson; Elizabeth Wein; Ian Whates; Kit Whitfield; Conrad Williams; Neil Williamson

# Chapter 1:
## *Do you consider yourself a writer of science fiction and/or fantasy?*

# 1989

The Mexicon questionnaire was an attempt to define British science fiction, and as such it seemed obvious to start by asking if people did, indeed, see themselves as science fiction writers. It was Christopher Priest who pointed out one obvious problem:

> You shouldn't have asked a question like this first. If you're in my position it makes answering the rest a bit pointless. A "yes" answer raises or confirms numerous expectations; a "no" answer encourages people like me to sound pompous.

Pompous or not, Priest and Josephine Saxton were the only people who responded to this question with a "no." This at least allows us to know that every other respondent regards himself or herself, at least in part, as a science fiction writer. But it is the extent to which they regard themselves as science fiction writers that is of interest.

Several people simply replied "yes," in the main newer writers like Lee Montgomerie, Simon Ounsley and Alex Stewart. It would be tempting to see this as a consequence of their relative lack of experience within the field. After all, another newish writer, Ian McDonald, said:

> Yes: to the extent that I haven't yet written anything outside the genre, but I would not want to say that I will always be only a writer of sf/fantasy; what I would want to be is a writer who writes about what interests him, regardless of genre boundaries.

So, may it not be that these people see themselves as operating within the genre boundaries merely because they have not yet had the opportunity to go beyond them?

But such a theory begins to fall apart the moment one starts to consider the response of those who took the question as demanding an either/or response. Brian Stableford was to the point: "Yes (both)," Colin Greenland was even more succinct: "And," while Diana Wynne Jones spelled it out: "I do consider myself a writer of science fiction and fantasy, preferably mixed."

Those who came down firmly on the side of science fiction were Brian Aldiss, Barrington Bayley, James White and Paul J. McAuley, who added, presumably in reference to an editorial in *Interzone*, "Radical Hard Science Fiction, actually."

The straightforward fantasy side was made up of Robert Irwin and Samantha Lee.

The overwhelming majority of replies, however, showed a distinct unease with these categories. Some were uncertain about the terms involved, a position perhaps best summed up by Mary Gentle: "Yes, I consider myself a writer of sf and fantasy, among other things, and provided I'm allowed my own definitions of both terms."

Gwyneth Jones also found the terms unsatisfactory:

> And/or seems to sum up the situation quite well. If I had to choose one it would be science fiction. I don't like a lot of what is called science fiction; equally I don't like a lot of what is called fantasy. But I can think of an alternative significance for the term "science fiction" that satisfies me, whereas the plight of the term "fantasy" seems hopeless (for my purposes). It's a bit like choosing between "black" and "coloured." However, I also change my mind about this ranking from time to time.

For some people it was necessary to define terms before they could say where they saw their writing fitting. David Redd was one example:

> I am an sf writer. Not because of hardware, but because I always want a sense of underlying logic, a rational basis for everything even if the sf content is no more than abnormal psychology. Barbarian swordspersons and the like just aren't logical.

While EC Tubb went even further into the question of what makes science fiction, jumping the gun more than somewhat on what should appear in the next chapter:

> Yes – but to answer this presumes some sort of definition of just what science fiction and fantasy is and the basic difference between them. To me science fiction is what is not demonstrably impossible but is something which has not yet been achieved. As an example: a hundred years ago transatlantic flight would have been science fiction if incorporated into a story. The use of antibiotics the same. Stories which now are based on Man's flight to the Moon are no longer science fiction – we can make them so only by extrapolating from the known into the realm of surmise. So science fiction is basically a "what would happen if?" type of literature. It deals with events and situations which

> are not present today but which could be given certain scientific discoveries or political changes.
>
> Fantasy is something else. Basically it demands a total suspension of disbelief but the degree of that disbelief is not consistent. Fantasy dealing with magic, i.e.: sorcerers, wizards, magicians, etc., with their accompaniment of spells, charms and mighty esoteric powers is not the same as that which asks you to accept just one piece of "impossibility" in order to enjoy the story. As an example of what I mean; it is a mathematical and biological fact that, on Earth, ants cannot grow to the size of horses. It has to do with the weight growing by the cube and the support tissue by the square, so if the thing gets too big it can't support its own weight. Stories which are based on horse-sized ants do, therefore, carry a degree of fantasy. You are asked to believe the impossible in just one respect. Much of science fiction, especially the adventure type of science fiction, operates on that premise. So, yes, I do consider myself a writer of science fiction and fantasy.

As well as redefining their terms, there were some who came up with a new name to define their work; John Christopher, for example:

> Jay Williams once did a piece in Signal titled "John Christopher, Allegorical Historian"; I liked that, even though I wasn't sure what it meant. I'd say, in my definitions of the terms, I've done a little science fiction, more fantasy.

Others chose to revive another term for what they write. Graham Dunstan Martin said: "I prefer to describe my work as 'speculative fiction', but since that is the purpose of sf and fantasy, I suppose the answer is 'yes'." An opinion that was echoed by Robert Farago: "I consider myself a writer of 'speculative fiction', but I have no trouble with term 'science fiction'." While James Corley, who is of the generation that coined the term "speculative fiction," had this to say:

> A difficult question. I haven't written fiction of any sort for about the past eight years. But it's only a hiatus, I'll get back to it some day soon. Yes, I did write straight science fiction, but most of my "serious" output was pretty much on the edge. Do you remember when "speculative fiction" was fashionable? I always thought it was an excellent label, it had the right initials, avoided arguments about where science, or even pseudo-science, ended and fantasy began (it's sufficiently vague to cover almost anything), and best of all it couldn't be abbreviated to sci-fi. The answer to your question is that I'm a writer of speculative fiction temporarily resting.

Corley's reference to writing that was "on the edge" brings us to the other main cause of unease evinced by the various respondents: generally they did not want to be tied to any one genre. John Brunner, for example: "I consider myself a writer, *tout court*. I happen to have produced a lot of sf and fantasy, but a great deal of other stuff has appeared under my name, and some of it I'm very proud of." Much the same sort of comment was made by Jane Palmer: "My work is probably fiction which extends into sf or fantasy. I do not intentionally set out to write either."

Several of the responses emphasized that the authors worked, or wanted to work, outside the genre. Kenneth Bulmer said that he wrote sf and fantasy "inter alia"; Leigh Kennedy replied: "I sometimes write science fiction"; Iain Banks defined his output as "90% science fiction, 10% fantasy (where it isn't obvious that the work concerned fits into neither category)"; and David V. Barrett remarked: "Amongst other things, yes. I am a writer first, and one of my preferred modes of writing is to employ the tropes and styles of sf and fantasy."

One of the clearest expressions of this unease at being labelled came from Neil Gaiman:

> I don't know. I'm not really sure *what* kind of writer I am. I suppose I feel more at ease with the fantastic, with "imaginative" literature than with any other kinds. And certainly half of what I read for pleasure falls into that kind of category. But I'm just a writer, and any pigeonholing makes me uncomfortable.

One gets the clear impression that these writers feel trapped by genre labels not because they object to the label but because it restricts what people expect of them, and, just possibly, what they feel able to write as a consequence. It is the writer's job to put words down on the page, anything that is read into them beyond that is the job of the audience, or the critic. Such, certainly, is the import of Alasdair Gray's response:

> I write books which use the devices of realism and of fantasy. Occasionally I have used some scientific speculations in a book, speculations of a far-fetched but possible sort, at other times I have applied scientific analysis to worlds which have never existed. I have no wish to attach a label to myself. That is the critic's job.

It's not that writers are in any way ashamed of science fiction or fantasy, as Garry Kilworth points out:

> I am not ashamed of science fiction and fantasy (as genres) and will admit to being a writer of both, but much of my work is on the fringes or outside either of these genres. I consider myself a writer of fantastic fiction, which encompasses sf, fantasy and certain kinds of bizarre mainstream fiction.

Lisa Tuttle is equally happy to admit to being a science fiction writer:

> Yes, although I also, and equally importantly, write non-fiction and non-science fiction-fiction. On social occasions, I'll often identify myself as a science fiction writer because it provokes a more definite response ... someone who has never heard of you and asks what you write isn't going to have much to say to an answer of "novels and short stories." Standing up for science fiction is potentially confrontational – although in my case it is the softer option; I don't always feel up to identifying myself as the author of the *Encyclopedia of Feminism*.

It's not so much that authors are denying science fiction, more that they are reulctant to see it as anything more than an element in what they do. As Stephen Gallagher put it: "I consider that my roots lie in sf and fantasy, although the links with some of the stuff that I'm doing now won't always be immediately apparent." Paul Barnett made the same point:

> I write very little straightforward sf/fantasy (although I'm currently working on a series of four, possibly twelve, kids' fantasy novels), but a great deal of it is tangential to sf/fantasy, appealing to much the same readership, and probably could not have come into existence had the two genres not existed. For example, and without wishing to plug: my *Sex Secrets of Ancient Atlantis* parodies the kind of pseudoscience so much beloved of certain sf writers (among others!); my *The Truth About the Flaming Ghoulies*, while in theory a satire of the rock industry, has androids as its central characters as well as various other sf devices; *Earthdoom* (with Dave Langford) parodies the disaster novel; and so on. Among my non-fiction, *Encyclopedia of Walt Disney's Animated Characters* is, by its very nature, devoted to a certain type of fantasy, while *A Directory of Discarded Ideas* has a sort of sf "feel" to its subject matter – or, at least, I think so.
>
> So it's hard for me to answer this question with a simple yes/no.

Some of the respondents specified their interests outside science fiction. Kim Newman, for example, described himself thus:

> Primarily, I'm a film critic. I'm not ashamed at parties to own up to writing science fiction and/or fantasy. I also admit to writing horror, which even your questionnaire seems to find beyond the pale. I also write humour.

John Brosnan is in the same camp: "I'm basically a humourist who at different times pretends to be a science fiction writer, horror writer, etc." And there are others who see their main work lying outside the genre, or outside fiction in the case of John Clute, who answered: "Only secondarily; primarily a critic."

Alternatively there are those who put priorities in a different order, like Elizabeth Sourbut: "Primarily I write science fiction, though some of it verges on mainstream work with very little sf content." Or Christina Lake: "Yes, primarily, though I'm also interested in writing non-sf for teenagers."

Douglas Hill, though, is at pains to point out that children's fiction is not a separate genre:

> Yes. But principally of sf and fantasy for "children." Not that there's all that much difference. Tom Disch said that all sf is children's fiction, but he meant it sardonically, I don't. Adult sf fans retain that old cliché, the "sense of wonder," mostly intact – and remain child-like (not childish) in that respect. If they don't, they're probably reading sf for the wrong reasons.

In the end it comes down to a question of what one actually writes. As David Langford shows:

> Sometimes, when I happen to be writing sf or fantasy, which isn't often enough at present. On this year's output, I can only call myself a critic in the field ... unless you count futurological "non-fiction" as sf.

The split seems to be fairly even between those who are happy to proclaim themselves a writer of science fiction and/or fantasy, without much need to qualify what they mean by the terms; and those who are happy to write science fiction or fantasy, but feel wary of being limited by the term. The general impression is that sf is one way of writing what they want to write, but not the only way; and no-one wants to be prevented from writing anything else by genre expectations. Whether this is a distinctively British trait might become clear by the end of this survey, but it may help explain why both Christopher Priest and Josephine Saxton chose to say that they are not science fiction writers. Science fiction appears, in Britain, to be seen as one literary mode among many, and writers are defined not by the mode they most use to express themselves, but by the fact they are writers. I suspect, therefore, that practically all of the respondents would find common ground with Keith Roberts:

> I think I just write books. If there are elements in them that fit into the categories of sf or fantasy, then so be it, I wouldn't like to categorise *Grainne*, for example, as falling into any particular camp.
>
> There of course lies the problem. I think if the twentieth century survives in memory at all, and we don't all blow ourselves up, die of skin cancer through reduction of the ozone layer or any other of the jollities we've laid in store, it will probably come to be known as the Age of the Pigeonhole. Everything has to have its label, which of course is very handy. It saves reviewers from thinking; they can get on with Criticism instead. I think the thing was summed up as neatly as anybody by Doris Lessing when she said that the social novel is a relatively new form anyway, it's only been around about four hundred years.

Before that, fiction was "wonder tale" by definition; something that holds true for everybody from Lucian to the Gawain Poet. Jane Austen, though an estimable lady, in a sense did a lasting disservice; what tends these days to be forgotten, or conveniently shoved under the carpet, is that romanticism, the other equally valid strand of literature, continued unabated. It's salutary to remember that Charlotte Bronte was born the year before Austen died.

Regardless of that, the situation is that today the Social Novel Rules, OK? Although there's excellent work being done in the field it's really one of the most restricted of genres. You can write about anything you like as long as it's randy college professors (Malcolm Bradbury) or anthropologist's secretaries (Jean Rees). Anything else, and you're probably beyond the pale. As I've said before, *Lord of the Flies* is probably the finest sf novel of our times, but if Golding had come in via the pulps he'd have been stopped at one low-selling book; he certainly wouldn't have picked up his Swedish pot.

# 2009

In September 2009, it's impossible to not indulge in a wry grin as I sit down to write about how writers self-identify. For 2009, whatever else it may be for science fiction, is an Atwood Year, with all the festivities that brings. A couple of weeks ago, in *The Guardian*, Ursula K Le Guin wrote this as the opening paragraph of a review of Atwood's latest novel:

> To my mind, *The Handmaid's Tale, Oryx and Crake* and now *The Year of the Flood* all exemplify one of the things science fiction does, which is to extrapolate imaginatively from current trends and events to a near-future that's half prediction, half satire. But Margaret Atwood doesn't want any of her books to be called science fiction. In her recent, brilliant essay collection, *Moving Targets*, she says that everything that happens in her novels is possible and may even have already happened, so they can't be science fiction, which is "fiction in which things happen that are not possible today." This arbitrarily restrictive definition seems designed to protect her novels from being relegated to a genre still shunned by hidebound readers, reviewers and prize-awarders. She doesn't want the literary bigots to shove her into the literary ghetto. [1]

Le Guin's review – not so much this part of it, actually, but later and snarkier paragraphs, which fully acknowledge Atwood's literary prowess without hesitating to ding her for such taxonomic tap-dancing – was quickly and widely linked to within the sf blogosphere, and beyond. It's noticeable that Le Guin, I have to assume deliberately, never mentions Atwood's preferred term for her own work: "speculative fiction."

No matter that four years ago Atwood held out an olive branch, acknowledging that "terms are fluid. [...] I have written two works of science fiction" [2]. No matter, indeed, that some writers within the sf community have used and – as we shall see – continue to prefer the same term. The myth of Atwood is alive and well and waiting to be attacked, for the honour of science fiction. Fredric Jameson, in the *London Review of Books*, perhaps went even further than Le Guin in his review:

> [Dystopia] has also been the one science-fictional sub-genre in which more purely "literary" writers have felt free to indulge: Huxley, Orwell, even the Margaret Atwood of *The Handmaid's Tale*. And not unpredictably, the results of these efforts have been as amateurish as analagous experiments in the realm of the detective or crime story (from Dostoevsky to Nabokov, if you like), but including a message or thesis. So-called mass cultural genres, in other words, have rules and standards as rigorous and professional as the more noble forms.
>
> But Atwood can now be considered to be a science-fiction writer, I'm happy to say, and this is not meant to disparage. [3]

I mention all this by way of introducing the first striking difference between this year's BSFA Survey and the 1989 Mexicon Survey. Then, Paul Kincaid could write that "The split seems to be fairly even" between those writers who happily self-identified as science fiction or fantasy writers, and those who, like Atwood, "feel wary of being limited by the term." Now, only about one in five writers put themselves in the "wary" camp. For the rest, answers such as these are typical:

> **Joe Abercrombie:** Yes, of fantasy.
>
> **Tony Ballantyne:** Nearly exclusively sf.
>
> **Iain Banks:** Sf, basically. Not always very scientifically correct sf, mind.
>
> **Chris Beckett:** I am definitely a writer of science fiction.
>
> **Eric Brown:** I consider myself a science fiction writer – certainly not a fantasy writer.
>
> **Susanna Clarke:** I'm a writer of fantasy.
>
> **Jaine Fenn:** Yes: soft science fiction.
>
> **Rhiannon Lassiter:** I consider myself an author of science fiction and of fantasy fiction.

**James Lovegrove:** Very much so.

**Ken MacLeod:** Yes – science fiction.

**Juliet E McKenna:** A fantasy writer.

**Katherine Roberts:** YES (a fantasy writer).

**Justina Robson:** Yes.

**Charles Stross:** Yes.

**Adrian Tchaikovsky:** Fantasy, definitely, although with a touch of steampunk.

In all, nine writers simply said, "yes"; fourteen writers said "yes, fantasy"; fifteen "yes, sf"; two "yes, horror" (Ramsey Campbell and Conrad Williams); a further fourteen "yes, both"; and eleven some version of "yes, plus some other things." Some, like Jaine Fenn and Adrian Tchaikovsky above, even went into details of subgenre. (Interestingly, although ten respondents are probably best known for their YA or children's writing, and a fair number more have written for that audience, only one writer – Frances Hardinge – claimed it as their primary writerly identity: "I consider myself primarily a writer of children's books with a strong penchant for speculative or supernatural storylines"; although NM Browne did qualify her "Yes" with "although currently I only write for a YA audience." Maybe it was the way the question was phrased.) As Keith Roberts suggested, twenty years ago, we do appear to now be in the Age of the Pigeonhole: but self-accepted, as much as imposed from without.

Many responses, of course, contained nuances that this bald categorisation elides, and there were, to be sure, some signs of wariness. Few were as bold as Stan Nicholls: "Yes. And I'm proud to be thought of as such." A couple deployed the passive voice, including Colin Harvey – "I've written both sf and fantasy" – as if to say, *but that's not* quite *the same as being a* writer of *science fiction and/or fantasy*. John Meaney resorted to extended metaphor to suggest both the shift that may have occurred over the last twenty years, and a resistance to being pinned down too firmly:

> In the world of martial arts – bear with me: you talk to a writer, you get a fistful of metaphors – the ultimate fighting test is MMA, sometimes called cage fighting. The fighters are all-rounders operating in simultaneous modalities – jiu-jitsu, wrestling, kickboxing. Under those conditions, most martial artists fall to pieces.
>
> In the nineties, the field was dominated by one Brazilian family, working from their core art of Gracie Jiu-Jitsu. Nowadays, the light-heavyweight

champion of the major worldwide circuit (the UFC) works from my own core system of shotokan karate, taking it into other modalities at world-class level.

Some of my work spans multiple genres – two of my novels are published as fantasy in the US but science fiction in the UK (and a different publisher offered to market them as police procedurals); while my novelette "Whisper of Disks" is *almost* pure literary fiction.

As a writer, my core discipline is science fiction; I take it with me wherever I go.

Brian Stableford was fatalistic – "Yes, alas" – while Ricardo Pinto was sly: "Yes – though probably with the usual caveats." Michael Moorcock's response felt careful: "When I'm writing it, yes." But the overwhelming majority of respondents either claimed some part of "a writer of science fiction and/or fantasy" as an identity for themselves, or stated that they were happy to have it applied to them. Graham Joyce, indeed, seemed to wish more people would apply the label to his work: "Yes, but most readers of sf and fantasy don't."

Nor was this comfortableness evident only among writers published by genre imprints (although it was, perhaps, more common there; see below). Stephen Gallagher thinks of himself "as a mainstreamer with an sf/f background that tinges almost everything I do." Toby Litt sounded comfortable with multiple identities, more than wary of being fixed with one, when he responded "Yes, but not full time" (particularly in the context of the rest of his answers); Andrew Crumey said, "No, but I have no objection to being considered one by people more knowledgeable of the genre than I am," adding, "I consider myself a writer of philosophical fiction."

China Mieville also took the knowledge of readers into consideration:

> Yes, though how I describe what I do depends almost entirely on who I'm talking to. If it's someone who doesn't know the field, I tend to say sf, for simplicity. If they know a bit more I might taxonomise a bit more precisely – though such categories are always grey-edged, of course.

Relatively few writers, too, adopted Ian R MacLeod's line: "Yes, I do ... The and/or bit is something I'd like to get rid of, though. Sf is just fantasy with a technological twist. I mean, starships are about as realistic as dragons, aren't they?" Or at least didn't adopt it wholesale. Al Robertson replied, "I write both; I tend to describe myself as a writer of weird fiction, because it seems to include science fiction and fantasy. It's also a nice nod to the various pulp visionaries, who have been key inspirations." And Mike Carey, if not quite seeing sf and fantasy as two flavours of the same thing, certainly came out in favour of mixing it up:

> I consider myself a writer of fantasy, or more usually horror/fantasy – almost never of science fiction. Although it's true in general terms that the

> boundaries between genres have become more permeable, they're still there in some form – and the one between sci-fi and fantasy will probably be the last bastion to fall. It takes a writer of rare talent – a Michael Swanwick, say, or a China Mieville – to mix and match sci-fi and fantasy elements and not end up with a nightmarish mess. But everything from fantasy through horror to crime fiction and romance is now to a large extent part of a big genre cross-dressing party. And on the whole I'd see that as a good thing.
>
> One exception to the above: I write superhero comics, and I tend to see the superhero genre as a sub-genre of science fiction. It can include magical and supernatural elements too, but it more often leans on scientific explanations and rationales both for its characters' existence and powers and in the elaboration of its plots. When I wrote *Ultimate Fantastic Four*, I took the book in a very science-fictional direction, with time-travel stories, alien invasions, other dimensions and what-not else.

Although this confidence in and comfortableness with identity as a science fiction or fantasy writer was common, and although it would be nice to believe that it is the result of the so-called "British Boom" of the 1990s – since many of the participating writers are of the generation that flowered in that decade – or even indicative of a new and more general cultural confidence in the literatures of the fantastic, as manifested in defenses of genre identity in such high-profile mainstream venues as the *Guardian* and *London Review of Books*, it was not universal among respondents to this survey. Stephen Gaskell did state that he, like Atwood, prefers "speculative fiction":

> Both. I prefer to use the umbrella term "speculative fiction" when talking about my own work. It is useful for at least two reasons. Firstly, "science fiction" and "fantasy" in the popular mindset refer to tired genres populated by spaceships and aliens, and quests and dragons respectively, and so by using the term "spec-fic" I avoid the prejudice that many readers experience when they hear those terms. Secondly, "speculative fiction," as a label, is not widely known outside the community, and it immediately triggers a question in the average reader's mind: what is *that*? This is very useful for re-calibrating people's expectations of sf and f.
>
> Taking the question in the spirit that it's intended, I would categorise my work closer to the sf side.

Susanna Clarke was clear on her identity as a writer of fantasy, but equally clear that, for her, the battle has not been won:

> There is a second reason I tell people I'm a writer of fantasy – a political one if you like. Many genres are considered second-rate; the genre of literary fiction is sometimes seen as the only first-rate one. This seems to me nonsensical.

> Good fiction and good ideas don't depend on genre or on the furniture of the story. Some of the best stories in English were and are written for children. So I am very happy to be considered a writer of fantasy.

She also touched on the next major theme of this chapter:

> That said, I am not a writer of fantasy in the sense that I live and die within the genre. In the privacy of my own head I think of myself as a writer of stories – and the genre I use depends on the needs of the stories – if I started to think of stories that fitted better with the crime genre, I'd switch to that. As it is, when writing I often look outside the fantasy genre and borrow ideas and styles from other genres – from literary fiction or non-fiction.

Of those writers who couldn't make "a writer of science fiction and/or fantasy" sit comfortably on their shoulders, or chose not to, only a handful claimed no alternate identity. For Will Ashon it is perhaps a question with no clear answer:

> Not really. I write things which draw on sf, I guess. I try to collide genres and see what happens ... Do I? Not sure whether that's not a pat answer. Maybe it's more accurate to say I write books which come out as they come out, regardless of genre. (On a side note, it seems to me that all fiction is genre fiction – including "literary fiction.")

Nick Harkaway does have a label for himself, but otherwise finds himself in a similar bind:

> I'm a storyteller – by which I mean my job is to tell stories which entertain and, if I'm very lucky, enlighten. My first and so far only novel, *The Gone-Away World*, definitely deals with the unreal, with an imagined circumstance, and with science – albeit loosely. I didn't know when I was writing it what category it would fall into. I'm happy with that. I think if something isn't clearly within a pre-existing genre, the only reason to try to define it more thoroughly is for convenient shelving. That's absolutely respectable, of course, but it isn't helpful in actually describing what a book is about. There are stories I'd like to tell which are clearly within the sf genre, and others which are equally clearly outside it. My second novel is probably another tricky fit. Am I an sf/fantasy author? I've heard readers of those genres say "yes," and I've heard them say "no." So I have no idea.

More directly, Christopher Priest's response was simply, "no," and M John Harrison replied, "I'm quite consciously against the categorisation of fiction." Mark Chadbourn is another one who resists categorisation of his work, although he does recognise the existence of the categories:

> I'm not interested in labels designed by marketing people to sell books. When I was growing up, I read sf, fantasy, horror, without making any distinction among them – they were simply "my kind of story." I write with the same approach – fantasy that hides sf or horror, or sliding across the genres in novellas and short stories. But my editors call me fantasy at their meetings, so if you're going to press me to take a stand I'll go with that.

Something similar is true for Kit Whitfield, who, as a writer published as mainstream in the UK and genre in the US, has perhaps more reason than most to be conscious of where her books get shelved:

> Yes and no. If you classify books by content, mine could certainly fit in that category; I've written one with werewolves and one with mermaids, and those are pretty traditional staples of fantasy or horror. But it's my belief that genre classifications aren't really that good for either writers or readers. The main purpose they serve is to make it easier for booksellers to pitch to shops. That's useful for business, but it can be rather cramping for books, and a writer who feels they have to fit too precisely into this artificial category is probably going to limit their own writing. My first novel, for instance, was published by a science fiction imprint in the US, a literary fiction imprint in the UK, and wound up in the Crime section of Borers, and that feels comfortable to me: the idea that a book has to fit in one category and one category only seems kind of reductive. So I'll happily classify myself as a sci-fi/fantasy writer if I get to classify myself as a literary writer and a thriller writer as well. If I have to pick just one category, I tend to dig in my heels and say that I just write books.

(The contrast between these writers and Richard Morgan is, however, irresistable: "Yes, I do. I can rattle on about noir crossover and slipstream with the best of them, but in the end, what I'm writing is quite recognisably sf, and pretending otherwise would just be deeply *sad!*")

Perhaps the dominant theme among this group is a desire to be a writer, without categories; to be able to say "I just write books." For Liz Jensen, science fiction and fantasy is simply "too narrow a label for what I do"; For Patrick Ness, label-avoidance is a pragmatic matter of ensuring creative freedom as much as anything else:

> I don't, but only because I don't consider myself a writer of *any* particular label. When I personally have tried to write any kind of Adjective Novels in the past, it's been a disaster every time, because my loyalty is to the Adjective and not the Story. Which for me is a very bad idea. So now I just ignore all labels and expectations and write what I myself would want to read. Then I figure out

> what it is later. This sounds glib, but it's just a way of giving myself complete freedom to use everything that's available. I regard *The Knife of Never Letting Go* as just as much a western as it is sf. And both were surprising.

Although I've generalized about the survey respondents, and am comfortable those generalizations are valid, there is still, as we've seen, great diversity between responses. Moreover I don't think that, this year, there is a reply with which every author could find something to agree, as Paul Kincaid suggested was the case with Keith Roberts' response twenty years ago. Whether the decline in the size of the "just a writer" contingent, and the apparent increase in confidence in genre, is a genuine change or sample bias we cannot know; although if it is a genuine change, I'd suggest it might be interesting to consider whether it has been driven by readers, or publishers, or writers themselves. (Or more likely, driven in what proportion by each of those three.) But the response that came from one of the newer writers to participate, Nina Allan, is probably one that Margaret Atwood, at least, could agree with, and seems to me to usefully draw together a number of the threads running through these responses, with a tellingly different emphasis to Roberts – there's that faith in the fantastic, again – and in a way that neatly anticipates the themes of the next couple of chapters. So we end here, back once again at speculative fiction:

> If you were to ask me what I am I'd say a writer, and if you were to ask me what I write I'd say speculative fiction. I grew up with sf – as a child and a young adult I was a massive fan of writers like Wells and Wyndham and then later Keith Roberts and JG Ballard and the Strugatsky brothers. I loved the dystopian novels of Orwell and Huxley, Zamyatin and Kafka. All the stories I tried to write in my teens involved aliens or monsters or penal colonies in harsh environments. I can honestly say that it never occurred to me to write stories that did not include some element of the mystical or fantastic. I read widely in what you might call the mainstream, but mainstream literature seemed to me then – and still does – to be missing some vital element, some extra layer, to be concerned more with the surface of the world rather than its murky interior.
>
> I often feel my stories are not organised enough to count as "proper" sf – so if I am a science fiction writer I am a very wayward one. On the whole I am wary of genre labelling, because too often people either have preconceived ideas about what sf is or what it should be, which can lead to them either dismissing your work out of hand or else having false expectations of it. I understand that genre labelling can be useful and is often necessary, as a means for facilitating discussion, and as a guide for readers and publishers. I just don't like it when these boundaries become too rigid.

**Endnotes**

[1] Ursula K Le Guin, "The Year of the Flood by Margaret Atwood," *The Guardian*, Saturday 29 August 2009. Online at <http://www.guardian.co.uk/books/2009/aug/29/margaret-atwood-year-of-flood>.

[2] Margaret Atwood, "Aliens have taken the place of angels," *The Guardian*, Friday 17 June 2005. Full quote: "Some use speculative fiction as an umbrella covering science fiction and all its hyphenated forms – science fiction, fantasy, and so forth – and others choose the reverse. I have written two works of science fiction or, if you prefer, speculative fiction." Online at <http://www.guardian.co.uk/film/2005/jun/17/sciencefictionfantasyandhorror.margaretatwood>

[3] Fredric Jameson: "Then You Are Them: *The Year of the Flood* by Margaret Atwood," *London Review of Books*, Vol. 31 No. 17 (10 September 2009). Online at <http://www.lrb.co.uk/v31/n17/jame02_.html>.

# Chapter 2:
## *What is it about your work that makes it fit into these categories?*

# 1989

How do you define science fiction? It's a question that people have been trying to answer since we stopped being "scientifiction," to no very satisfactory effect. There are dozens of definitions, from "anything that has sf on the spine" to "cognitive estrangement," all of which cover most of the ground satisfactorily, but somehow manage to miss out some book that most people would happily call science fiction.

But there we have a problem: this survey is intended to find the defining characteristics of British science fiction, and we're not going to be able to do that without a clear idea of what we're talking about. If no-one else has been able to define "science fiction" it seems unfair to ask: "What is science fiction?" This question, therefore, tied with the first one, is a back door attempt to get to the same place. Not, of course, that people were unaware of what I was doing. John Brunner's only response was a heart-felt: "(OUCH!)" Others avoided the question. John Clute wrote: "The fiction I do write is clearly generic"; Barrington Bayley replied: "It isn't anything else"; and Josephine Saxton said: "It has no other category." None of which actually gets us anywhere.

Fortunately, other respondents were more forthcoming. Brian Aldiss attempted to define sf by excluding what it was not: "A rejection of optimism and dragons." That rejection of optimism could be very significant in the light of the common view of British science fiction, but everyone else defined their contribution to the genre more positively.

Some went the route of the publisher's label. For Lee Montgomerie it was simply because it was "Written for sf mags." For Christopher Priest:

> The literal answer is that publishers frequently (but not always) put my stuff into their sf category. I never encourage this, but never actively discourage it. I'm more resigned to this than I was in the old days; they have to make a living.

However, Mary Gentle, who started off down the publisher's label route, clearly shows that this is a much deeper and more intractable problem:

> The short answer is publisher's labels. The long answer is the presence of surreal, unreal, speculative, irrational, realistic, and metaphysical elements; necessitating that it not be read in the (now about defunct) tradition of the 19th century realist novel. (I just realised this definition allows *Hawksmoor* which was published as mainstream. Oops.)
>
> Try again: use of *genre* furniture, because I enjoy it.
>
> Try yet again: inclusion of the impossible, currently managing to get away from *genre* roots.
>
> It's a form of fiction which, in being read, allows nothing to be taken for granted?

It's what she calls "*genre* furniture" that seems to be the defining principle for most of those who replied. Often in terms purely of the technology, as with David Langford: "Spaceships. Megalomaniac computers. Black holes. Matter transmitters. Time travel. Ultimate weapons of universal destruction. Subtle literary nuances like these." Or Eric Brown: "The usual 'property' of sf – futuristic settings, a use of technology not yet invented, aliens, ray guns ...!" Or Garry Kilworth: "The reason my work sometimes fits into sf or fantasy is because I deal with themes (time travel, marvellous children, strange societies) which are commonly held to be within these genres." And, again, James White: "The plots have a present or future basis in science, usually medicine, space travel, communication with non-human life-forms, societies or philosophies, and the characters are affected by these backgrounds."

Kim Newman is another who refers to the detail of his stories:

> In the past, I've written about aliens, zombies, future societies, personalised death, vampires, ghosts, technological extrapolations, black magic, demons, monsters, etc. I think that earns me a place in the category. However, I've also written about private eyes, telegram girls, life in North London, and plenty of other things. I like science fiction, and I like being able to write it from time to time, but I have no great sentimental attachment to the genre.

And from the angle of fantasy there's Robert Irwin:

> Novels featuring half-men, dream control, talking apes and treasure hunting somnambulists (*The Arabian Nightmare*) or intellectual bits of fluff and grime (*The Limits of Vision*) are difficult to square with the tradition of the mainstream novel.

Elizabeth Sourbut refers to the devices in her stories, but points out that there's more to it than that:

> Usually my stories are set at a putative future date, with social and political conditions extrapolated from the present. They tend to contain the trappings of sf: communities in space, FTL ships, alternate realities, advanced gadgets – though sometimes used for comic effect, I try to explore the possibilities of human culture or the possible outcomes of trends visible now.

Iain Banks also has something to say about the attitudes underlying the use of hardware in science fiction:

> Behind sf – even where it includes FTL drives and the like – there ought to be a respect for the scientific method, for causality, for the quest to answer the question, How does it work? That doesn't seem to be there in the vast majority of the fantasy I've brushed up against. In all my books – non-sf as well – I'd claim that feeling of ... practicality is there. This is not to disparage fantasy, just to point out that that's the way I se the difference, and the way I want to work. Fantasy is, anyway, still there in several of the books – specifically *Walking on Glass* and *The Bridge*, though in a form which is as much a commentary on "conventional" fantasy as fantasy itself.

It is this concern for what I suppose we might call the "reality" of their interventions that lies at the heart of the attitude many of the writers displayed towards their writing. It is very much a view that is tied up with the way they define science fiction. Thus, from Paul J McAuley:

> SF? The literature of the possible (which is not to say, of the probable; we should not confuse sf with Rand Corporation forecasters). Despite implausible embellishments, my own work is rooted in what we know about the real Universe.

Or, as John Christopher puts it:

> My definition of science fiction is speculation based on scientific probability, carefully avoiding any defiance of the same. Thus you could write about interplanetary travel before we knew too much about the solar system, but it's dull stuff now; no Fantastic Venus, Dying Mars etc. Interstellar travel, and most of the other contemporary trappings, fail to suspend my disbelief. So latterly it's largely been fantasy, following soberly and logically (I hope) an initial wild jump.

A view which chimes closely with EC Tubb's definition of science fiction in the last chapter. But this interface between science fiction and fantasy is something which concerned a lot of the respondents. David Redd, for instance:

> Everything I write is set in a possible world (if you accept the initial assumptions of the particular stories). Fantasy worlds with dragons and suchlike are not possible. I do like going to the very edge of the possible on occasions, though. In these cases I think of the non-logical elements as "mythic" rather than "fantasy." This Zelaznyism is a world-view I developed in the 60s and haven't changed for the 80s.

It is precisely this question which led Brian Stableford to construct a succinct but useable definition of science fiction and fantasy:

> The fact that it consists of stories set in hypothetical worlds which, although intelligibly connected with the world in which we believe ourselves to exist, are differentiated from it by the incorporation of some novel factor (or coherent set of factors); the novel factor in question will characteristically be a product of the scientific imagination (in sf) or an aspect of a once-believed but now discredited world view (in fantasy).

That, essentially, is a restatement of "cognitive estrangement," but in clear, accessible terms and extended, possibly for the first time, to encompass fantasy, and differentiate fantasy from science fiction. It begs a lot of questions, of course, but this really isn't the place to go deeper into the question of what exactly is meant by "scientific imagination," for example. As it stands, however, it seems to be a pretty handy definition.

One explanation of "scientific imagination" might conveniently be derived from Leigh Kennedy's definition of her science fiction, which "has elements of scientific extrapolation or deals with future possibilities in science or society," or from Robert Farago's: "My stories revolve around the human impact of a speculative premise, usually based on a projected scientific advance." Graham Dunstan Martin proposes yet a third perspective: "My work falls within the sf and fantasy categories because it always contains either (1) departures from the supposed 'Laws of Nature', or (2) 'thought experiments' about future human societies ... or both."

This isn't taking us away from the idea that the stories are defined as science fiction by the devices they employ, but it is expanding the definition of "devices." At its broadest this is as stated by Christina Lake: "Future settings and/or introduction of elements that aren't an accepted part of the world we live in today." EC Tubb puts it another way:

> My stories are not set in any recognisable setting, i.e.: cities are futuristic, installations are not as we know them, etc. The overall backgrounds, social,

> financial, cultural, are also different though all are based on changes in the familiar, ie: a world in which charity is unknown is not totally alien to us, neither are societies which are based on peonage, slavery, etc. The acceptance of these conditions together with the working out of means of survival within them form stories based on the "what would happen if?" framework. The situations, developments, characters, etc, could not exist within the accepted constraints of our known world.

Or, as Colin Greenland put it: "The material, which is fantastic. The fact that I make up not only stories, but the worlds they happen in."

But it is as much the way these elements are written about as the elements themselves which can define science fiction. Simon Ounsley talks about "an element of fantasy which is vital to the story," and Alex Stewart of "Elements of the unreal in plot or setting, treated as though they're perfectly rational." Diana Wynne Jones repeats the point, and again a distinction is drawn between science fiction and fantasy:

> The books that I write always contain at least one element which is not normally thought to be present in the everyday world. In fact most of the elements I draw on are taken from what most people regard as science fiction, not from what most people regard as fantasy.

A neat sidestepping of the problem, there.

James Corley is another writer who looks for something beyond the hardware in science fiction:

> As far as the science fiction went I wasn't very adventurous, I just followed the tropes. If black holes were in vogue I'd throw in a bucketful. Now the "serious" books, well one was a near future novel where I was writing about Britain under a far-Right government, urban riots commonplace and unemployment over three million. This was at a time when a Labour administration was getting crucified for a dole queue just approaching half a million. I've never understood why some think-tank didn't snap me up as an ace economic forecaster. I wouldn't call it science fiction (though I've seen books under that label with far less justification). It might be "speculation," it might not. Alternatively I also wrote a scurrilous novel about God, since I wasn't struck down by lightning that might be fantasy, but personally I'd definitely call it speculative fiction. To approach the point of your question my sort of speculative fiction has to have something of the stuff of dreams about it, a touch of myth, poetry and transcendentalism but reconciled with rationality. That's not to say, though it sounds it, that it has to be pretentious. My old and tattered copy of Voltaire's *Candide* is the seminal work as far as I'm concerned.

Transcendentalism reconciled with rationality seems a very good summing up of what people have been saying about their science fiction. You get a sense of it also in Ian McDonald's reply, and he's another writer who finds himself drawn to the term "speculative fiction."

> While I still firmly believe it's possible to write an out-and-out sf novel about the here-and-now, Britain 1989, without straying outside the boundaries of the actual (interesting that mainstream writers, particularly in Britain, have been venturing more and more into pretty straight sf without having the courage to call it that; there's a tremendous amount of "near-future Britain/ Dystopia" around, and if Bruce Chatwin's *The Songlines* described by himself as an "18th Century novel of ideas" isn't an exercise in anthropological sf, what is?) I think that what would mark my work as "science-fictional" is that, while I am concerned primarily with the relationship between people and change, I'm not afraid to push that change beyond the bounds of the probable into the possible, or even improbable. Isaac Asimov said in the introduction to *Nebula Award Stories 8* that "of all forms of literature, science fiction is the only one that deals principally and basically with change ... It is not the function of science fiction to predict the actual future, but rather to present alternate futures of any degree of probability from one hundred percent to zero, and to do so as intricately as possible." To be horribly pious about the thing, I would rather say that I write (to rehash that hoary old cliché) *speculative fiction* rather than sf or fantasy. To finally answer the question, I wouldn't want what I do to fit too comfortably into the categories of sf or fantasy, overcategorisation is the curse of the genre.

Something to be borne in mind when considering these things, of course, is that the categories are actually changing. Lisa Tuttle offers a case in point:

> Most of my fiction fits somewhere into the region of the fantastic – horror, fantasy, science fiction – but individual pieces can't always be neatly categorised. I don't think I write genre fiction, as such; I think of science fiction as being an attitude rather than a genre. In the 1970s, when I was still living in the US, I often thought – and the reasons sf editors gave for rejecting some of my stories confirmed – that I wasn't really writing science fiction. But these same, marginal-sf stories, collected and published in one volume by The Women's Press in 1987, have now acquired an identity as "feminist sf." They weren't viewed that way ten years ago ... and they are the same stories ... but I think the definition of sf has become much wider. And, as a result, it suits me better.

Given the way sf and fantasy have been distinguished by the various respondents so far, for example, where do we place this from Kenneth Bulmer:

> At the moment I am writing fantasy with ramifications of internal logic; does not contain unpronounceable words; is concerned to illuminate the human condition; has a consistent geography and various glossaries etc. researched by other hands than mine.

Which leads us neatly to a comment by Jane Palmer: "The category is dictated by the needs of the plot. The more fantastic the idea the more likely the story will fall out of the constraints of general fiction." In other words, the category is determined by the story-telling needs of the author at that point, and if your needs are, as Samantha Lee describes them, "Imaginative themes out of the normal space/time continuum," or, as David V Barrett puts it, "A strangeness, a side-stepping from mimetic straightjackets; and a use of mythic archetypes" then the chances are that what you write will find itself described as science fiction or fantasy.

And this can have deeper resonance in one's writing than a simple matter of which mechanical devices are incorporated into the story. As Stephen Gallagher says:

> Underlying theme rather than surface detail. I'll still use extrapolated technology or supernatural elements, particularly in short stories; but the main thrust of the work at present is to tell a straight tale with deeper resonances.

The point, which Neil Gaiman makes clear, is that a device which seems clearly science-fictional may not necessarily result in a story that is unambiguously science fiction:

> I suppose because it's easy to point to things in my work which are easily categorisable, although even those tend to blur the borders. For example, concentrating on my longer graphic work, *The Sandman* is somewhere on the border between high fantasy and low horror, *Black Orchid* is a film noir crime story with an sf McGuffin turning it into an ecological fable, and *Violent Cases* is either a ghost story or not a ghost story (I incline towards the latter view). I love the metaphors of fantasy, horror, sf, crime, gothics and such, and I love the territory.

And ambiguity comes with the territory when you're writing fiction. Note that Gaiman only "inclines" toward one interpretation of *Violent Cases*, he no more has one definitive explanation of his work than anyone else does. And the same it is very much true of the way writers choose to make certain points, and the way it is read and interpreted. It is a "subtle question of emphasis," as Gwyneth Jones puts it:

> a) Historical accident, b) A subtle question of emphasis. Plenty of mainstream fiction has "science" in it, sometimes as background, occasionally as foreground; often more realistic and better integrated into the fiction than the science

> in most "sf." More and more mainstream fiction is set in the future, a place which has taken over the function of all other "otherworlds" as setting for speculation, political comment, etc. Some mainstream fiction even ranks the scientific or ideal content of the fiction above any other interest. Maybe the only difference is that most sf, unlike most mainstream fiction on "sf" topics refers to and acknowledges a particular set of possible futures (those treated in the body of genre works) as if they already exist.

Not, of course, that such subtlety relates to every work of science fiction, or its author. I'll leave the last word to Douglas Hill who is, I am sure, speaking for more people than himself when he treats my question to the following robust response:

> Silly question. My stuff lies nowhere near any of the blurred boundaries between sf and other fiction. It's unashamed space opera or sword-and-sorcery, set in universes that don't and can't exist (yet).

# 2009

For most respondents, there is a sense in which the question posed in this chapter has a simple, if recursive, answer. What is it that makes these writers' work fit into these categories? Me. If I didn't think it possible that a given writer's work could be understood to be science fiction or fantasy, after all, I would not have sent them a copy of the invitation to participate. The roll-call for this survey is as close an approximation as I could manage of what I point to when I say "science fiction and fantasy."

But to usefully contextualise the answers to the rest of this survey what is needed, of course, is a version of what Damon Knight actually said: a map that describes what *we* point to when *we* say science fiction (and fantasy). No one definition is ever considered sufficient, but in the aggregate of the responses collected here we can get a sense of what is considered sufficient at this time, and in this place, and by these people. It is interesting to note, for example, that of the forty-nine writers who indicated that at least some of their work could be considered science fiction, only twelve specifically mentioned the future as a defining characteristic; while of the forty-eight writers who indicated that at least some of their work could be considered fantasy, only twenty mentioned magic or the supernatural.

This is not to say that I consider anything reported here to be, as it were, a definitive statement. I'm not planning to hold anyone to anything. Apart from anything else, answers to questions such as this (and indeed those making up the rest of the survey) will evolve naturally over time, as a writer's career progresses and they produce new work. What was true for their fiction of twenty years ago may not be true now. But there is still, I think, some wisdom to be had from this crowd, a sense of which answers are most popular at the moment, which spring to mind first, and why that might be.

For some, the category is imposed from without. As Tanith Lee puts it, "I've been categorized as fitting by others. For myself, I don't really know if it *does* fit. Or if any sf/fantasy *fits*, in that sense." This categorization can, it seems, take place at several points along the journey from writer to reader. Tim Lees was one of those who noted that the venue has an effect:

> In part, it's where a story is published. A piece with a slightly weird element, if published in a mainstream book, might be considered mainstream (ghost stories, for example, are a fairly mainstream sub-genre). If it appears in *Interzone*, then it's f/sf. How do you categorize fiction? Is Harry Potter genre fantasy, children's or mainstream? Is the Russian writer Victor Pelevin f/sf? Quite clearly, in some stories, but he's not published as such.

It's an observation borne out by Paul McAuley's reply: "I was first published in science fiction magazines. Pretty much guaranteed that everything I wrote thereafter would be classified as science fiction (even my crime novel)." But there are two parts to the effect of venue on categorisation, I think. First, there's marketing – or, as Alan Campbell says, "that's where they put it on the bookshelf." And the system of categorisation we have today is, at least for Christopher Priest, a damaging fiction in and of itself:

> Ask the people who put it there. I wrote my first novel (*Indoctrinaire*) self-consciously thinking of it as science fiction. That was forty years ago. Since then I have been restless, trying to push the boundaries a bit. I believe the genre tradition we inherited from the USA has been for the worse, that literature has always contained elements of the fantastic, and that the fantastic presents metaphorical possibilities to the writer that are important and special. Falling back on genre attitudes is to be avoided (as is thinking about books in categories).

But there's also the role of readers, either adhering to a given category, or trying (like me, shamelessly) to pull things over to a category that they are in sympathy with. Will Ashon reports:

> My first two books were interpreted as "near future" fiction, but *Clear Water* was set in 2001 and *The Heritage* in a kind of parallel present. I guess people (journalists in particular?) like to categorise things.
>
> People have been very keen to draw comparisons to Ballard. I think if you try to write vaguely serious books about "now" that aren't Booker-style lit-genre about university lecturers of the sons of vicars (or vicars themselves) then that's the obvious comparison. And Ballard is still considered sf, by the sf

> community at least ...

So perhaps what's most damaging, or at least limiting, about the process of categorization is that it's a self-reinforcing feedback loop. Chaz Brenchley appears to describe something of along these lines:

> Um. Something between authorial intent and marketing decisions made by other people? I became a horror writer almost by accident, because bookshops did keep putting my thrillers on the horror shelves so I thought I might as well play up to that – but even then there was an element of authorial choice, I did introduce supernatural elements to what had been mimetic fiction. With the sf and fantasy it's been more deliberate – mythic elements introduced into reshaped history for the fantasy, interplanetary travel, body-swapping and other classic tropes for the sf – but it has still been suggested to me that my crime was really horror all along, the horror was really fantasy, and the fantasy does have strong elements of crime ...

Ricardo Pinto answered that his work fits because, "It is a work in which the setting and events are entirely made up – although as good an alternative answer might be: because that is what the English language publishing world seems to demand – this rather crude characterization." Which does rather invite you to consider whether the solution would be no classification, or at least a more nuanced and multivalent system, along the lines suggested by Kit Whitfield in the previous chapter. Per Frances Hardinge's response, the latter probably has some problems:

> All three of my books ask the reader to accept some otherworldly premises. Two of them are set in alternative worlds, and while the third is set in our world there is a dominant supernatural plotline. My first book is something of an oddity, since the alternative world in which it is set features nothing obviously or provably supernatural, but it is convenient to classify it as fantasy since the "picaresque mock-historic magicless alternative-world crime romp" genre probably won't be taking off any time soon.

The argument that books get classified out in the world, though, while true, does to a certain extent dodge the issue. At some point, the decision as to how to categorize a work gets made, by someone: and on what basis are such decisions made? Charles Stross hedges his bets and gives both answers:

> Two things: a) The notable presence in all my writing of technologies, social phenomena, and/or magic, all of which are dealt with in a literalist (non-metaphorical) mode, and b) My works are filed under sf/f in the bookshops and marketed as such by the publishers (genre pigeon-holing, in other words).

Indeed a majority of respondents, sf writers and fantasy writers, YA writers and adult genre writers and "mainstream"-published writers alike, gave some form of content-based answer, Andrew Crumey, for example, stating "I imagine it is predominantly the content (which is sometimes manifestly scientific), and perhaps my professional background as a physicist"; or Ian Whates' explanation that, "there are invariably elements of the narrative which are not yet possible in today's world and which, more often than not, never will be." In the broadest sense, two elements in particular came up repeatedly: the world, and the things within the world. Joe Abercrombie, for instance, was typical of the self-identified fantasy writers: "It takes place in a secondary world with some magic and a pre-gunpowder level of technology. And it has many genre staples such as kindly wizards and magic swords"; similarly, Sarah Ash: "The world in which the stories are set is invented (although it has certain parallels with our own) and in this world, angels, daemons and dragons exist." Susanna Clarke emphasised the fit between the raw materials of fantasy fiction and the ideas in which she is interested as a writer:

> My work contains:
> - fairies
> - old books and libraries
> - magic
> - magicians
> - connections to an idealised past
> - roads that possibly might take you physically to other worlds.
>
> These things are some of the usual furniture of fantasy literature.
>
> My work also contains: trees, hills, and landscapes which sometimes are alive in some sense and which possess importance and value to people; objects, landscapes or situations that have meanings beyond the obvious – meanings which may or may not be comprehensible to human characters; a sense that human beings are not always and not necessarily the centre of the world.
>
> These sorts of ideas (it's by no means a definitive list) seem to go rather deep with me. You could certainly explore them in other genres or forms – in poetry or literary fiction to take two at random – but fantasy fiction seems a natural home for them. (All of the above are ideas you'll find in Tolkien and Lewis). So fantasy seems to be the most natural form for me.

The relationship between the worlds of fantasy and our own also came in for some scrutiny. Katherine Langrish describes her books as "history with the beliefs put back in." For Mark Charan Newton, it's very simple: "the fact that it is set in a secondary world prevents it from being other than fantasy." Adrian Tchaikovsky, on the other hand, seems to feel that simply being set in a different world is not sufficient, pointing to the *kind* of world: "An entirely separate world, with different rules and laws, including magic [and written with] a general disregard for the more inconvenient laws of nature." This departure from the rules of our reality also seems significant to Kari Sperring, who echoes some of Susanna Clarke's points about landscape:

> I write with an historical sensibility, I think, rather than an overtly fantastical one, but I also work with a framework of reality that differs from the mundane and which has implications for the events and characters. My up-front plot interests are usually political, but the world building is dependent on a sort of "magic" (though I don't call it that – it's more a kind of environmental and elemental sentience which is accepted as myth or fact by characters, depending on their background). This is hard to explain; it's a "feel" thing. Plus I love to write ghost stories.

Tim Lebbon suggests that his work spans a spectrum:

> All of my work has elements of the fantastic – that is, aspects that don't necessarily fit into today's worldview. From subtly supernatural work, to novels set in completely alternate universes where I'm free to create flora, fauna and societies as I wish. So generally I'd use "fantasy" as a broad name for what I do.

If, on this spectrum, we can understand the world of any fantasy fiction as to some degree a mixture of our (present or historical) reality with impossibilities, then full secondary worlds such as those of Abercrombie, Sperring and Tchaikovksy would be at one end of a spectrum, Langrish's books would be somewhere in the middle, and the work of a writer like Suzanne McLeod (and with her, much contemporary urban fantasy) would be at the other: "Although set in the real world, my cast of characters include mythological figures, such as vampires, faeries, trolls, goblins, witches etc and some aspects are explained by magic." Mark Chadbourn seems to be working from a similar perspective when he states: "Fantasy is about mapping the landscape of the unconscious – myth and legend, symbols and archetypes. I like to write stories at the point where outright could-never-happen fantasy crashes up against the real world." Stephen Gallagher admits that he "can't say it without sounding pretentious, but I try for a sense of mythic resonance in the mundane," and Ramsey Campbell considers his impulse towards myth-creation in a bit more detail:

> It uses the supernatural in various ways, often as a metaphor, sometimes as an odd light to shine on the way we live now. The characters don't take it for granted (as I take to be a defining characteristic of magic realism) but usually react to it as a disruption of the mundane. I suppose that as an atheist tending increasingly to agnosticism (which may just be another phrase for growing old) I regard the stories that touch on an after-life as more speculative than the others (especially the idea that as far as consciousness is concerned one's dying

> dream may seem to last forever). I'd prefer to invent a myth (or at least believe that's what I've done) rather than reinvent existing myths, but I wouldn't be too surprised to find that's what I really do.

That "odd light to shine on the way we live now," the idea that the fantastic genres have a unique point of view to offer, is an idea that recurred in a few other responses. Keith Brooke, for instance, reported that he likes "to sidestep contemporary reality in various ways in order to give myself a fresh perspective on whatever I happen to be writing about," and noted that the sidestep could be into either fantasy or sf as seemed more appropriate for the story at hand. For Steve Aylett, it is precisely the pursuit of that perspective that renders his work fantastical:

> My writing is basically satire, but some of the techniques of satire involve exaggeration and taking arguments to their conclusion – this often puts things into the future, into strangeness, or at least among sf furniture. *Fain the Sorcerer* and *Rebel at the End of Time* are certainly fantasy satire. My stuff tends to be called slipstream or Bizarro or some other recently made-up label.

Whereas for Nina Allan, the effect is more delicate, leading to one of the more appealing definitions of near-future science fiction I can remember encountering:

> All my work involves some element of the fantastic. Sometimes that element is very slight, and is more of a shift of emphasis, a tampering with reality rather than any easily definable objective change in it. I like the term hyper-reality, because this seems to suggest a deepening rather than a broadening of the fantastic element, that it has to do with the particular visions and insights of the narrator and/or character.
>
> I have also produced work where the external characteristics of our own world remain largely intact, but where there has been some political, social or environmental change that either affects the way people carry on with their lives in a practical sense, or else affects their belief systems, their sense of the possible. I suppose the shorthand for that is that I write near-future sf.
>
> Not that I have anything against monsters. I would like to write a great big gothic monster novel one day!

And for Paul Cornell, that "odd light" compensates for an absence perceived elsewhere – and as for Allan, covers the entire range of fantastic fiction:

> I think I look at "realism," especially the representation of modern British life you see on television and in literary novels, and find it staggeringly wide of the mark when it comes to depicting reality. It's almost as if it's felt that that's not actually what realism is meant to do. So I like to pick up on one particular

> thread of the many failings that encompasses, the lack of a presence of what might be called the numinous, the fantastic, from dreams to religion to the actual situation of human beings as standing on a planet in a spiral galaxy, and pick at that, and find all the ways that talks about the human condition.

Ah, the human condition. For Gareth Lyn Powell, how that thorny subject is tackled marks the difference between fantasy and science fiction:

> I think I use more sf tropes than fantasy ones. Plus, my work is intended to be science fiction. Whether it succeeds in that aim is something for someone else to decide. To me, the difference between sf and fantasy lies not so much in technique or subject matter as in application. Broadly speaking, I see sf as a tool for exploring what it will mean to be human in an increasingly strange and baffling future; whereas I see fantasy exploring what it means to be human (or superhuman) in worlds which plainly do not, nor ever will, exist – a hotline into our archetypal dreams and superstitions, where mighty heroes vanquish armies of grotesque sub humans and beautiful vampires fall in love with their food.
>
> Of course, there are exceptions to these categories, and the borderline between them is fuzzy and hard to pin down. Not every story can be slotted neatly into one category or the other. Perhaps it would be more helpful to think of science fiction and fantasy as two ends of a spectrum, with all the various shades of grey in between. Most of my work falls towards the sf end of the spectrum but that's not to say there aren't a few shades of fantasy in there. So to sum it up in a neat sound bite: Sf and fantasy are exercises in exploring what it means to be human – sf explores scenarios which could plausibly occur while fantasy maps those which never could. However, both genres can be employed to a greater or lesser extent within a single story.

It is, I have to say, rather noticeable that most of the attempts at formal *definition* came from the self-identified science fiction, rather than fantasy, writers. Years of habit, perhaps. And, when fantasy writers took that tack, they tended to emphasize the similarities between the forms – "My writing explores societal, philosophical and political questions by way of adventure stories set in entirely imagined, secondary worlds drawing on historical sources," wrote Juliet McKenna, "rather than looking forward to an imagined future with a focus on the impact of technology on those societal, philosophical and political questions, which would be science fiction" – while Powell's definition was almost alone amongst those offered by sf writers in doing so.

Some writers, of course, were as straightforward as Abercrombie and Ash in defining their work as sf by virtue of its tropes. Iain Banks, for example: "Humungous space ships? Sarcastic drones? Plethoras of aliens? Stuff like that." (Banks is an interesting case when it comes to the role of "the future" in defining something as science fiction, since at least some of the Culture stories are contemporaneous with our history.) And Richard Morgan: "Well, take your pick – space travel, alien worlds, dystopian futures, jacked up gene engineered super-soldiers, exotic weaponry and tech ... it's all in there somewhere." In contrast, Ken MacLeod, mirroring Mark Newton, picked the setting as sufficient to mark a work as sf, without necessarily requiring familiar tropes: "Future and/or present settings – sometimes a present or recent past seen from a scientifictional angle."

But most common in this group were responses like Eric Brown's that defined the terms of the science fictional world: "I write fiction that is set in a world in which my characters understand that the underlying basis of reality is scientific, not occult/ magic etc." Gary Gibson took the same approach: "The implied idea that a mastery over nature and an understanding of the same has led to the fantastical technologies, rather than restricted knowledge being allowed by magical figures." Alastair Reynolds pinned down the distinction a bit more precisely:

> The type of sf that most appeals to me is set in a world – be it Earth or the galaxy, be it the near future or the far – that is linked to ours by a roadmap, a series of steps that take us from here to there. If this goes on ... this is what might happen. I don't care whether it's a likely roadmap, or a highly improbable one – but I do want that roadmap. That's why alternate history doesn't particularly appeal to me, although I've dabbled in it, and why I'm not all that interested in fantasy, or even that type of sf that takes an impossible premise and runs with it (e.g. there are still swamps on Venus). Ultimately I'm a rationalist, and I see sf as the literature of rational enquiry. It's a fiction that subscribes to the notion that the universe is fundamentally unknowable, whereas fantasy doesn't. I'd be uncomfortable writing something that didn't have a rational foundation, however opaque it might be to the reader. If I was going to be nasty, I'd say that fantasy bears the same relationship to sf as pseudo-science does to science. It sort of looks similar to the uninitiated, but there are deep conceptual differences. However that's not to say I can't enjoy some fantasy.

The perception – or not – of those "deep conceptual differences" is at the heart of the disagreement between those who see fantasy and science fiction as fundamentally one form, and those who, like Reynolds, see them as separate. Graham Joyce noted that he sees "Sf as essentially a rationalist mode of writing, closer to realism in that it rules out the magical or the supernatural, which are the province of fantasy." A slightly different attitude-based approach to definition was put forward by Jon Courtenay Grimwood, who suggested his work fits the sf/f categories as a result of "A refusal simply to write or accept reality and a desire to look at both sides of every question, even when there's only one side." And then there was Adam Roberts, who answered that what made his work science fiction is "Its cultural Protestantism." Tony Ballantyne's definition perhaps hews closest to traditional notions of what science fiction is and does:

> My definition of sf:
>
> 1) It has a sense of wonder
> 2) It extrapolates (unlike fantasy, which reflects)
> 3) It is cutting edge
>
> The last probably needs some explanation. Consider a book such as *The Time Traveler's Wife* by Audrey Niffenegger. Whilst an entertaining read with many sfnal elements in it, I don't think there was anything genuinely new in her treatment of the idea of time travel.
>
> This is not a problem; the book works well as a romance with a touch of sf in the background. Granted, if you took away the time travel the story wouldn't work, so by some definitions it's a science fiction story, but I would argue that ideas such as time travel have expanded out of sf and into the mainstream (think about all those James Bond films with a science fiction weapon as the plot driver). This is why I think sf needs to be cutting edge. If we keep going around and around the same ideas and not adding anything new, then we are missing that indefinable part of the genre that we all recognise from when we first began to read sf aged 11 or 12.
>
> I try to bring something new or cutting edge in my writing, in my treatment of sf themes. Whether I succeed or not is down to others to decide.

I have to admit that reading the Mexicon survey, and seeing Ian McDonald, among others, comment on "mainstream writers ... venturing more and more into pretty straight sf," I'm a little more sceptical of the idea that genre walls are breaking down. And yet, in the last eighteen months Michael Chabon won Hugo and Nebula awards; and *Interzone* regular Chris Beckett (whose answer also emphasised that in sf the world is "at least nominally explainable in terms consistent with scientific rationality") won the Edge Hill prize with a collection of science fiction stories. But we'll have time to investigate this question more thoroughly in later chapters; for now we should just note that whatever else is going on, plenty of writers appear to be having fun *within* the field of the fantastic. At least, neither James Lovegrove nor Ian Watson seemed to evince much ambivalence when reporting that, in Lovegrove's phrase, they are unable to avoid including "some element that elevates the narrative into the realm of the weird," even when they *try* to write realistic fiction. The sense of a community was also present in China Mieville's response:

> i) That the stories are predicated on something(s) which is not true, and very probably impossible, in reality. ii) That the stories are predicated and constructed on a familiarity with the protocols of fantastic fiction, sf/f/h.

I can't help wondering how closely that connects with the *emotional* aspect of science fiction identified by Patrick Ness (the only writer other than Tony Ballantyne and Paul Cornell to address such an aspect):

> Chaos Walking is set on another planet and deals with humans interacting with native species, so that's the easiest fit. But sf in particular has a kind of yearning to it that really grabs my heart, and I think that's definitely present in my writing as well. Yearning to reach out and explore and connect. A hopeful kind of yearning.

What really struck me, reading through the responses to this question, was the diversity of thought behind them; the same elements may recur in different answers, but usually in different combinations, and often with different arguments leading to or flowing from them. (Though I was also surprised how infrequently some elements came up: I would have thought more writers would have made the extrapolative, or roadmap, aspect of sf explicit. Does this say anything about the kinds of futures being written now? Or is it not, after all, a significant change from the Mexicon survey?) The (incomplete) sampling above has been something of a random walk, an attempt to pull out associations and resonances that struck me as I read through them. My hope is that other such links have struck you, ones that I haven't explicitly mapped; because I can certainly see two or three other ways I could have organised this material. This is not to say that I don't bear in mind M John Harrison's warning that each book is its own definition:

> We talk about f/sf as if its product – i.e. the meaning or meanings carried by any given example of it – is itself. When you ask me if I write sf, you are pretty much disabling any meanings my book was intended to have, and substituting sf-ness for them.

But I think the responses printed in this chapter merely bear out the truth of his comment, in that each reveals as much about its author and their work as about sf or fantasy in any categorical sense. This is what 84 writers point to – and write – when they say science fiction or fantasy.

# Chapter 3:
## *Why have you chosen to write science fiction or fantasy?*

## 1989

It's a logical progression. Having found out what it is that people think they are writing, the next step is to find out why they are writing it. But, as Elizabeth Sourbut showed, the two questions are inextricably linked:

> As I see it, fantastic fiction is the whole, and mainstream or "Establishment" fiction is only one genre within the whole. I don't like to be limited by supposedly realist fiction; some things can be said better if the setting is removed to a different place or time. I try to limit fantastic elements to those which are absolutely necessary to the story, which is why my work is often on theborders of the "mainstream."
>
> On a more mundane level, sf is what I was reading as an adolescent, and I got hooked – I wanted to do it too!

One of the most remarkable things about the responses to this question was the uniformity. That last paragraph from Elizabeth Sourbut set the tone for a remarkable proportion of the replies. In fact, nearly everyone agreed to some degree. James White said: "From an early age I read more sf than anything else, got more from it, and it seemed natural to write it rather than any other genre." Leigh Kennedy repeats that sentiment: "I used to read it, enjoy it and therefore naturally wanted to write it when I began to write seriously." John Brunner echoed her: "I enjoyed reading it as a kid; it was natural for me to attempt my preferred genres when I started to write my own stuff." Colin Greenland put it more or less the same way: "Because I like to read it, and large (enough) numbers of other people do too." And EC Tubb added:

> I chose to write what I liked to read. My tastes have altered over the years but I still like to read what I have written even though I know that, now, it could have been written somewhat differently.

In other words, writers from anywhere along the spectrum were saying exactly the same thing. As Samantha Lee phrased it: "Because I love it, mate."

Occasionally, this affection for the genre may be expressed differently, as in the case of Brian Aldiss:

> My disposition as a small boy was towards the unlikely, because nothing seemed to me more unlikely than the world in which I found myself living. Then I fell in love with distance.

But it amounts to the same thing, the child is father to the man. Ian McDonald put it like this:

> It was what I was brought up on, from being bought my first copy of the *Eagle* through exposure to the likes of *Thunderbirds, Doctor Who, Star Trek* (quite possibly, if Mum hadn't forced me to watch *Mike Mercury and Supercar*, I wouldn't have been an sf writer), then, moving from the televisual to the literary (if you can use the term with respect to some of the following) in the company of EE "Doc" Smith and Frank Herbert and Larry Niven and Jack Vance and Silverberg etc etc ... it was kind of difficult for me to write anything else. Also, and this is more important than one might think, there are almost no openings for absolute newcomers in any field other than sf, particularly in the short fiction market.
>
> Perhaps the question should be rather, why do you *continue* to write sf; to which I would answer that it gives me an intellectual and emotional thrill and a great sense of satisfaction to literally create a whole new world out of nothing, and also, the freedom of expression of the imagination that the mainstream denies; sf should be like jazz, or a sonnet, within the thematic framework you are free to improvise whatever you like.

In this, he raises two points that were taken up by a number of respondents. One, which I'll return to later in this chapter, is the commercial opportunity presented by science fiction. The other, which is obviously very important to judge by the response, is the freedom that science fiction gives to the creator. Robert Farago phrased it thus: "The genre allows a free play of imagination." Eric Brown said:

> Because I like reading it. Also it allows the writer a freedom not granted in the mainstream. As an sf writer I can set a story anywhere/anywhen in space and time; the only restraining factors are my imagination and knowledge.

Paul Barnett has a much more down-to-eath, pragmatic way of saying the same thing:

> Because I enjoy reading it. Because it allows me to explore ideas I can't in mainstream fiction. Because I'm too lazy to do the research for other forms of fiction (it's easier and more fun to create a new world than to check out the details of Victorian England or even contemporary Washington).

Or, as Jane Palmer puts it:

> Using fantasy or sf elements takes away the necessity to prove details that are historical, geographical, political etc, which mainstream fiction must deal with. The term fiction can often be a contradiction because to be accepted as such it will, to some extent, have to deal with facts the reader can verify. The obvious benefit of the sf and fantasy categories is the way they can liberate the reader from those constraints without making the work any less valid.

It's a theme that cropped up constantly in the replies to the questionnaire. Brian Stableford calls it: "an intense and enduring interest in the utility and aesthetics of imaginative creations." David V Barrett feels that "It allows me to view reality, and my place in and reaction to reality, from a different perspective. It is one of the few mediums remaining which allow the artist to be subversive." And indeed it is this subversion, this feeling of breaking the rules, that appeals to James Corley:

> Principally I think because it lets you break the rules. There's a freedom in it you can't have with other kinds of writing. If I couldn't be a rock musician I always wanted to be an sf writer. Environment played a part, I took a psychology degree under a professor who'd known Aldous Huxley and still believed in the psychedelic exploration of consciousness (this was just before they tightened up the law on hallucinogens). Also the first Moon landing was on my 21st birthday, it seemed very profound. What else would I want to write besides speculative fiction?

We can't escape it, whatever else may prompt the writing of sf, it seems to have its foundations deep within early life.

And there were others who commented on the freedom that comes with sf. Graham Dunstan Martin had clearly thought the matter through carefully:

> Because (a) my starting point is usually "What if ...?" This is what turns my imagination on; and, importantly, my desire to write (since a strong driving impulse is needed to sustain one through a full-length novel).
>
> (b) I suspect that the world is not really quite the way it appears to be, so that – ironically – "realism" falsifies the nature of reality.
>
> (c) Sf is a wonderful vehicle for ideas. Both fantasy and sf are the modern crystal ball, through which we see into the dark places of our mind, or even

> scry the future. Jung was right to suggest that our nightmares should be made conscious, lest they happen in the real world, as fate.
>
> (I should like to add to this last comment that one of the most irritating things about some mainstream critics and writers is their strange prejudice that thinking is out of place in a novel "because it drives out feeling.")

Simon Ounsley is another:

> To be honest, when I first started writing I had very little experience of life and I've always been a lot more interested in writing than researching so, for these rather negative reasons, I was drawn to sf and fantasy. But it does seem to be natural for me. I recently wrote a story which was based to a great extent on an incident in my own life and even here I introduced a strong fantastic element. I was recently reading Brian Stableford's *The Way to Write Science Fiction* and I was surprised at how different my motivations are from his. He is interested in extrapolating known facts to create viable futures whereas I have no interest in that sort of thing at all (as a writer, not as an editor) For that reason, I think I'm inherently a writer of fantasy rather than sf (even when I'm writing work which would be identified as sf). I'm interested in writing about the condition of human beings and I find that the best way to do that is to use some element of fantasy to bring a new perspective to bear on that condition. Whether that element appears to be "sf" or "fantasy" is really irrelevant to me.

And Diana Wynne Jones says something much the same:

> I chose to write science fiction or fantasy because in writing either or both of those the main point is to tell a story. This I regard as my main objective, but I also find that I can use the fantasy/science fiction element as a kind of metaphor with which to say a great deal about human beings or the society in which we live. Though I would hate to regard any of my books as having anything so dreary as a "message."

Interestingly, Diana Wynne Jones was the only one of the respondents (other than Neil Gaiman) to say anything about telling a story. But quite a number picked up on the usefulness of science fiction to get across a message, whether or not it is within quotation marks. Iain Banks for one:

> I love it. I grew up with it, and I still think, even more certainly after 85-86 – an sf year if ever there was one: AIDS, Chernobyl, Challenger – that it's the only literature remotely capable of dealing with the *present* properly, let alone the future.

It was, I believe, JG Ballard who first said that science fiction was the only literature capable of talking about today. It may be what lies behind John Clute's enigmatic response: "No knack for conceiving of the world as not ending." Someone else who shares Ballard's feeling is Christina Lake, who also brings us back to Ian McDonald's comment about the opportunity sf offers to new writers.

> Partly because of the support group – the sf community provided the Orbiter groups, workshops, etc, that I became involved with. On the other hand, that was only because of a pre-existing interest in science fiction (kindled now I think of it by plunging into writing a sub-*Blakes Seven*-type soap opera). Originally, I guess, I was attracted by the possibilities for grand drama, of putting characters in situations which would be impossible in modern day realistic novels – and letting them face choices and contemporary problems in a setting that gives them more significance. More and more though it's coming to seem that you can't write the world we live in without some recourse at least to a science fiction mentality because so much we live through nowadays is seriously bizarre.

There were several writers who looked back to the time they were starting out when answering this question. For Kenneth Bulmer: "It's the way I got started"); for Josephine Saxton: "30 years ago it seemed a good idea"; and for Barrington Bayley: "I wouldn't have become a writer otherwise. Can't write anything else." Of course, once you become known as an sf writer, that's how you're constantly regarded. It's what Christopher Priest and Josephine Saxton were fighting against in Chapter One, and that subject crops up again here. Gwyneth Jones harks back to her two-part response to the last question:

> a) Historical accident. If I had had a mainstream novel published early in my career I'd probably be writing mainstream novels now – which might be set in the future and deal with scientific topics.
>
> b) A feeling about the proper place of the artist in society. The relationship between readers and writers in sf appeals to me – maybe more than anything else about the genre.

Not, of course, that being typecast as one sort of writer is necessarily a bad thing. Douglas Hill reports that a little publishing encouragement was helpful in starting to write in the genre:

> Because I've been an addict for 40 years, and a professional writer for twenty-four. Because it seemed a natural step; and a publisher or two encouraged me to take it, ten years ago.

Garry Kilworth also says that he writes what he used to read, but his response takes us down yet another path:

> I began writing the sort of fiction that I like to read and from there a development took place which led me to the kind of fiction I write today. I do not consciously sit down to write within any kind of category. I get an idea, or rather series of ideas, and allow the fiction to shape itself.

Judging from the response a lot of writers are led by their fiction. If the story turns out to be science fiction, then that is what they are writing, but they are not deliberately (or possibly even consciously) working within the boundaries of the genre. Picking up on the phrasing of the question, a typical response came from John Brosnan: "Choice doesn't come into it." Alex Stewart echoes this: "I haven't. I write what interests me, and that just happens to be what most people identify as sf, fantasy or horror." As Stephen Gallagher puts it: "Who chooses? I write the stuff I enjoy writing, tell the stories I want to tell, and let the genre demarcation ilnes fall where they may." And Lisa Tuttle also lets the demarcation lines be decided after the story is written:

> One answer is that I didn't choose – I write what I write, and it then gets identified and marketed as science fiction or fantasy ... and if it can't be so identified, I find it harder to sell. The other answer is that when I was a teenager writing stories and sending them out the positive responses came from science fiction editors. *The New Yorker*, *Mademoiselle*, et al, returned my stories – unsurprisingly – with printed rejection slips. Harlan Ellison, Ed Ferman, Damon Knight, Ted White, Charles Platt also sent my stories back, but included some encouraging words. So I concentrated on the likelier-seeming markets and was soon successful.

Again we get back to it being easier for writers to start in sf.

But there's still the matter of not choosing what you write. Robert Irwin has an elegant way of putting it: "There is a case for claiming that fantasy chose me to write it – a great deal comes unbidden from dreams and reverie." David Langford is somewhat cruder: "It's not a matter of choice: what comes out happens fairly frequently to be sf if it's fiction at all. ('Why have you chosen to produce turds?')"

For some, the reason they have no choice goes back to how things started in this chapter with the influence of early reading. David Redd, for instance: "I didn't choose to write sf – it chose me. Before I was ten I'd started reading sf, scribbling little schoolboy stories in little schoolboy notebooks." Or Paul J McAuley: "It chose me, worming its way into my nervous system via early exposure to John Christopher, HG Wells (a cheap complete edition in the school library with dingy dark green covers and microscopic print), John Wyndham, Asimov, Clarke ..."

For others it is tied in with the freedom afforded by science fiction. Kim Newman, for example:

> On one level, I'm not so sure I have a choice – the subjects that interest me, the ideas I have, can only be expressed in these ways. On another – from my critical background – Im interested in notions of genre, and find it stimulating to play about with them. I've recently written a hard science fiction ghost story ("Twitch Technicolor"), for instance.

While still others admit that it's all too complex to allow of a simple answer. Mary Gentle, for instance:

> This varies from *because I like reading them* to *some of the best world literature is fantastic* to *what makes you think I* had *a choice*? depending on what quarter the wind's in, and who's asking. The short answer is John Webster.

There were other responses. Lee Montgomerie said that she was "too alienated from real life to write straight fiction." John Christopher pondered the question and decided: "I don't know. Partly for the bread, partly, obviously, because I have an affinity for it." But the simplest answer of all came from Alasdair Gray: "Because I enjoy doing so."

# 2009

As twenty years ago, so today, it seems. After reading through Paul Kincaid's analysis of the Mexicon survey responses to this question, Peadar O'Guilin's answer to this iteration sounded familiar –

> It chose me. I doubt if this answer will turn out to be unique. So many of us read the good stuff at such an impressionable age, that we had no choice in what we eventually became.

– and proved to be prophetic. The impressionable age wasn't quite as dominant this time around as it seems to have been last time, being cited by about a third of respondents; but that absence of choice was cited by another third, and the two were linked quite frequently. A number of writers found that, as for Ian Watson and James Lovegrove in the last chapter, the material can have a mind of its own. Jon Courtenay Grimwood, for instance:

> It's what everything I write turns into, even when I start out writing something else. *neoAddix* was meant to be a straight crime novel that ended up in a

> 22nd century French empire, with hovercraft. *Pashazade* started out straight alternative history and germ line manipulation forced its way in there anyway. I think it's a sensibility, combined with a mindset, I like collecting facts and shuffling odd narrative shapes together in my head to see what comes from the random patterns.

Mike Carey *can* write realistic fiction, but to start with found that it went against the grain:

> It's what I read for pleasure, most of the time, and it's where my mind naturally goes when I think about possible stories and projects. To me, writing in an entirely realist mode is actually very hard. I've done it twice – both times in YA books – and I think I made a reasonable fist of it, but it felt strange at first.

Tony Ballantyne similarly acknowledges that when he says he "didn't choose" to write sf, what he means is that it's as much the way he thinks as anything else, and he's just going with the flow:

> I didn't choose to write sf, it chose me. It's the extrapolation thing: there is something in my nature that looks at a dragon, a ray gun or a love affair and thinks "Now how or why would that work?" (and if the answer is it wouldn't, I write a story about something else.)

Reading through the Mexicon survey's responses to this question, the other thing that struck me were responses like Ian McDonald's, that "More and more though it's coming to seem that you can't write the world we live in without some recourse at least to a science fiction mentality because so much we live through nowadays is seriously bizarre." In part this struck me because although it's a common enough argument – that the present moment somehow uniquely *demands* science fiction as a response – only one person made it, this time around. (Colin Harvey: "Nothing apart from fantasy and sf really interests me enough to write about it ... that's probably because to a large extent we're living sf – certainly as viewed from, say, 1959. Mobile phones, laptops, genetic modifications to crops, holes in the ozone layer, pandemics – and we're probably only a few years from the beginning of the end of cheap oil.") And in part it struck me because it made clear how naive it can seem, singularity or no, once the present moment has passed. There is, of course, a more nuanced version of the argument to be put forward, as Nina Allan made clear:

> I can't ever imagine not writing it, watching it, reading it, thinking about it. It has always struck me as peculiar and a little arrogant that so many "mainstreamers" – both writers and readers – dismiss sf as "unrealistic" or "impossible." Today's sf has always been tomorrow's reality. If you were to

> take a Victorian scientist along to PC World he'd think he'd travelled forward a thousand years instead of a mere hundred or so. We have only been here a short time and have barely scratched the surface of our universe. It seems to me that sf has more to say about the world we live in than any other kind of literature, both in terms of what goes on inside our heads and what might go on out among the stars. Sf is not just the true literature of the twentieth century but of every century.

That is: *every* present moment demands sf as a response. This is not quite the same as JG Ballard's notion that sf is always *about* the present, I think. Rather, it seems to me now, that it's something approaching a definition of a science fiction *writer*, rather than science fiction itself, to say that they approach the world in a certain way, in possession of certain habits of thought, such that the nature of the stories that occur as a response to their experience bend in a certain direction – leaving apparently no choice in the matter.

Something similar should be true for fantasy. Juliet McKenna suggests that it might be, that she fits fantasy particularly well because she thinks about certain subjects, when she says, "I'm a historian by inclination and education. My love of that subject is only rivalled by my love of literature, from the classics to contemporary popular fiction. That combination makes fantasy the ideal genre for me." And Kari Sperring is direct:

> It's how my mind works. I don't think I've ever seriously considered any other kind of fiction writing. As a professional historian, I find the idea of writing historical fiction to be far too much like work (and probably unengaging). A fantastical setting allows exploration of the things that interest me – swashbuckling, ghosts, permeable realities – I can't imagine writing elves, dragons or vampires, though – steampunk is more appealing, if I were to expand within the genre categories.

Where these habits of thought come from: well, there, of course, we're back into youthful indoctrination – and again, this seems to be as true for the fantasy writers as for the sf writers. Joe Abercrombie "was a huge fan of fantasy as a kid, and had always dreamed of writing my take on the classic fantasy trilogy," while Paul McAuley "stumbled over science fiction at a very young and impressionable age. I've been trying to recapture the feeling I had then ever since." Katherine Roberts cites an experience that is no doubt familiar to many in the UK who are of a certain age:

> I think it chose me! Most of my reading as a teenager was in the fantasy/SF genre. I used to look for the Gollancz yellow spines when I graduated to the adult library, because they had the best stories. Then I read *The Lord of the Rings* about ten times and I was hooked! I read a greater variety of books now, but

> I always return to sf/fantasy for a good story that stretches the imagination. Myths and legends also inspire my work, particularly where ancient history overlaps with these.

Similarly, Toby Litt:

> Science fiction and fantasy novels were what got me reading in the first place. I was a devoted TV watched until won over by *Dune*, *Lord of the Rings*, *The Glass Bead Game* and *Splinter of the Mind's Eye*. For a long while I found any other kind of fiction boring. And while I changed my mind about non-fantasy fiction, I still tend towards books that give me the world plus something else.

Paul Cornell recalled the moment of discovery:

> I think it was chosen for me at the moment I opened a crate in my parents' loft, and found my older brother's books, which included runs of *Galaxy* and *Worlds of If*, *Eagle* Annuals and the sf of Captain WE Johns. And when I felt that I had to be brave enough to watch *Doctor Who*, something that led between the playground, the social world, and that very solitary experience of reading books that even smelt different to everyone else's books.

While Tanith Lee evoked the sense of enticement and compulsion most romantically:

> As with all the other genres I work in, they seemed to choose *me*. They just opened their doors and lured me in. For me a wonderful experience, which it still is. In the case of sf, the impulse probably began because I read such a lot of sf when young – my eclectically well-read mother was also a most intelligent and discerning fan of the genre. Our flats/rooms were less full of furniture than of books, including mountains of early US sf magazines, and paperbacks of Ray Bradbury and Theodore Sturgeon, and many other geniuses. With such wonderful giants in the water, how could one resist trying to swim?

NM Browne, Peter Dickinson, Ramsey Campbell and Deborah Miller, among others, expressed similar sentiments. As Stephen Gallagher said, "When you start writing, you imitate what you love." You have to feel a little for Chaz Brenchley, though, illustrating just how inhibiting love can be: "For the longest time, I didn't. I wrote everything but fantasy and sf. I was scared of sf, I think, because I lacked the scientific background that seemed to be essential in the '80s; I held back from fantasy because I didn't want to be yet another Tolkien clone. It was twenty years before I had an idea I thought original enough to be worth pursuing."

Brian Stableford put it more cynically – "I was young and stupid when I started, and knew no better; it's far too late to do anything about it now that it's turned into an obsessive/compulsive disorder" – but in doing so was not alone. Several writers noted the ways in which market realities, or even simple chance, intersected with their ultimate careers. Michael Moorcock pointed to the importance of an editor being in sympathy with a writer's work:

> It was easy for me to do. If [John] Carnell hadn't asked me to write for him, I probably would have written for some other editor doing totally different work ... And if Carnell hadn't recommended me as editor of *New Worlds* I would have edited anything from political magazines to books.

Which makes me recall responses like Lisa Tuttle's from 1989; is it only that *The New Yorker* is objectively harder to break into, or is it partly that the editor of *The New Yorker* may be in sympathy with different kinds of writing?

Andrew Crumey replied that "I have chosen only to write novels that interest me. The choice of genre is one made by readers, and they are entitled to it"; M. John Harrison went further, saying

> You should ask why (or if) I chose f/sf as the apparent medium for a given book. Even then, the answer might seem blunt. *The Course of the Heart*, for instance, is not a fantasy novel. It's The *Course of the Heart*. *In Viriconium* is not a "dying Earth" novel. It's *In Viriconium*.

Liz Jensen's response to why she's chosen to write sf or fantasy was just as blunt: "I haven't." Nick Harkaway felt similarly – "Well, I didn't. I chose to write the story. That came first. Everything else followed" – as did Patrick Ness, though he noted, "I'd never take anything off the palette. [But] it has to be, for me, all about the story, and not being a snob (either way) about what fits the story best." Will Ashon's way of putting this, after noting that he himself just writes, was pragmatic: "Not going to bite the hand that feeds, though."

Adrian Tchaikovsky identified himself as a genre reader, but was also clear-eyed about his career prospects: "It's what I like, what I tend to read myself and, frankly, what I can write." Once again: is the suggestion here that sf or fantasy is easier to write (and sell), or that it's easier *for him* to write? Similarly, Tim Lees was another of those who reported that it isn't a choice, but cited external forces, of the sort that Chaz Brenchley commented on in the previous chapter, as much as any personal appreciation of the form:

> I didn't make the choice. When I was starting out, I sent stories to all kinds of magazines. I got the best response from the sf mags, so I concentrated on that area. Now I've published a fair amount of short fiction in the field, but the few novels I've written (all non-sf) I can't get anyone to look at. So I think my path

> is being decided for me. It may also be, of course, that whatever my personal tastes and ambitions, f/sf is the thing I do well. Editors may have recognised this long before I did.
>
> I think we sometimes imagine writers as fiercely independent creators, unfettered by commercial pressures, doing whatever comes into their heads. In reality, a writer's career is more like an actor's. He probably starts out with a game plan ("I'll play romantic leads, get established, then do a really serious movie to show I can act, then do a stint at directing ..."), but in reality, he goes where the work is. This can be frustrating, but it's not wholly a bad thing: it pushes you into areas you never imagined yourself going, and reveals strengths you never knew you had. (Or let's hope so, anyway...)

Mark Charan Newton, on the other hand, made the decision before editors had a chance to, and is perhaps closer to Tchaikovsky's position:

> I don't feel that I'd have much to offer – or indeed many writers can offer these days – to the realms of mainstream fiction. What is left to cover that hasn't been covered well enough already, by some remarkably talented people?
>
> But I've not just chosen the ugly girl of fiction! First and foremost, I adore the genre. I have done for years, and have never lost the power of imagination, or a sense of what fantasy can offer. Fantasy is liberating in the way that you can do absolutely anything you want; you're not restricted by conventional rules. However, it is also a challenge in the sense that a fantasy writer (in a secondary world) is cut off from casual and obvious cultural references in language and plot. That challenge makes the writing process extremely interesting – and fun.

Fun, for many of the writers surveyed, now as twenty years ago, seems to inhere most often in the freedom that science fiction and fantasy offer, particularly for those who *do* feel that they've made some kind of choice to write these types of fiction. Iain Banks said simply, "It lets my imagination extend itself," and Neil Williamson that "I have what they used to call a 'vivid imagination', and writing speculative or fantastical stories allows me to exercise that. And, well, it's fun." Ian Whates elaborated:

> I could write an essay on this question alone. Principally, because fantasy and, in particular, science fiction, excite me; both to read and to write. I've described science fiction in a past interview as the literature of potential and that really sums it up for me. Within genre fiction, imagination can run wild to produce joyous, fantastical excess, but it can also be controlled and focussed to suggest something chillingly plausible. Strands can be teased from the fabric of current society or latest scientific theory, isolated, taken forward a few years or decades or centuries, often expanded to an extreme, then rewoven with

> other elements to create a tomorrow which might be oddly out of kilter yet uncomfortably familiar, or completely whacky and out there. Against such backgrounds you introduce characters and watch them cope, interact and develop as your plot unfolds. What could be more fun than that?

Bob Lock, too, said that he's "chosen to write sf/fantasy because of the huge scope that those two genres offer. Each can be moulded to any type of story you want ... The choice is infinite, only your imagination governs your voyage"; or as Jaine Fenn put it, "It's fiction without frontiers." And Charles Stross came at the same point from the opposite direction: "You can draw these categories as a Venn diagram of concentric circles; mainstream *non*-sf/f is the narrowest, most tightly circumscribed circle on the dart-board. And I'm just not terribly interested in minute detail; I'd rather look at a bigger picture." Adam Roberts feels

> Caught between answering this question autobiographically (saying: ever since I could first read I have read and loved sf and fantasy, and it has never really occurred to me that there is anything else worth writing) and answering it instrumentally (saying: sff is the mode of literature that allows us the greatest imaginative, metaphor and intellectual latitude, and these are the qualities in which I am most interested as a writer) I discover I cannot choose one over the other.

Or as Chris Beckett puts it, perhaps: "Fiction is about making things up. Why not make up the world as well as the characters? It's more fun." For Al Robertson it's the most sensible course ("To some extent, I see all fiction as fantasy; it's ink on paper, pretending to be worlds ... Thus, I've never seen the point of restraining its possibilities by limiting its content to 'things that could happen' or 'things that have happened'"), while Justina Robson gets bored with anything else, as does China Mieville: "I don't tend to sustain interest in writing things without impossibilities, the fantastic, monstrous, weird, what-have-you, within them."

For Kit Whitfield, on the other hand, the freeing pleasure of sf and fantasy has two aspects (one of which recalls the "habits of thought" argument I was pushing earlier), and is in part down to the fact that these genres are not *just* about fun:

> I like writing about imaginative scenarios for two reasons. One, the world itself is a magical and numinous place; we get used to it, but when we really stop and look, reality is extraordinary. Writing an imaginary situation allows me to caricature the extraordinariness of reality, to create that stop-and-look effect by presenting a world that's as new and strange to the reader as reality can be to all of us when we see it with fresh eyes. Two, it makes it easier for me to be a bad girl. If I steer too close to literal reality I start getting conscientiously worried about whether I'm portraying it accurately. If I'm portraying stuff I

> just made up, that gets me off the hook: I can write whatever I darn well please. It's disinhibiting. Writing non-realistic scenarios gives me a more direct line to my subconscious, and that's where the fire is. On the other hand, if I get an idea for a non-science fiction or fantasy story, I'll happily write that, too. I just go with whatever ideas seem likely to come out best.

More didactically, perhaps, for Stan Nicholls that seeing-it-fresh can be part of a more-or-less conscious agenda:

> It's a lot to do with the fact that I've loved these categories of fiction since I was a kid, and the passion hasn't really gone away. I've travelled the classic fan to professional route, I suppose. But that aside, I genuinely believe imaginative literature is a wonderfully flexible vehicle. It's a great platform for straightforward, page-turning storytelling, but it's also capable of bearing weightier concerns. Social commentary's something sf's been doing since the year dot, of course, but fantasy's growing maturity means it's taking on that mantle too. I've always admired Iain Banks' assertion that science fiction belongs in the gutter, in the sense that unregarded forms of literature can get away with more. Much as we'd like to see our genres given the respect they're due, there's something to be said for being under the radar of the literary establishment. That's part of the fun of it.

The potential of science fiction to be more than "just" a story in several other areas was also mentioned, for example by Paul McAuley – "I'm extremely keen on science, and science fiction has a good tool set for embodying wild speculations that take off from bleeding edge science" – and Martin Sketchley – "Science fiction offers the writer the ability to examine, confront and discuss the world humans have created by proposing alternatives and/or potential outcomes, as well as the direction of the human race based on current conditions." (Although Vaughan Stanger noted that "I chose to write sf because I wanted to fuse my fascination with science and technology with a love of, and deep concern for, people. Too much sf focuses mainly on the former. I wanted to write something more balanced.") Less specifically, Gary Gibson replied that he tried to explore "What some European critic called 'cognitive estrangement'. I was always drawn towards weird stuff," a sentiment echoed by Conrad Williams: "I'm attracted to the weird and the dark and the atmospheric. I love monsters. I love planting characters in strange, desperate situations. I guess I find realistic fiction boring. We live the banal every day. Let's have some odd." Chris Butler would find sympathy with that position: "Normal life can be experienced by living it, but sf and fantasy worlds are only available to us through fiction."

For Paul Barnett, this time around, deeper study of the potential fantasy seems to have led nearly out the other side again:

> A long time ago, in my teens, I wanted to be an sf writer: I thought they were all gods, and I wanted to be like them. A long while later, after I'd published a few stories, I got the opportunity to write some high-fantasy tie-ins. Near enough to sf, I thought, buckling down. But as a result of writing those, and of working on the first *Encyclopedia of SF* and of course the *Encyclopedia of Fantasy*, I became really interested in what fantasy could *do* – so sf kind of got edged out. I'm still experimenting with the potential of fantasy (although at the far extreme from high fantasy!), which is why these days I tend to think of my fiction more as mainstream work that's using tools from fantasy.

Although you suspect that Barnett is something of an exception, and that for many writers it's as straightforward as it is for Ken MacLeod, for whom the reason for writing sf was simply: "Because so far I don't have any ideas for anything else!"

# Chapter 4:
## *Do you consider there is anything distinctively British about your work, and if so what is it?*

# 1989

This is where we come to the meat of the survey. British science fiction has a reputation for being gloomy, doom-laden. The truth, or otherwise, of that should emerge during the course of this chapter; but such an attitude does suggest that British science fiction is seen as being in some way different from American science fiction. Since the intent of this survey was to discover what that difference is, it was a logical first step to ask writers their opinion.

The long response from Colin Greenland – above and beyond the call, if anything is – amounts to a short essay on the distinguishing characteristics of British sf and fantasy, and would be, on its own, enough to justify this whole exercise.

> Yes, its idiosyncracy. I write by stirring together odds and ends from here and there, from music, from manners, from memory. I present this mixture as if it were coherent. With luck, time and effort, some of it sometimes is. The key to its in/coherence is me, not any generic formula, fashionable model or prevailing myth.
>
> Whether this idiosyncracy is specifically British or generally European I don't know. I can only talk about America and Britain. Contemporary British fantasies do seem to have little in common. I think this is to do with space. America is very big. South and west of New England, people are very spread out. They need to affirm their similarities to find any sense of community. Britain is very small and comparatively crowded. People need to affirm their differences to secure a private identity. Fantasists in America invent groups to belong to. Fantasists in Britain don't. This theory begins to crumble quite quickly if you look at it too hard.
>
> 2nd try, later:

I sometimes have a notion that there are two traditions of fantasy in English: the canonical one that goes Spenser – Malory – Tennyson – Tolkien and all stations west including most of America; and another one that for ages is just an aspect of the national literature, of Shakespeare and Bunyan and Swift and Dickens, and doesn't really emerge until (?) Carroll. Then it goes TH White and Mervyn Peake – Moorcock – Harrison – me.

The first tradition is about ideals; the second about verities. The first lot would like to replace the world. They yearn upwards towards nobility and justification. The second lot seize upon the world, are flabbergasted by the world, give the world a good talking-to, tease the world about its follies. Hence, tales of moral commentary in which ordinary, everyday people and bizarre, signifying grotesques mingle freely, or rather, inextricably. Here the 2nd tradition starts to resonate with the work of people like Angela Carter or Alasdair Grey, who are out of somewhere else altogether, and with South American magical realism as British readers interpret it. But it doesn't accord very well with the map of genre fiction, with its organised clusters of conventions and formulae. (Moorcock's *The Golden Barge*, *Gloriana* and Corneliana are different *kinds* of book from his genre sword-and-sorceries.) Tradition 1, on the other hand, was made generic very easily, because it is hierarchical, conservative, and, like all genres, fundamentally consolatory.

And, I was going to say, America is where contemporary sf and fantasy were both industrialised, codified into genres out of idiosyncratic European originals (Verne and Wells; Morris and Tolkien) ... and nobody can yearn towards nobility like an American ... but when I look for other current exponents of the 2nd tradition, I think of Jim Blaylock and Richard Grant, and, more decorously and obliquely, John Crowley, rather than Brits. So the distinction holds even if reality is out of step. That is, I mean, um.

Blast.

3rd attempt, a couple of weeks later:

I think what's distinctively British about my work is its matrix: the context out of which it comes, my reading, my society, my upbringing, my experiences, my language; my sense of what things mean what, and of what stories there are to tell. (More about this in answer to question 5.) Maybe this is tautological. But all my books have a theme of disgust with imperial assumptions – *Thin Ox* and *Other Voices* obviously, and *Daybreak* is the story of a glorious culture decaying in isolation until it discovers that there's a world out there which has been carrying on regardless. And I have a recurrent image which I suspect is more than personal: a solitary character wandering round a big old deserted building, looking for something or someone that might make sense of themselves.

The Britishness of all this is the assumption that value is inherited, is defined by the past, and has to be redefined. In America, what confers value is the future – even now, especially now, that the future is Japanese, or Korean, or

> whatever it is this year. In Britain, the nearest source of value is the lost empire. Perhaps what Americans (and Charles Platt) identify as downbeat, unaspiring, depressive in British fantastic fiction is actually the axiomatic cultural matrix, the dead empire; showing through whatever wallpaper we put up.
>
> They'll get there soon enough.

There are many points worth bringing out from that, most of which will be raised by other respondents. It is worth remembering at all times that, whether a writer is British, American, Japanese or whatever, each is independent, an individual, and the key to their work lies, primarily, in them. So, any British influences we discover in writers is separate from, and usually inferior to, whatever individual qualities the writer himself brings to his work.

Moreover, Greenland raises a question that others will raise: is the influence British, or European? It's a question that probably will not be answered without a far more intensive examination of the variety of influence that work on any author.

His identification of two traditions is something that others have noted, though his analysis provides a clear perspective on them. He applies it only to fantasy, but I feel that something similar holds true for science fiction. Though there are always exceptions to any rule, it seems that in this country science fiction has grown from the second, the literary tradition, by way of the scientific romance which, as its name implies, is an altogether less hard-edged form of the genre.

At the same time, Britishness comes from far more than a literary background. There are in fact a complex web of influences that affect any writer, cultural, social, linguistic – each of which will be picked up, to varying degrees, by other respondents. In Britain one of the prime cultural experiences seems to have been loss of empire, which provides a tone to British writing which crops up in an astounding variety of writers, and which is often sublimated in a personal image of loss, alienation, lack of meaning. Again we will see numerous references to this in what follows.

Perhaps this loss of empire is why Britain seeks value in the past, while America seeks it in the future. Hence American sf tends to the celebratory, optimistic, forward-reaching, sf adventure where the brave can grasp success. In Britain, on the contrary, sf tends to the elegiac, pessimistic search among the ruins of a past glory. Perhaps.

But as we seek out these traits and trends it is worth remembering that the writers themselves may be the last people able to provide a clear and certain analysis of the influences that shape their work. As Diana Wynne Jones says:

> Yes, I regard my work as entirely British not so much in vocabulary as in outlook. But this is very hard to pin down and I hope you get some definite answers from other British writers. It is almost an inborn way of looking at things.

"Not so much in vocabulary," she says, but in fact the language is one of the key instruments of British culture, one of the chief tools for shaping our thoughts and outlooks. When George Bernard Shaw described the British and Americans as two peoples separated by a common language, he was only pointing out that the culture shaped by the language has followed different paths in the two countries. Some respondents did indeed refer to the importance of language, from Josephine Saxton's laconic "Grammar, spelling," to Alasdair Gray's: "My British experiences, of which the language is a very great part."

What is important, of course, is the way the language is used, as Brian Stableford points out:

> Insofar as I am a product of British culture, so is my work; the principal manifestations of which I am aware are a frequent tendency to calculated understatement and an occasional tendency to heavy irony, both of which are more easily apprehended and appreciated by a British audience than an American one.

Is this simply a matter of taste? Irony and understatement are among the tools we use to spin a tale, capture atmosphere, and express humour. It may simply be that these things don't travel. Certainly Paul Barnett seems to suggest that another characteristic use of language, humour, does not have the same effect overseas as it does in Britain:

> The only distinctively "British" aspect of my work (so far as I know) is the sense of humour, which has made it difficult to sell in the US (although Holland and Germany seem OK). Curiously, my most widely distributed book in the US has been praised by reviewers, publishers and experts alike for its sense of humour. I can't explain why this should be.

Another parenthetical suggestion that we may be talking about a European rather than a British characteristics. But more of that later. Ian McDonald is another who lays great emphasis on the language:

> "Anything distinctively British"; hmm. Despite being born in Manchester, I would consider myself to be an Irish writer as much as (or, if it suits me, more so) than a British one; primarily because there are so few indigenous sf writers it's easier to be a big fish in a small pond. Pure arrogance, I know. So, pardon me if I substitute the word "Irish" for "British," and reply that, in the tradition of other Irish writers outside the genre, I enjoy verbal playfulness, I like to push the language around and bully it into strange and unnatural acts to say what want it to. This, I think, is my beef with the cyberpunks, for all their veneration of William Burroughs and Thomas Pynchon, the best their actual writing style achieves is a poor imitation of Ryamond Chandler. Where's the

> fractured imagery, the verbal inventiveness, the stylistic unconventionality? I enjoy playing around with style and format, tense changes, second person narration, embedded stories within stories, and, particularly in the longer fiction, where I have more room for expression, burying allusions and clues and stylistic parodies of other writers. I hope ...
>
> As a British writer, I try to identify with the British sf tradition of literary respectability. In some respects, this has been a burden, in others it gives British sf some value outside the genre (though the mainstream tries vehemently to deny this). To a greater extent than in America, British writers have made the successful crossing of the genre divide, Garry Kilworth, Chris Priest, Brian Aldiss, Keith Roberts, they are less tightly constricted by the limits of the genre.

Reference to Burroughs and Pynchon, of course, and thoughts of Alfred Bester, Steve Erickson and others, is sufficient reminder that linguistic playfulness is not the exclusive preserve of James Joyce and his heirs. But still, language does seem to be important.

And McDonald returns us to another of Greenland's points, the literary heritage. A direction also taken, from a different angle, by Mary Gentle:

> Yes for *A Hawk in Silver*, this having a British background in all respects. But heavily into Celtic myths of many varieties. Yes in *Golden Witchbreed* and *Ancient Light*. Both heavily American-influenced, but: GWB is structured around the experience of empire, drawn mostly from British experience (but used to comment on other present-day empires), ditto AL, the latter also being Jacobean sf; if that isn't English, I don't know what is ...

Ah, yes, Celtic myth (the Matter of Britain?) and Jacobean tragedy; but end of empire comes into it again, and a timely reminder that anyone writing sf today is bound to be heavily influenced by the American form of the genre. Still, even in what Greenland suggests is a very British form of fantasy, the literary tradition, there is no need to be British influenced, as Robert Irwin points out: "I don't think there is much that is particularly British about my writing. Sterne and Peake may have been influences, but they are heavily outnumbered by foreign writers."

It is worth, therefore, turning to the suggestion that we are really talking about a European rather than a British tradition. Gwyneth Jones takes that view:

> I write as someone brought up in a small, sophisticated, old country; and as someone brought up in Utopia and forced to watch as Utopia is dismantled by time, chance and human villainy. I also write as someone conversant with a tradition of scientific romance and idealist fantasy which is perhaps distinctively European rather than distinctively British. Maybe European would be a better word for what you're asking here.

As does Garry Kilworth:

> There appears to be something distinctly *European* about my work, since I sell extremely well in places like Italy, Germany and France, and very badly in the States. It's possibly a stylistic difference, coupled with a reluctance to go for the kind of optimism expected by American publishers. I'm not even sure their readers agree.

And from Brian Aldiss:

> I try to see the world as it is, in all its grim array. I try to depict the nature of personal relationships. I espouse the view of the underdog – or, to put it another way, I am a socialist with a small "s." I do not let false hopes intrude in my view of human life. I do not peddle fake optimism. I am a follower of Wells and Stapledon. All of these qualities may be regarded as English if contrasted with the more meretricious American sf; but they are, of course, traditionally European qualities, and not European alone.

All of which qualities also define exactly the view of British sf expressed by Charles Platt and others (and one wonders, incidentally, if espousing the underdog comes with experiencing the role of underdog, for instance by losing an empire?). But again and again this reference to the pessimistic viewpoint came up in the responses, as from Christina Lake: "A slight tendency towards pessimism – no glorious futures for mankind, only people who don't quite manage to solve their problems. Is this British? I don't know." Or Simon Ounsley:

> My stories tend to have unhappy or unresolved endings. That just usually seems the most realistic way to leave things. If I try to stick a happy ending on them it feels like a cop-out. Is this distinctively British or have I paid too much attention to Charles Platt and George Scithers? Isn't there a danger that this question may simply endorse existing fallacies?

The common ground – other than an uncertainty about their own defining characteristics – is the quest for believability, the determination that a twist of happy fortune is generally unacceptable in a story because it fails to chine with most people's experience. There's more of the same from Iain Banks:

> I guess the down-beat nature of some of the stories – especially their endings – and the equivocal nature of the moral grammar informing them – makes them more distinctively British (or maybe European) than the seeking for grand effect (the Wide Screen Baroque – thank you, Mr Aldiss, sir – approach) makes them obviously US influenced. Also, and thankfully, you get a different

> perspective on what being British means when you come from Scotland.

Oh what a pregnant phrase: "equivocal ... moral grammar," yet one more succinct summing up of the nature of British science fiction. The American form, at least in the celebratory, optimistic manner, tends to have a simple moral stance. Good succeeds over bad, right over wrong, right over left. It is a black and white generalisation but holds true of a surprising number of works. British sf, however, springs from a more sophisticated, complex world where shades are grey not black and white, where seeing both sides of the argument is honoured as a tenet of Old World liberalism and moral arguments therefore have to be more equivocal. And as writers strive for truth, or at least some form of realism, that is what comes out in their protagonists. James White, for instance:

> I have been told that my writing style is British, possibly because my principal characters are more unsure of themselves than any self-respecting sf hero should be, and the problems he, she or it faces are never solved easily; but the answer to that one is I don't know.

David Langford is another:

> After the spelling, a general gloomy lack of conviction that (as in much *echt* sf of today) libertarian survivalist loners equipped with unfailing bloodlust and nuclear handguns are really the people of the future.

In other words, there often seems to be a political dimension to this defining characteristic, a dimension that David V Barrett makes clear in his answer: "Mood, character, mythic qualities, sense of place, general lack of technophilic emphasis, politically subversive (or at least *open*) as opposed to right wing." But behind the politics lie an awful lot of other things, like mood and tone, as Neil Gaiman says:

> I'm British, so undoubtedly it's there in my work. *Violent Cases* is a very British story – intrinsically so.
>
> I do feel that there are obvious differences in the graphic area between British and American writers (I'm thinking of writers like Alan Moore, Grant Morrison, Jamie Delano, myself and others – British writers writing American comics) – generally a willingness to take things further, to compromise less, and to try and expect more of the medium.
>
> In general terms (in and out of comics) I would hate to presume to generalise, but I suspect on the whole the British are slightly more jaded and less easy to please, which either means you get something lifeless but worthy, or it means you get something that treads new territory.

It's easy to be jaded, Britain has a long history and it weighs heavily upon us. There are all manner of experiences, perceptions and assumptions fed into us from childhood, and they are bound to come out in our writing. Elizabeth Sourbut makes this point, and is the only respondent, curiously, to mention class, supposedly that overwhelming characteristic of British fiction.

> Almost certainly, because I'm very British, but I haven't travelled widely enough to get a decent perspective on it. I think I'm strongly affected by class structures and by a feeling of having very deep roots – my own family is Anglo-Saxon and I live in York, a city with a very obvious historical heritage. Also I have an ingrained, gut feeling that Britain is the centre of the world.

We cannot escape what is ingrained within us, as Alex Stewart says:

> The way I see the world, and select the themes I feel I want to explore, are bound to be influenced by the culture I grew up in. Stylistically, I think, the most obvious thing is the way I find myself implying or alluding to things without describing them directly; a very British trait.

For Christopher Priest, his fiction is recognisably British because: "Most of it is set in Britain, has British people in it and is permeated with British assumptions." While Graham Dunstan Martin remarks:

> "Britishness" is probably felt rather than perceived, and is impossible to define, particularly by the writer himself. However, I can say that:
>
> (a) My sf work is British (and often specifically Scottish) in its settings, and hence its atmosphere.
>
> (b) But let me make another rather different point, in the context of Charles Platt's claim in *Interzone* that British sf is (by comparison with American sf) gloomy, defeatist and pessimistic. (What nonsense! Who could be more ironically pessimistic than Vonnegut?) My fiction is none of these things; it simply attempts to handle serious questions in a serious (and ironic) way. But that's not exclusively British, is it?

Again, a quest for reality comes into the picture. But, interestingly, both Priest and Martin consider the settings important. It's something we'll come on to in the next chapter, but for now several others seemed to share this feeling. John Clute, the only non-British respondent who gave a positive response to this question, said: "Yes. It's all set in Britain after the rain." John Brunner said: "I happen to be British, and it shows. I often use UK settings and characters. That's distinctive – I suppose." John Christopher also seems to feel that his nationality is sufficient to presuppose the assumptions in his work: "Well, I am British; that seems distinctive enough." While for Stephen Galagher, a novel set in a vividly realised America might be seen to count against him: "I'd like to think so, but after *Valley of Lights* I'm probably on a loser if I try to prove it."

Kim Newman makes the point that foreign cultures in which we are interested can have an equal effect upon what we write:

> I don't set out to be British, but one or two of my pieces have been rooted in contemporary or futuristic British societies. However, I did recently write a story ("Famous Monsters") set in California (where I've never been) simply because I'm interested in American culture/history etc.

But when we come down to it, "Britishness" seems to be, as Graham Dunstan Martin said, more felt than perceived. David Redd, for instance, felt "less 'British' than Cowper, more 'British' than Clarke." While Barrington Bayley replied: "Some people say so, but I'm not aware of it."

What's more, there was an emphatic "No" from Eric Brown, Kenneth Bulmer, Paul J McAuley, Lee Montgomerie, EC Tubb and Samantha Lee (who preferred "Celtic"). Non-British writers John Brosnan, Robert Farago, Leigh Kennedy and Lisa Tuttle, perhaps inevitably, did not feel British. Lisa Tuttle, considering whether there was anything distinctively British in her work, decided: "Only the post-mark."

And there were some who objected to the idea that there might be, or should be, distinctively nationalistic characteristics in a writer's work. James Corley declared: "It is possible to recognise the 'Britishness' of most UK authors but I think it's something we should struggle to rise above. I subscribe to the 'literature should be universal' school." While Douglas Hill said: "I am an expatriate Canadian. And I find insularity distasteful in sf as elsewhere. (Do I mean parochialism?) Though the Americans are its main practitioners ..."

# 2009

What difference does two decades make? That, to my mind, is the question behind the question for this chapter.

Some landmarks may be helpful. When the Mexicon survey was carried out, Britain was deep in the Thatcher years; George HW Bush had just become the forty-first President of the USA; and Eastern Europe was in turmoil, culminating in the fall of the Berlin Wall at the end of 1989. In science fiction and fantasy, CJ Cherryh's *Cyteen* took home the Hugo, while Lois McMaster Bujold picked up her first Nebula, for *Falling Free*; in the UK, Robert Holdstock won the BSFA Best Novel Award for the second time with *Lavondyss*, Ramsey Campbell was awarded the British Fantasy Society August Derleth Award for *The Influence*, and Rachel Pollack accepted the Arthur C Clarke Award for *Unquenchable Fire* – the third presentation of an award that has since become an institution of the field.

Looking at respondents to the first survey, Iain Banks, Ian McDonald and Paul McAuley had published only two novels apiece, while Neil Gaiman had barely begun *The Sandman*. (Only eight Discworld novels had appeared.) *Interzone*'s editorial cry for "radical hard sf" was only a few years previously; cyberpunk had more or less burned out; and Bruce Sterling's essay on (and definition of) slipstream had just appeared in *Science Fiction Eye*. In his review of the year for *The Orbit Science Fiction Year 3* (ed. David Garnett) John Clute continued to document the die-off of the "dinosaurs" of First SF, and the emergence of a new generation of writers; and he wrote (it is not hard to see why) that "Lately, what has begun to happen is history. The Cold War, after clutching Time deep-frozen to its winter heart for longer than we dare remember, has finally cracked open, and a million clocks have begun to turn" [1].

So there is a sense that 1989 may have been the end of something, or the start. Now, at the end of 2009, British science fiction is often described as being in as vigorous health as it's ever been. In the interim we have had the "British Boom," that ambiguous, diverse efflorescence of sf that began at some point in the 1990s, and of which the careers of a majority of the respondents to this iteration of the survey (the generation of writers that I have grown up reading) could be considered part. We have had a trend – "New Space Opera" – and something resembling a movement – "New Weird" – both usually seen as, in significant part, driven by British writers.

Indeed, Paul Kincaid has argued that the traditional characters of British and American sf have swapped around:

> What I want to suggest is that, quite simply, British and American science fiction have changed places. [...] The truth is that the overall mood of the majority of British science fiction has become upbeat, much like American science fiction was when it felt able to take on the world in the 1950s. American science fiction, on the other hand, has started to develop a sour, uncertain view of the present and of the near future, and the result is a mood not unlike that of British science fiction in the days of the cozy catastrophe. Neither position is necessarily a good or a bad thing; both have produced superb work and horrors. But if, as I believe, imaginative fiction provides a significant reflection of the social and cultural milieu from which they emerge, then this switch is saying something very interesting about the state of Britain and America write now. [2]

The letter from which this quote is taken was published in *The New York Review of Science Fiction* in September 2001, and so is now a historical document of its own. It comes from New Labour's first term of office, and before the events of September 11th. But the subsequent decade has seen remarkable success for British writers that may reflect this sort of a shift in the character of British sf and fantasy. In 2003, in his essay "Thirteen Ways of Looking at the British Boom" [3], which attempted to capture the heterogeneous nature of the moment, ex *Vector*-editor Andrew M Butler pointed out that *Harry Potter and The Goblet of Fire*'s Hugo win in 2001 made JK Rowling only the third British writer to win a Hugo Award for Best Novel, and the first to do so since Arthur C Clarke in 1980. The subsequent decade has seen three more Best Novel wins for British writers – Neil Gaiman in 2002 and 2009, and Susanna Clarke in 2005 – plus short fiction Hugo wins for David Langford, Charles Stross, Ian McDonald, and (once more) Neil Gaiman. In all, it represents a higher British fiction Hugo tally than any other decade – although it's interesting to note that all of the Best Novel wins were for fantasy works.

Both sf and fantasy continue to enjoy good coverage in the British national press (particularly *The Guardian*), and significant commercial success, from Pratchett and Gaiman and Rowling and Peter F Hamilton to the latest potential addition to that stable, Alastair Reynolds, who earlier this year signed a ten-book, one-million-pound contract with Gollancz. In many ways, then, we are a long way from 1989, and such success may, go some way to explain the confidence in claiming a genre identity seen in chapter one; but do writers detect any change in the *character* of British sf?

Richard Morgan, another writer to have achieved both commercial and critical response, argued that Britishness may not be a particular shaper of his work:

> A pervasive sense of cynicism and despair, maybe?
>
> To be honest, I think the overall flavour of my work probably owes far more to American templates than it does British. Noir is largely a US invention (with a little focal help from the French), violent anti-heroes have had their modern testing bed in American fiction since at least the thirties, and so really has science fiction as a mass market dynamic. And what's often forgotten these days is how dynamically subversive all of that stuff was. Currently, we have this perception of American sf as a bit staid and conformist/conservative, while the UK is the powerhouse of brutal malcontent genre work full of edgy political and cultural content. But most of us included in that stable are actually mining the rich seams of style and subject matter laid down by former practitioners on the other side of the Atlantic – guys like Sheckley, Heinlein, Bradbury, Bester, Pohl and Kornbluth, and of course the whole cyberpunk crew, who in turn owe a huge debt to old style American noir. I don't think there's anything specifically British in my influences that can stack up against all that.

Gary Gibson tells a similar story ("I think I was probably more influenced by US writers without realising it: you don't consider the nationality of an author when you're a kid pulling books off the library shelf"), as does Alastair Reynolds:

> Not really. I grew up in the UK, but I was exposed to American sf from an early age – *Star Trek*, Asimov, even the "Americanised" worlds of Gerry Anderson. With the exception of Clarke, James White, and later Bob Shaw and JG Ballard,

> most of the writers who were important to me were American – Niven, Haldeman, Varley, Gibson, Sterling, Wolfe etc. I was late coming to the British New Wave, and did not read the likes of M John Harrison or Christopher Priest in any great depth until my thirties.

We'll be revisiting the question of influences in more detail in chapter six, but one thing that's immediately obvious from the responses to this year's survey is that, compared to twenty years ago, far fewer British writers consider themselves part of a European tradition – including Morgan, only six respondents gestured in that direction at all, and only Liz Jensen went so far as to say say outright that she considers herself a European, rather than a British writer – and far more, like Morgan, referenced America. How such influences might work themselves out through a British mindset is an immediately fascinating question (and you also wonder how many of the contemporary American writers Kincaid was thinking of would list British writers as influences); although of course the caveat from the original survey, that any Britishness will probably for most writers be subordinate to their individual character, still applies. But Charles Stross' response does suggest that it's not going to be as straightforward as British writers having simply appropriated the furniture of American sf:

> Only insofar as I'm British. (At least to the extent of being the second generation of my family to be born on British soil.) It's interesting to note that when I write American protagonists, I get annoyed mail from my fans – who detect bogus, foreign notes in the writing. (I've decided to give up.)

On the other hand, Eric Brown writes that

> Much of my science fiction is pretty mid-Atlantic, certainly my recent stuff which has been published in the States. There are exceptions: *Kethani* was infused with Britishness, or even Yorkshireness. What is it that makes it British? Apart from the setting, certainly *Kethani* was slower in pace than my mid-Atlantic sf, less reliant on gadgetry and sf tropes, and more character-driven. And maybe even more pessimistic. My *Starship* novellas have a British feel, I think, even though they're set on an alien world – but that's because they're influenced by the work of Michael Coney.

The suggestion that British sf is linked to pessimism creeps back here, as if to say any change in the character of sf by British writers is precisely *not* a change in Britishness. John Meaney's response hints at a similar argument, and mentions that idea of "transatlantic" sf again:

> Sometimes yes; sometimes no. It's American critics who say that I've written

> about class-ridden culture – in my Nulapeiron books – with a sensibility only a Brit could bring to bear. But the Tristopolis books are purely transatlantic, with a dark gothamesque setting that comes straight from my love of New York.

Mike Carey goes further, and suggests that any attempt to obtain a hard-and-fast distinction is doomed, at least on his patch (and his response is interesting to compare to Neil Gaiman's, in the Mexicon survey):

> No, I don't think there is. I grew up on American comic books and American movies as much as – if not more than – their British equivalents. I don't think my creative sensibilities are any different from those of a US writer.
>
> There was a time, relatively recently, when British comic book writers had a name for being more imaginative, bolder, more iconoclastic than their American counterparts. Alan Moore, Neil Gaiman and Grant Morrison all made their comic debuts at that time, and of them it was very largely true. I don't believe it's true any more. The paradigm shift happened: all writers, on both sides of the Atlantic, learned those lessons, and although we apply them in different ways, you can't any longer do a sheep and goats thing, if you ever could.

Peadar O'Guilin is another who takes influences from both side of the pond: "I'm Irish, but my biggest influences growing up were people like Brian Aldiss, Ian Watson and Bob Shaw. Actually, sod that, ten years programming by the staff at *2000AD* probably had a greater effect on me than any amount of novels I might have read. No doubt it comes through in my themes and my subject-matter. But there'll be a lot of American influences too from the likes of Harry Harrison and a few seasons of dodgy *Battlestar Galactica*."

It's also worth considering here the responses of the four American-born UK-resident writers who responded to the survey, which start to introduce a theme common in the Mexicon survey – that of language. For Tricia Sullivan, for instance, the answer is straightforward: "I'm not a British native and my work is American in setting and tone." Patrick Ness is equally clear – "No, but that's probably because I'm an American ex-pat living here" – but goes on to say that, "The American publishers complain my colloquialisms are too English and vice versa, so I can't really win there." Lisa Tuttle, who twenty years ago took the same sort of line, was more contemplative this time around:

> I don't know. I think that kind of distinction is generally discovered – or imposed – from the outside, rather than being felt by the writer ... at least, by me. I'd have to give a similar answer to a question about whether or not there was something ineluctably female about my writing ... well, since I *am* a women maybe I write like a woman – but maybe I don't! But since I'm not

> actually British ... I've now lived in this country for about as long as I lived in America, but since I grew up in the US, it shaped me. And I'm still an American citizen, despite being resident in Britain for so long.

While Elizabeth Wein felt her work *is* somewhat British, although again invoked the idea of work being "transatlantic":

> Well (um) I confess that I'm American, and though I've lived in the UK for 15 years and Scotland for the last ten, my books are only published in North America! And yet, *yes*, there is definitely a distinct Britishness to my work. The setting of several of my books, for a start – the northern Engilsh landscape, and of course, the Arthurian slant. I have a short story in Sharyn November's most recent *Firebirds* collection (*Firebirds Soaring*) that takes place during the battle of Britain (it was rejected by the editor who originally asked for it on the grounds that it would be "of little interest to American readers"). In fact, come to think of it, many of my short stories are set in British landscapes: Oxford, Dover, Orkney ... I also work hard to keep my writing neutrally transatlantic.

Location is the subject of the next chapter. However, Chris Butler noted his belief that "the British landscape is deeply ingrained in our collective psyche," and as in the Mexicon survey, a number of writers singled it out in their answers to this question as a possible source of Britishness in their work, including Nina Allan, NM Browne, Alan Campbell, Elizabeth Counihan, Rhiannon Lassiter, Tim Lebbon, James Lovegrove, Suzanne McLeod, Justina Robson, Conrad Williams, and Neil Williamson. Stephen Gallagher noted that his work tends "to alternate between closely-observed British settings and closely-researched foreign landscapes, usually (but not always) with a British character for point-of view," but there was, interestingly, little of the Brit abroad in other responses. Nick Harkaway tried to get around location entirely, for his first novel, *The Gone-Away World*: "To my delight, Americans tend to assume it's the UK, and Brits tend to assume it's the US. I'm not sure what Australians think, but I understand mostly that it's not Australia." Transatlanticism taken to its logical conclusion, perhaps.

Harkaway also noted that, "That said, there's a flavour of the writing which I think is identifiably British – a Wodehouse ish feel, maybe. I hope so." Again we must postpone the question of influence, but his answer does encapsulate two of the most common responses to this question: that it's a matter of language, and therefore voice, and that a particular sense of humour is common. It's not a surprise that other writers, such as James Lovegrove, also linked them: "Over and above the use of British characters and settings, which I seldom stray from, there's also a sense of reserve and a reliance on satire and irony in my work that are, I feel, peculiarly British traits, not to mention wordplay and use of extended allegory."

To stay with language, for now: Jaine Fenn replied, "I don't try and emulate the

American use of language, so I think anyone reading my stuff would be able to identify it as written by a Brit. Other than that, no, I don't think so"; similarly, Mary Hoffman insisted she makes "no concessions on vocabulary ... And I am an absolute stickler on grammar and punctuation, which is quite British." Paul Meloy and Bob Lock also picked language as a distinguishing feature of their work. Sarah Ash tried to pin down what, for her, the difference in language means, and where it comes from:

> Only in that I suspect that the rhythm of the prose and the richness of the language that I absorbed and adored as a young reader has inevitably shaped the way that I write, so that the style of the Brontes, Jane Austen, Tolkien and Alan Garner (to mention but a few!) underpins the text.

Mark Chadbourn also tried to specify what the "British voice" might sound like:

> My work is distinctively British in setting and character, but also, I think, in tone. There's a peculiar British voice – slightly oblique, wry, ironic – which is also one of the reasons why British fiction doesn't travel as well as American fiction, which tends to have a more universal tone.

Many writers made similar diagnoses. Joe Abercrombie, for instance – "Perhaps a slightly British sense of humour – sarcasm, cynicism, and not taking oneself too seriously" – or Ian Watson – "Sense of humour, I hope, though this has become steadily more surrealistic." Colin Harvey thinks his writing displays "a healthy dose of cynicism compared to the idealism of a lot of American sf," as does Stephen Gaskell. Colin Davies reports being told that "my work has a streak of dark humour which Americans seem to identify as distinctively British," while Stan Nicholls remarked that "there's a distinctiveness about British wit. Not that it always travels well."

The idea that the tone of American fiction is more "universal" is interesting, however; it's tempting to take it as further support for the idea that if British science fiction has become more successful – and in the context of many of the institutions of the science fiction field, such as the Hugo Awards, a large part of the definition of "successful" has to mean "noticed and praised in America" – it may be as much because it has adopted some of the traditionally American clothes of the genre as because its distinctive qualities have come to be appreciated. Justina Robson's experience, however, may suggest otherwise: "I used to think that my less than dashing heroines and dysfunctional relationship quotient was too high to be classed as American, but now I'm not so sure." But this is another case of this chapter's answers throwing out tendrils to other questions: we will revisit the question of how writers' work is received in different markets in chapters seven and eight. (Though perhaps now is the time to note Steve Aylett's response: "My stuff is very rich, concentrated and imaginative. This is all despite the way things are in Britain/America, in which individual thought, imagination and genuine creativity are damn near illegal.")

How much further can the character of British sf and fantasy be pinned down than the generalities we've identified so far? China Mieville suggests not that much further:

> I think I'm a writer indelibly and obviously stained by my Britishness, but I'm not sure that's the same thing. I don't really believe in "distinctive Britishness," so would distinguish between being able to place me as a writer obviously top-to-bottom a product of his environment, and being a "distinctively British" writer, which strikes me as a bit of a meaningless chimera. You can generalise, and such generalisations aren't always useless, but I'd abjure anything like British essentialism.

Certainly plenty of respondents demurred from diagnosing their own Britishness. For Iain Banks it is "A wood/trees problem. I think I've come to accept that it's for those with a more objective view of this to comment." Ken MacLeod felt similarly, as did Ian Whates ("Consciously, no; inevitably, yes"), Adrian Tchaikovsky, Juliet McKenna, Deborah Miller, Ricardo Pinto and several others (some of whom have been quoted above, such as Lisa Tuttle). And Andrew Crumey underlined Mieville's point about the usefulness, or rather lack thereof, of generalisations: "I don't know what 'distinctively British' means ... National identifications are ultimately political and economic rather than artistic. As a way of extracting meaning from art I find them reductive."

Still, a few more points did emerge from the aggregate of responses that may be worth noting, even if they highlight what is distinctive about some of the British writers who responded to the survey more than what is distinctive about British writers in general. Compared to twenty years ago, for instance, empire was almost absent as a consideration, and even some of those who mentioned it doubted its potency. Will Ashon, for instance: "I can't remember who I read recently, but they said that British fiction was more exciting than US fiction precisely because we were a tired, dying imperial power. It's not true, but it's a nice idea." Two biographical responses from younger writers are interesting, however. First, Gareth Lyn Powell:

> I was born in Bristol, twenty-five years after World War II. The last vestiges of the British Empire were falling away into history and we were caught in the middle of a Cold War, sitting between two superpowers with itchy trigger fingers and enough nuclear weapons to wipe out the human race. Given all that, I guess it's understandable that the collapse of civilization and the end of the world form recurring themes in a lot of my work.
>
> Aside from that, I find myself identifying more with British writers than American ones. At the moment, I'm drawn to and inspired by the work of a lot of British writers – Richard Morgan, M John Harrison, Jon Courtenay Grimwood, Ken MacLeod, Iain M Banks, Alastair Reynolds, Ian McDonald, Chris Beckett, Stephen Baxter – there's something about their work, a quality that

> speaks to me at a deep level and which I feel when I read my own work, but I'm not sure what it is.

Powell's answer I find interesting for suggesting both a continuity with previous generations of British sf writers, and clearly indicating that the British Boom itself is, at least for some, a source of influence, even a dominant source. And second, there is Kit Whitfield, who was almost the only writer to bring in contemporary politics – perhaps surprisingly given British sf's reputation for being political, and left-of-centre in particular:

> Well, my work is distinctively me, and I'm British, so inevitably my novels are distinctively British in some way. They probably have a British sensibility (or rather an English-Irish sensibility, those being the two nationalities I was raised by). I'm a member of a country with a tremendous history of imperialism and bad karma that I love nonetheless, that's currently fallen from its power and has spent a lot of time truckling to the dangerous superpower that was Bush's America – a nation that seemed rather to despise us and everyone else who wasn't a member of the fatherland, which meant we got a certain dose of what we'd dished out in previous centuries, although on a smaller scale. The politics of that situation have influenced my writing: there are a lot of moral incompatibilities and power dynamics in there.
>
> Also, as a writer I tend to resist easy solutions. Having parents from two different countries, and countries that have historically been oppressor and rebel (English father, Irish mother, and the struggle for peace in Northern Ireland was very prominent during my teens), has probably influenced me: I grew up in a house where there were two completely different ways of looking at the same situation, and where you came from made a big difference to how you thought. That's a truth about human thought that tends to shape my stories.
>
> None of this is really conscious, though. At least in my own experience, deliberate point-making tends to leads to heavy-handed writing. I just try to write as honestly as I can and let my nationality influence things how it will.

Like Whitfield, a number of other respondents emphasised the importance of history and of Britain's mongrel nature – factors that are clearly linked to empire and its absence, even if the link is not made explicit. Mark Charan Newton wrote that he hoped in his work "to show appreciation for the sense of history that's ever-present in British life: old buildings in which we may work, some of our curious customs, our multiculturalism." NM Browne mentioned the importance of British history to her stories, as did Juliet McKenna, who also made the point that familiarity guides some of her choices. Frances Hardinge summed up much of this very well. She was one of the few writers to attempt to construct an idea of "Britishness," and echoed several points already made, including Whitfield's desire for complex responses to situations:

> I suspect that my work is pretty heavily infested with Britishness. My humour has doses of understatement, irony and surrealism. I've also noticed in my writing that slight streak of cynicism which isn't exactly pessimism or misanthropy, but which makes the British suspicious if they're being offered something too good, too gleaming, too neat. I don't write purely happy endings – in fact I don't entirely write endings.
>
> In addition I have a fascination with history, particularly British history, and I often draw on this for purposes of plotline or to give my locations depth and atmosphere. The British have an attic-culture – we can't bear to throw things away, so we're loaded down with inconvenient tiny thoroughfares in city centres, utterly illogical spellings, centuries of chintz and a romantic appreciation of the shabby. I would fight to the death for all these things.

Although neither Hardinge, nor anyone else, could quite match Paul Cornell's enthusiasm:

> Hugely. The exasperating nature of the British, and the problems of Britishness, and indeed the nature of all nation states, leading on from that, is almost all I write about. I'm frustrated with what are these days taken to be inherent characteristics of Britishness (being uncomfortable with success, preferring a hard fought loss to a win, a general pessimism and cynicism) in the way only someone who thinks of themselves as very British can be. Of course, this means I want to go off and live in America, where I can be much happier watching Britishness from a distance. But at least I own up to that.

Ben Jeapes, on the other hand, is happy here: "As a matter of national pride I want to perpetuate some of the things I consider good about the UK: we are far from perfect but I wouldn't want to live anywhere else."

Intriguingly, quite a few writers argued for their work as distinctively English, such as Ian MacLeod – "I'm not so sure that 'Britishness' means much these days" – and Adam Roberts:

> I consider my work to be more distinctively English than British, and that in terms of its emotional repression, its violence, the way its pessimism is leavened by its particular modes of irony and humour, its conflicted relationship with its own intellectualism and its hospitality (I hope) to cultural and artistic diversity. These things approximate a definition, actually, of 'English' as a cultural category.

Or Susanna Clarke, whose *Jonathan Strange & Mr Norrell* was described by Neil

Gaiman, with infamous precision, as "unquestionably the finest English novel of the fantastic written in the last seventy years," and who described her work as "English, and self-consciously so," primarily for its emphasis on English landscapes. Emphasis on Scottishness or Welshness was less common, although a few writers, such as Katherine Langrish and Suzanne McLeod, noted the use of English mythology in their work, and Kari Sperring suggesting quite a deep influence of her study on her fiction:

> There's a strand of material drawn from my specialism as a historian of the Celtic-speaking peoples and notably the Welsh, though it may not be obvious in terms of clichéd "Celtic fantasy" – it's more at the level of nomenclature, social structuring, language elements (there is Anglo-Saxon English in there too) and there are a few early medieval references thrown in for my own amusement (mostly in names, but sometimes elsewhere).

Toby Litt suggested, "in comparison to American writers, there is a British sense of limits – social limits, spatial limits. We are reluctant to believe in total and successful self-reinvention. I might not like this, but I have this trait." Tim Lees took the analysis further, and suggested that another angle on Paul Kincaid's contention that British and American sf has swapped roles:

> An Australian reviewer considered my work very British, with a sense of – I can't quote this directly – characters being constantly watched and checked up on. We're a small, crowded island after all, and the vast open spaces of, say, the US create a wholly different mind-set in which eccentricity can thrive. (I'd even count the extreme conformity of certain US communities as a form of eccentricity – they really should get out and mingle more.) I know the Brits are meant to be eccentric, but we're not, not these days. I've seen some very strange behaviour in the States, barely remarked upon by locals. There was a guy prophesying in front of the Capitol, for example. He did not appear to be mentally ill. In Britain, we have our share of crank religious groups, but it's all behind closed doors. Start proclaiming your vision in front of Parliament and you'll end up sectioned. Or worse.

As we shall see next chapter, for some writers this sense of limits is tied into the British landscape, and our status as an island nation; but the idea of class that Litt invokes, of course, also goes back to empire, as Jon Courtenay Grimwood outlined:

> The arrogance is probably English; so too the acute awareness of class as a cultural signifier. My characters are usually fighting their class first, themselves next, the world afterwards.
>
> I suspect the tightness of my scope is also quite English. Someone once said I write the fall of empires, seen from the kitchen. My feeling is the inside

> of one person's head is more interesting than the behaviour of crowds or the simultaneous thoughts of a hundred thousand people's heads. I tend to regard American science fiction and fantasy as doing (very well indeed) epic and exciting huge set pieces and the assorted UK versions as either afraid to try this, or being unable to stop a tighter focus on character from sneaking in. (A gross generalisation, and Reynolds does space opera as well as anyone, possibly ever.)

As we have seen, Reynolds considers American influence on his work to be very significant, so perhaps Grimwood is on to something here.

So what difference does two decades make? Not much, and all the difference in the world, depending on which writers you are talking to. A few writers did mention the British reputation for pessimism, but often as something imposed on their work from outside, such as Chris Beckett – "I've been accused of 'British miserablism'. Obviously I dispute this" – and Keith Brooke – "I like to think that my work has positive outcomes, but sometimes I have to really work to convince people of that." Although not always; Paul McAuley suggested that his work had "a faint but pervasive sense of English melancholy, perhaps," Roger Levy said, "Yes, it is British. It's bleak. Maybe it's European. Maybe it's just Levyish, a microsubset of British," and Martin Sketchley most fully endorsed the traditional dichotomies: "There is a general focus on the more negative aspects of life, and people's endeavours often fail. For those reasons I would say it has a distinctly British feel, as opposed to more upbeat and right-wing American material." But not many other respondents took this line, and for most of those who did it was linked to a sort of dark humour, as we have seen.

My overall sense of the responses is that beyond the basic generalities discussed earlier – language and location – they illustrate a wide range of factors in play that can all, to a greater or lesser extent, be said to interplay with notions of "Britishness" (or "Englishness," and so forth), but not define them; and this, in turn, strikes me as evidence of a healthy and diverse writing population. It is, in the end, as Nina Allan shows, an unanswerable question; it is what we point to when we say it, and it's always a moving target.

> I didn't realise how important England – and my own Englishness – was to me until I started writing seriously, and then it became obvious almost at once that I am a distinctively English writer. I think the thing people have most often commented on in my work is its English ambience, that "it's so English," or "it reminds me of how England was when I was growing up." Even my future Englands seem to remind people of their childhood! This is something I am truly proud of, that my work has this kind of resonance with my readers.
>
> I have a very intense sense of recall – I prefer to call it recall rather than nostalgia, because I'm not saying "this was better," but "this is how I remember it" – and I think it is this fondness and concern for detail that gives my work

> this quintessentially English flavour. I am English, I grew up in England, it's where I live now, to it's not surprising if the things I dwell on and choose to describe are influenced by that. I would even go further in stating that I believe that one of my main "jobs" as a writer is to try and capture the image and essence of England as I have known it and to preserve that the best I can. The world I grew up in is changing – you could almost say it is disappearing – and my work at least in part is gradually becoming an elegy for a lost kingdom.

This is, if nothing else, a contrast to Tony Ballatyne's view: "I think that sf should be about getting away from the certainties of childhood. I think that those certainties and habits instilled at an early age are what make us British or French or Japanese or whatever. They are fascinating, they should be examined, but they are not what sf is about." Perhaps it's safest simply to anatomize the question, as Christopher Priest did: "Landscape, literature, culture, attitudes, family, language, scientific heritage, weather, spelling, history." And the rest.

**Endnotes**

[1] Clute, J. "Year Roundup: 1989," in *Look at the Evidence: Essays and Reviews* (Serconia Press, 1995), p. 139.

[2] Kincaid, P. Letter to NYRSF (response to Judith Berman's essay "Science Fiction Without the Future"), in issue 157, September 2001.

[3] Butler, Andrew M. "Thirteen Ways of Looking at the British Boom," in *Science Fiction Studies* 91 (November 2003).

# Chapter 5:
## *Do British settings play a major part in your work, and if so, why (or why not)?*

# 1989

The responses in Chapter Four showed that a lot of authors equated British characteristics with British settings, at least in part. It's as if the spirit of place affects all else, as if our Britishness seeps into us from the landscape we inhabit.

Be that as it may, it certainly seems that one of the distinguishing characteristics of British science fiction is the use of landscape. There are innumerable works – exemplified, for instance, by the run-down cities of M John Harrison's stories or the depopulated West Country of Keith Roberts' – where the landscape seems to assume the role of a character. It was natural, therefore, to follow up that last question with this one. The responses were wildly varied, from John Brunner's "Yes," to Samantha Lee's "No – I don't like to pin myself down," though where people positioned themselves on this spectrum was sometimes a little unexpected.

Given the nature of his work, it was probably inevitable that Keith Roberts should come out strongly in favour of using British settings:

> I think if writing is to have any validity it has to reflect real situations and surroundings. I wouldn't for instance try to set a story in America because I've never been there. Not as a serious piece, anyway. A bit of a paradox perhaps when it comes to sf; but the creative trades are full of them. (Not how carefully I step round that nasty little word "art.") The plain fact is though that any writing, however seemingly way-out, has got to be based, ultimately, on our own experience; because reality is the only input we have. Everybody, whether they wish to or not, reflects their own life and times. Griffiths' Babylonian slave girls are quite definitely Edwardian flappers. The other day I saw an interesting night shot of Los Angeles. Invert the image, and the vast, flat panorama becomes the underside of Spielberg's great space ship. So, American

stories are American, British stories are British; there's really no escaping it.

Where it goes wrong of course is where it becomes self-conscious and parochial. I recently summed up the Scottish sf scene as "Nudge-nudge, wink-wink, tee-hee, Sauchiehall Street," which of course didn't go down too well. But I was disappointed; I'd looked for something much bigger and broader based. If the aliens always landed in the Strand, London fans would rapidly get bored; even if the writer could reel off the names of all the shops.

What I suppose I'm saying is that though national and local influences exist, they're best used with caution. My own Kaeti is quite definitely a Londoner, and the locales are real enough; but for the most part they're played down. That was the intention anyway. All too easy to reel off lists of street names, and get a sort of cheap buzz from it.

Time of course is the other great factor, as I've hinted by mentioning *Intolerance*. When I was writing the Anita stories, a year or so ago now, I thought I was recording aspects of Northamptonshire. I was, in a way; but now I find the pieces curiously dated. There's a story of "Nudge-nudge, look, mum, I'm being naughty" quality that seems to me redolent of the sixties; at least, the sixties as I perceived them. The decade, after all, sprang from the austere fifties; there was a lot of looking back. It certainly wasn't the golden, freewheeling time it's been painted since. The real break came later; certainly, Kaeti and Anita couldn't exist on the same printed page. The world has moved on.

Roberts is readily identifiable as a very British sf writer, though if anyone fits the common description of a typical British sf writer it must be Brian Aldiss so it is, perhaps, a little unexpected to find that his response comes from the other end of the spectrum:

> No. I rarely use English settings, except in my non-sf novels. I have set stories in Scandinavia, France, Belgium, Germany, Jugoslavia, Czechoslovakia, Poland, the Soviet Union, India, Burma, Sumatra, Singapore, China, Brazil, and elsewhere on this planet. I would imagine I have covered the globe as widely as any author. And why, you ask. Because I have always regarded sf as a literature of exile; this conclusion is fortified by my understanding that many of the readers of sf – or at least those met with at conventions – find no other place in society; they are internal exiles, seeking a literature to meet their needs. It is perhaps not without significance (an English double negative) that my writing is continually branded "pessimistic" in the States; that complaint rarely arises in this country; after heavy losses in two world wars and the loss of empire, not to mention economic conditions, the British are naturally less sanguine than their American cousins.

Interesting that Aldiss should cite that familiar loss of empire in support of a literature set largely outside this country. Still these diametrically opposed positions, with their counter arguments that a writer must write about what he knows, and the sf readership is alienated, do come together in answering the purpose of this question: they suggest that any national characteristics British sf may possess do not come from the settings.

However, it may not be quite as simple as that, as Colin Greenland suggests:

> Not in the sense you mean. But, yes, of course, it could hardly be otherwise. The prefecture of Eschaly in Luscany is built out of bits of the Ashmolean Museum and the Bodleian Library; the alleys of Calcionne run aslant through Leeds and Ramsgate. For my current novel, *Take Back Plenty*, the abandoned colliery at Chislet has been transplanted to the moon. My next novel may entail the more subtle fictive imposture by which Ramsgate appears in the text as "Ramsgate," London as "London." It just depends what I'm writing.

This is an attitude that finds support from Iain Banks:

> Scottish settings in *The Wasp Factory*, *The Bridge*, and *Espedair Street* matter to a varying degree; in ascending order of importance to the feeling and timbre of the book, they'd be ranked TWF, ESt, TB. Partly it's just easier to write about someplace you know well (especially when you're writing about childhood or adolescence), and partly I think the old place deserves to be written about. *Walking on Glass* has a London setting; I was living there at the time and wanted the real bits – the non-castle scenes, especially the parts concerning Graham Park – to be grounded as closely as possible in the mundane reality of a London day ... and come to think of it, the whole last half of *Consider Phlebas* was inspired by the London Underground, so there's a ghost of an influence there.

In other words, the spirit of the place does seem to seep into a work even when it is superficially set far away and long ago. Gwyneth Jones is also aware of this hidden influence:

> Sometimes, sometimes not. In a sense "British settings" may always be found hidden under the futuristic trappings; and maybe this is perceptible to the investigative reader. I try to write about places I know. Therefore, if I say it's Cairo, it's probably Cairo. If I say Bangkok, it's Bangkok. If I say Mars City, or New York 2020AD, then under the wallpaper it is probably Brighton or Manchester.

Alex Stewart put it another way: "Yes, simply because it's an environment I know, and can evoke easily. Even the imaginary settings tend to be based on something I'm familiar with." Or, as David V Barrett chose to phrase it: "Not necessarily, though the 'sense of place' in my work is certainly influenced by British settings and my own British upbringing. 'British' is an attitude, not a place."

An important final sentence there from Barrett, because it does more and more seem that British landscapes appear in the fiction as a result of background, familiarity. And hence British assumptions and attitudes probably appear for exactly the same reason. Alasdair Grey remarks on how much goes into the beliefs and experiences that come out in the writing:

> British (or to be more precise) Scottish settings are the ground of most of my work for economic reasons – I could not buy a convincing Japanese setting with less than a lifetime's experience. So when I want an exotic setting I usually fantasise.

And as Graham Dunstan Martin suggests, it is that lifetime's experience that is far more important than the locale, though the one does tend to imply the other. "This is because fiction should be a mirror for people to see themselves more clearly in. Fiction is often a clearer mirror than fact, e.g. Orwell's *Animal Farm* is the clearest possible account of Stalinism."

But this, of course, raises another point. Without that lifetime's experience there would be nothing for the writer to write, and locale is part and parcel of that experience. By inference, then, some writers might not be able to write if not for the setting their stories take. Diana Wynne Jones certainly takes this position:

> I use British settings almost entirely though not all the time because I find this is what I naturally visualise, and if I fail to visualise the setting then I fail to write about it. You might say that I need a British setting in order to write at all.

And there are others who share this attitude. John Christopher writes about Britain "because I am happier with the settings I know," while for Elizabeth Sourbut it's:

> Mostly because I haven't been anywhere else for long enough to absorb the atmosphere. I learned three or four years ago that one (or I at any rate) can't write nearly so effectively about a place one has never been to. If I'm not in Britain I'm in another reality or on another world – then no-one can say me nay. But if I set a story in Algiers someone's going to come along and say you can't see that from there because of the gasometer in the way – or whatever.

Stephen Gallagher is another who shares this feeling:

> The more comfortable I feel with what I'm doing, the more I feel able to draw on settings that are closer to home. In the past I've done a lot of travelling and

> research on faraway locations; maybe I felt I had something to prove, I really don't know. Now I'm trying to use the traveller's attitude of mind on my own territory. What I'd hope to avoid is the pitfall of provincialism, which is the first and deepest pitfall that seems to await the British writer.

There are writers who use British settings for purely practical purposes, as Christina Lake says: "I tend to base my settings on places I actually know – except where it's an alien world entirely." And Jane Palmer also finds the familiar important:

> Through necessity many settings of my stories are in this country, otherwise they tend to exist in places where any criticism of the geography would have to come from an alien. I would like to broaden the choice of Earthbound locations, but do not have the required background knowledge.

But there are others who fight shy of it for precisely that fear of parochialism mentioned by Stephen Gallagher. Ian McDonald is a good example:

> Living in Northern Ireland, and having been regrettably exposed to some of the local publishing scene, I know the dangers of pious parochialism. I've set a story here if it's right for the story I want to tell, I set a story in Britain if it's right for that story, I'll set a story in never-never land if it's the right place for that story. For me, theme and general *feel* suggest the place. Apart from those places which no-one has been to, I like to try and write about places I have been to, or which are similar enough to places I have been to for the substitution to be valid. I like to be able to *smell* my locations. So, while I don't reject British locations out of hand, neither do I subscribe to the Dan Dare/Brittania Rules the Spacewaves school of thought.

Again there is an example of that age-old advice: writers should write about what they know. But McDonald also makes the very valid point that the setting needs to be right for the story, which is why some writers, like Eric Brown, find it difficult to set their fiction in Britain:

> I find it hard to write about where I'm living. And there's also, to be honest, the technical difficulty of setting straight sf in an "English village," let's say – it presents problems of tone, believability ... though that won't stop me trying.

That's the sort of viewpoint that's probably behind Barrington Bayley's response: "I try to use wholly invented settings. Am not much into contemporary realism," and EC Tubb's: "No. I worked on a wide canvas which encompassed worlds." And there's much the same point from James White:

> When a story isn't set off-Earth, I try to make the background neutral, say a hospital or research establishment in an unspecified location, unless the location is well-known to me. The background for the recent *Sanctuary*, for example, is just across the road.

There are others, however, for whom the setting is only occasionally important, if at all, and they may or may not set their stories in Britain more or less as the whim dictates. David Langford is an example:

> I tend much more often than not to assume a British setting, but have only worked to stress such a sense of place on a few occasions when the story seemed to demand it. I don't (if this is what you're getting at) try to fake up American settings for market purposes.

Douglas Hill takes much the same stance:

> Most of my settings are in outer space or a fantasy world. But I've set books in Britain as well as North America. (I chose the latter for one trilogy because I needed the continental expanse, and topography – not from patriotic fervour.)

There's more along the same lines from Lisa Tuttle:

> Not usually in my science fiction, but British landscapes and backgrounds have been important in some of my horror/fantasy stories – for example "The Dragon's Bride" and "Treading the Maze" – whereas in others it's simply a matter of detail, not vital to the story. The London of "From Another Country" could just as easily have been New York City (only I know London more intimately), just as the upstate New York background in "Riding the Nightmare" could have been swapped with the Gloucestershire setting of "The Nest" without drastically altering either story.

If Britain does feature in a story it could be for purely practical reasons that have nothing to do with the story itself. In general the practical reason would be simple familiarity, as with Kim Newman:

> I don't tend to write the kind of f/sf set on other planets or in totally invented worlds (I can't get interested in that sort of thing), and so I'm forced to use settings I know. I've not travelled widely, so naturally I tend to stick with British (mainly London) settings. In some stories, this has been important, but in others it's fairly minor.

And there's the same sort of response from Simon Ounsley:

> Real life settings haven't played a large part in my meagre output to date but two stories have used them: London in one and Yorkshire in the other. When I use a real life setting it will tend to be in Britain because that's where I've spent most of my life.

There's familiarity of a slightly different kind invoked by John Brosnan: "So far British settings haven't featured in the little sf that I've written but have in the horror novels I've written, mainly because my co-writer (of the horror novels) is British."

But generally, these writers use British setting only if the story demands it. Thus Paul McAuley uses British settings: "only occasionally, for purposes of historical resonance." Similarly, Brian Stableford:

> The majority of my early works were set on alien worlds or in a future sufficiently remote to make present-day political boundaries irrelevant, but British settings feature more frequently in more recent works and in projects currently in the planning stage, because the works in question are set in the past or the near future, and require a closer reliance on the familiar.

It is this historical resonance that also matters for Mary Gentle, and we are starting again to get the impression that it is what the landscape represents, an essence coming from the country, that is important. She says:

> Not a major part so far. They will and they won't, according to which book I do. (*1610* will be set in England, mostly.) If I'm allowed British history, that's a major setting; present day Britain not so much so yet; European history and present Europe are major settings (see it, steal it; the writer's motto). Where I set is what I've seen. When I want to do a truly depressing dystopia, guess where I'm going to set it.

Curiously, James Corley repeats that last point: "Britain unfortunately is an ideal setting for disaster stories. Off hand I can't think of a single sf novel with a British setting that isn't a complete dystopia." Maybe it's something to do with the end of empire?

Maybe, British settings only play a part in stories if Britishness is, to some extent, the subject. At least, that's the suggestion of Robert Irwin:

> British settings do not play a part in my work. Although *The Limits of Vision* seems to be set in South London, it is really set in the mind. However Britishness is an interesting and important theme (see John Fowles' *Daniel Martin*) and I plan in a future fantasy novel to tackle Britishness in a London setting.

Still, some people use British settings. Josephine Saxton admits: "Yes. Imprinting," which is as good an explanation as any of the effect Britain has on its writers; while John Clute has undergone the same imprinting because "I've lived here for 20 years."

But, as Neil Gaiman says, "I love British settings. I don't always use them." There were a fair number of respondents for whom British settings formed no significant part of their writing. Paul Barnett, for instance: "Not really, I don't think. But my British settings are usually Devon (where I live) or Scotland (where I came from)." Yet despite the attractions of familiarity, as Kenneth Bulmer says: "I am not chauvinistic enough to eschew other settings."

Nor is it just chauvinism, there are several British writers who don't even have much of that familiarity to call on. Garry Kilworth, for one: "My settings are pretty cosmopolitan. I have only lived a third of my life in the UK." Or Leigh Kennedy, one of a growing number of American writers now living in Britain: "Don't use British settings except in a glancing way (yet)." And we must always bear in mind the response of Lee Montgomerie: "No; not British by birth, don't feel British, not interested in Britain."

# 2009

If, as the first four chapters have suggested, the story of this survey is a story of British science fiction and fantasy as thriving, successful genres, what should we expect when it comes to the use of British settings? Should we expect a championing of the British landscape and environment? Or does the adoption of a more traditionally American idiom hinted at by several writers in the previous chapter run alongside a shift in the venues for the tales told?

There was, at least, less variety in the responses this year than in those of twenty years ago. Just over half (44) of the writers who responded stated that they regularly use British settings in their work; just over a quarter (22) said equally definitely that they do not; and the remainder (17) answered some variant of "sometimes."

Even for a question as apparently clear-cut as this, there is an element of subjectivity in the coding of responses. It is not the case, for example, that all writers of secondary-world fantasies were counted as eschewing British settings. For some, certainly, that seems to be the case. Adrian Tchaikovsky found the question easy to answer: "Not at all, as the books are set in an entirely secondary world." Similar sentiments came from Ricardo Pinto and Juliet McKenna, among others. McKenna emphasised that in addition to writing imagined worlds, she "consciously seek[s] out sources and inspiration from world-wide myth and history," as did Sarah Ash: "My recent work has been much more influenced by the legends of France, Eastern Europe, and Japan." Kari Sperring went so far as to say that "My default setting is French."

But others put the spotlight on the less conscious choices a writer makes, such as Mark Charan Newton – "Certainly not directly, simply because I'm writing in a secondary world. But I'm sure that indirectly my writing will be influenced by Britain" – and Stan Nicholls – "Not a big percentage of my work overall. Most of my stuff's set in completely imaginary worlds – though I'm sure something of the British landscape has worked its way in somewhere." Joe Abercrombie was a bit more specific: "Having grown up in the North of England and lived in Britain all my life, I'm sure there are some influences in there, particularly of the Lake District and Yorkshire Dales (how Victorian of me)." Science fiction writers, including Eric Brown, Jaine Fenn and Alastair Reynolds tended towards the literal interpretation that off-world settings are not British settings, although for some the refusal is more conscious. Ben Jeapes, for instance:

> Only one novel has been physically located in the British Isles, but as it dealt with the English Civil War that's not really surprising. Despite my answer to question 4, I try to make my futures as multinational as possible, in terms of setting and characters. Characters are generally multi-ethnic with names meant to imply mixed race ancestry. Why? Because my dream future would be like Cordwainer Smith's Instrumentality of Man: all of us quite unmistakably one race, with no superiors or inferiors, but at the same time able to draw on the marvellous riches of our many cultural heritages.

Paul McAuley echoed this theme, and introduced a couple of other notes:

> Not a major part, no, although I have written several novels set or partly set in Britain, and several others feature stubbornly British characters. Why not? I guess because much of my sf is set away from Earth, I'm a strong believer in trying to find other viewpoints beyond the white British/US ones, and anyhow, Arthur C Clarke and Stephen Baxter cornered the British-in-space meme. On the other hand, I've written a fair number of horror stories, and most of those are set in England. Perhaps because, for me, unease works best when rooted in something borrowed from my own life.

The notion that British settings lend themselves to particular stories was picked up by Chaz Brenchley, who also reframed the concept of Britishness to mean something more well-travelled:

> Oh, look: an easy one. No. I have been there and done that in other genres: the majority of my thrillers and horror novels have been set in Newcastle specifically or else near-analogues thereof. The sf is all about other planets, other orbits (or else, in the *Nature* stories, the getting-to-other planets; I suppose those have been set in Britain, but only in the sense of being somewhere to leave behind), because I am that kind of sf reader: I have no problem with inner

> space, all fiction worth reading is about inner space, but hey look, let's have outer space as well, eh? Because we can!
>
> And the fantasy is all about other places because my mind turns easterly – to Palestine, to Istanbul, to Taiwan – as if by nature, but more likely because I am my mother's son and my mother is a daughter of empire, born in Rangoon and raised in Kuala Lumpur and Singapore, and what could possibly be more British ...?

Other writers suggesting a productive link between the Britishness of their chosen themes and chosen settings included Conrad Williams ("I suppose a number of my characters are emotionally repressed, which seems to be a particularly British thing") and James Lovegrove, who noted that "Where I've written a novel or short story that isn't explicitly set in Britain, themes of Britishness (e.g. the class system, social stratification) still intrude." For other writers, in some books at least, the location *is* the story, or a big part of it; Will Ashon, for example: "Yes, so far, in a removed, twisted, cut and pasted kind of way. Why? Why not? That's what the books are about"; or M John Harrison:

> Yes. *Climbers* and *The Course of the Heart* are landscape novels; most of my short stories emerge from British landscapes. I see that aspect of my work as a development of two traditions – the ecstatic mysticism of Arthur Machen and the rural naturalism of HE Bates. More importantly, I spent two large tranches of my life – boyhood to twenty years old, and thirty years old to forty – outdoors in the UK. I'd rather be on a sea-cliff in a fog than walk down a London street in the sunshine; but I'd rather do either than read a book or watch a film.

Gareth Lyn Powell wrote of being "drawn back to the landscapes of my childhood: the muddy shores, seaside resorts and declining industrial landscapes of the Severn Estuary," and Toby Litt mused that "I find them more fascinating than elsewhere, because I believe I can see them in greater detail." Tanith Lee simply put, "I love the landscape, and cities such as London, Glasgow and Edinburgh." Kit Whitfield described the interrelationship of story and location in her work in this way: "It depends on the novel. The aesthetics of Britain tend to influence my backgrounds – grey English cities and beautiful English woodlands both spark my imagination at times – but it's best if I just let those chips fall where they will. The settings have to work for the story."

Of course, sometimes it's non-British landscapes that inspire a writer, as is the case for Richard Morgan:

> No – though British protagonists have, a couple of times. I think my problem with British settings is that I find most of the UK just too comfy to be useful as landscape. An American once said to me, on the subject of wilderness, *Yeah, you guys don't really have any of that, do you. The whole country is just like this big park*

> *owned by the Queen.* A little harsh, maybe, but I know what he means. Give me the deserts of Arizona, the mountains of the north Norwegian coast, Istanbul and the Bosphorus, the Peruvian altiplano or western Australia's coral coast; there's an exotic appeal to these places, a drama of place even before you start to tell a story located there. And then, of course, there's off-world, which is even better because it can be anything you want it to be.
>
> What I'm interested in exploring in my fiction is human intensity, whether that be via a dynamic plot or desperate characters or both. And I find that intense landscapes or exotic cities work best as backdrop to that kind of storytelling. Of course, there's no reason you can't tell an intense, dynamic tale in a British setting – many authors do so, and I've even done it once myself – but for me the inspiration of place just doesn't hit as often or as hard on my home turf.

Some writers reported simply not being that familiar with British settings, such as (not hugely surprisingly) Tricia Sullivan, and Jon Courtenay Grimwood: "I grew up in Malta, the Far East and Scandinavia. I didn't watch UK television as a child or really deal with British popular culture. I've set a short story for the BBC in Winchester, used London a couple of times as a location, particularly in *End of the World Blues*, but always the multi-racial areas."

A few writers were more negative about British settings. Steve Aylett wrote that, "Even with great imagination it's hard to picture anything interesting happening here," while Stephen Gaskell feared "it would make my work too depressing! In my day to day life I experience too many negatives of modern British living that I know would seep into my work if I used UK settings. I get a much bigger kick from setting my stories in unusual places (at least, unusual to me as a British citizen of the early 21st century)." Gary Gibson echoed that sentiment: "I have a hard time thinking of the place I live as somewhere where anything remarkable might happen," though he also noted that, "I've used British settings, mostly because I was aware there was no real reason not to, and I pushed myself to deliberately ignore my own prejudices."

The question of whether there is a "real reason" – a market reason – to use or not use British settings was raised by a few writers. Brian Stableford's reply was sardonic: "Yes, alas, because I feel reasonably comfortable with their marginal familiarity – although it does of course make my work commercially unmarketable, as I only have US outlets." More cynically, perhaps, Martin Sketchley wrote that "British settings do not play a major role in my work because, despite its British feel, I hope to sell my fiction in America!," and Colin Davies reported that "I have used British settings only occasionally as I target most of my stories at the American market (because it's bigger)." We'll have more to say on this topic in chapters seven and eight, but Sketchley and Davies' approach probably wouldn't meet with approval from Paul Barnett, at least:

> Most of what I write these days is set in the US, for reasons of self-discipline.

> I moved my life here in 1999 so that I could marry Pam, who's an American. It was a big step to take, obviously. I thought it was important to commit myself fully to my new life in the US, and that to continue setting my fiction in UK locales would be to betray that commitment.
>
> At the same time, I didn't want to imitate US writers, because it's usually pretty embarrassing when Brits do that; so I think my style is still distinctively British. On occasion this gives US reviewers a bit of a headache, but with by far the majority of reviewers I think it's to my advantage: they actually like it that my "voice" is somewhat atypical.

And Ramsey Campbell has been there, done that:

> They do indeed. When I was fifteen I started imitating Lovecraft, even down to setting tales in Massachusetts, where it was painfully obvious I'd never been. August Derleth put me right and insisted I use British settings. For a couple of years I made them up, but by 1965 I was using contemporary Liverpool locations, and I frequently have since. Whenever possible I like either to use a setting I've visited or to visit it before use – there's always some aspect of it that you couldn't have imagined and that will be thematically relevant or will add to the sense of place.
>
> I believe fantasy – my kind, anyway – benefits from being grounded in as much reality as possible. I learned from Fritz Leiber that contemporary urban settings can be the source of the supernatural rather than just where it invades, and they very often are in my stuff, where they're also often inextricably bound up with the psychology of the characters. I think this is especially true of my novel *Creatures of the Pool*, which mixes Liverpool history and legend and fantasy until at the very least the narrator can't separate them.

Tony Ballantyne, meanwhile, said almost the same thing from a science-fictional point of view:

> I return to two settings in my work: South Street, a reflection of parts of the East End of London where I used to live, and Bridleworth, a reflection of the area of the North West where I now reside.
>
> Much of my work is set on other worlds, so mostly the question does not apply, but two of my short story cycles are set in the near future, and I anchored them in the two locations above so as to lend them familiarity, to contrast the strangeness of the sf with the normality of everyday life. As they were what I knew best, I set them where I lived. They were British settings, then, because I am British and they reflect my unspoken assumptions and my unconscious prejudices. They are not intended to be an examination of Britishness, rather a realistic backdrop against which the sf plays out.

The two intertwined points here – that familiar settings can ground the fantastic; and that for many writers, British settings are used because they are familiar – recurred again and again in the survey responses. Charles Stross, for instance: "Where it plays a major part, it's because I've decided that a particular story is best set in a present day setting where I can give it a concrete grounding, so that the fantastic elements are highlighted by contrast. I'm too lazy and parochial (not to mention monolingual) to do the necessary groundwork to set such stories elsewhere with sufficient conviction to make them work." The same sentiment came from Rhiannon Lassiter, Al Robertson, NM Browne, and others; Ian R MacLeod spoke of using British settings, but not "unadorned reality," because "I think you do need a sense of distance from what you're writing about." For some, as for Toby Litt earlier, the familiarity of British settings provides an additional charge, even if they are subsequently abstracted as part of the creation of secondary worlds. Frances Hardinge wrote that

> British settings do play a part in my books, though usually in a distorted or disguised form. For example, Mandelion, the city in my first book, is actually a mixture of Chester, 18th Century London and Sighisoara in Rumania. The locations in my second book are all loosely based on real English villages and towns, but altered for the purposes of the story. Because of their familiarity, British locations have more resonance with me, so I can use that to give the imaginary locations more atmosphere and substance.

Ken MacLeod used the same word, "resonance"; or, as Alan Campbell put it: "Writers tend to soak up whatever is around them, and then use it in fiction – and I grew up here in the UK, so I think there's a British feel to my settings." This, at least, is not something that has changed in the last twenty years; Chris Beckett, Keith Brooke, Andrew Crumey, Liz Jensen, Tim Lebbon, Paul Meloy, Deborah Miller, Adam Roberts, Vaughan Stanger, Ian Whates, Neil Williamson, and others already mentioned spoke to this issue, to a greater or lesser degree. (Although it would be interesting to see an analysis of the *kinds* of British settings being written now as opposed to then; unfortunately, such lies outside the scope of this survey.) But whether writers are using British settings for fun, as Chris Butler does, or simply because it's the default, as Peter Dickinson put it, "Unless the story demands otherwise," there is the possibility that this question is not specific enough. China Mieville puts it this way:

> In a phantasmagorically mediated way, sure, but I'm not sure it's helpful to think of them as primarily "British" as opposed to, say, Londony, or North-West-Londonaic, or Kilburnian.

One response, I suppose, is to say that what this survey is considering is a group of writers who are members (to a greater or lesser extent) of the same culture, and that what this question is measuring as much as anything is how much that culture supports writers of the fantastic refracting what is immediately around them, as opposed to what their imaginations can create.

As Christopher Priest put it: "Yes. Mexican writers set their books in Mexico; French writers set their books in France ... and so on. (Or metaphorical versions of their own countries.) I was born, live, and presumably will die in Britain. You can only write about what you know, or about what you feel." On the other hand, Iain Banks, for one, would "generally rather imagine a new world than devote too much time to re-imagining this one – it's been pretty well covered already"; and Colin Harvey feels that "The universe is too big to limit it to one small, damp, overcrowded island." But at the same time, Mieville has a point. Suzanne McLeod, for one, identified herself as a London writer rather than a British writer: "It's a place I love, plus it has plenty of history and offers plenty of inspiration." And consider Nina Allan's response:

> A sense of place is fundamental to my work. I am proud to be a Londoner. It's where I was born, and I have recently returned to it as a smelly foot returns to a well-worn shoe. The city is a daily inspiration to me, especially the less-known and under-appreciated corners of South-East London, where I live. The coastal towns of South East England, which formed the backdrop to much of my childhood, also feature frequently in my stories. I love discovering new parts of England – I feel it would be quite possible to spend the whole of one's life in this country and never get to the end of it – and England's history, its invertebrate life in particular, has always been an obsessive interest of mine.
>
> So yes, British, and proud – though having said all that the story I am currently writing is set mostly in Germany...

British, and proud, she says; but her locations are not generic British, they are very *specifically* British, as are many of those above, and those of Roger Levy: "The first two books – *Reckless Sleep* and *Dark Heavens* – take place in part where I live and have my day job, and in part in a thinly disguised London teaching hospital where I trained. Why? To look at places with fresh eyes. To change my own perceptions." Many good fictional settings, you suspect, will be the same.

So beyond that basic cultural or subcultural fact, that many British-based writers of the fantastic currently feel comfortable using British settings, we should probably not attempt to draw too many conclusions. Maybe this is why very few writers attempted to define what a "British setting" means; and maybe Susanna Clarke's response provides the word we need:

> I read somewhere many years ago that in modern times there exists a romantic image of the American landscape, but not any longer one of the English landscape. The implication was that England was now a tawdry, mundane sort of place that couldn't inspire any interesting writing or film. I thought this was wrong and I also thought it ought to be fairly easy to correct, so I

> became interested in writing about English landscape and about the sort of emotions it inspires in me. I also had a lot of memories knocking about in my head of Northern England – specifically West Yorkshire where I spent much of my teenage years. Northern England seems to me a very vivid place. CS Lewis thought that conveying the atmosphere of individual places was very important. He called it "Donegality" – as in the Donegality of Donegal.

In the end it comes down, I suspect, to whether you think half of British writers of the fantastic routinely drawing on their on Donegality is too much, too little, or perhaps, just right.

# Chapter 6:
## *What do you consider are the major influences on your work?*

## 1989

It's an obvious question. Perhaps too obvious; like "where do you get your crazy ideas?," it's the sort of thing that every writer gets asked by every tyro interviewer. As a result responses are honed, considered, and probably vary depending on the time of day or the person asking the question; and we should bear that in mind when considering the responses given below. Nevertheless, it is an important question and one that, if answered honestly, could lead to very revealing insights into the sorts of impulses and ideas that go into the generation of their fictions.

Since we are examining science fiction writers, we would expect other sf authors to feature on the lists, but will they be the old guard (Asimov, Heinlein, etc.), or more modern writers (Wolfe, Shepard?), will they be primarily American, or primarily British (Wells, Wyndham?), will there be a difference between those who write hard sf and those who prefer fantasy, and will there be a difference between younger writers and the more established names?

But we are also attempting to define the unique characteristics of British sf (if there are any), so will we find any evidence for this, such as a preponderance of literary influences from outside the genre, an interest in the classics, perhaps, or even a shunning of all genre influences.

Nor must we forget the non-literary influences, for all sorts of things can go into a writer's work from childhood memories to last night's pub conversation. What can be drawn out of these, could there perhaps (*pace* the last chapter) be an influence drawn from the landscape, or from other distinctively British features such as the class system, or even our famed liberal education?

And at the end of it all, every writer is unique with a wealth of influences that no-one else could possibly share because they are not that person. Drawing common threads of shared experience from this survey is difficult for this very reason. In fact putting together this chapter I will abandon the practice I've used elsewhere, and use extracts from responses as they are appropriate.

Let's start with those who list other sf writers as influences. EC Tubb, for instance:

> I came to magazine science fiction at a highly impressionable age and I must have been influenced by the stories of Williamson, Verrill, Cummings, Smith and other creators of the outright adventure yarn. To me, then, they offered escape from a not too happy world.

Which is about as far back as anyone goes, though John Christopher names:

> Wells, of course, a whole host of thirties writers (there's a bit in the Tripods trilogy which, I realise, echoes a short story by, I think, Frank Belknap Long; and the Tripods themselves notably echo Wells) and a few others such as George R Stewart.

And James White does the list:

> Virtually all of the "Golden Oldies," Asimov, Clarke, Heinlein, Clement, Anderson, Del Rey, Simak, the Smiths, EE (for introducing me to the idea that visually horrifying BEMs could be Good Guys) and Cordwainer, and many others since.

Barrington Bayley goes for: "American magazine sf of the late 40s/early 50s. Also Stapledon." John Brunner prefers: "Kipling, Wells, Huxley. All the sf mags I read as a kid." And Douglas Hill quotes: "All the sf I've read in 40 years. Maybe especially the good stuff of the high "Golden Age," when I was consolidating my addiction. Also especially, the major humorists (Sheckley, Harrison)."

A good solid diet of good solid sf there, which does seem to reflect the sort of fiction produced by these writers. But plenty of newer writers have just as solid a science fictional background. David Lanford, for instance, gives: "the aftertaste of too many sf magazines (*Galaxy*, I think, mostly) read when too young," and to show that magazine sf continues to exert an influence, Lee Montgomerie, perhaps inevitably, names: "*Interzone*." David V Barrett has, with one notable exception, a very distinctively British list. "Delany, Priest, Kilworth, Holdstock, Cowper, Roberts ...," while Samantha Lee has more American influences: "*Amazing Stories* and Ursula Le Guin."

It's notable, however, that more of the newer writers have a broader spread of influences that extend outside science fiction into many other forms of literature. And not just literature, but other forms of artistic endeavour such as music, film, television, comics, criticism. In fact the term that seems to sum it all up is eclecticism. For instance you get Gwyneth Jones citing: "*New Scientist*. Joanna Russ. CS Lewis. Murasaki Shikibu. Mozart" and John Clute referring to: "Snatches of poetry. Music. Eddison, Pynchon, Wolfe." Mary Gentle's influences range far and wide:

> I can only answer for right now: Hernandez *Love and Rockets*, Dave Sim *Cerebus*, Peter Ackroyd, Stanley Weyman, John Webster, Ben Jonson, The Albion Band, Dire Straits (always *Brothers in Arms*), the National Portrait Gallery, comix, opera, the history of Early Modern science, and Hermeticism, RSC productions at The Swan, Tim Powers, steampunk ...

A response that shows, among other things, a considerable and distinctively British cultural awareness. Which comes out also in the response from Diana Wynne Jones:

> The major influences on my work often surprise me. I start with Edmund Spense, John Milton and William Shakespeare and then I find that apart from Jane Austen nobody has influenced anything I write until E Nesbit and possibly CS Lewis. After that I find I am influenced by the entire body of science fiction writers.

There is, in the main, a similarly British feel to the list supplied by Christopher Priest:

> The fictional work of Jerzy Kosinski, John Fowles, Graham Greene, Brian Aldiss, HG Wells, William Sansom, Anthony Burgess, Muriel Spark and a few others.
>
> The non-fictional work of George Orwell, Guy Murchie, Graham Greene, Cyril Connolly. The poetry of Ted Hughes, Philip Larkin, John Betjeman.

Not that the literary influences are always British. Christina Lake talks of: "an amalgam of influences from Stendhal and Dostoyevsky through to Philip K Dick and Diana Wynne Jones," while Robert Irwin lists "novels by Philip K Dick, Borges, Gogol, Calvino and Potocki." Garry Kilworth said: "At the moment probably Julio Cortazar, but at various times, Wells, Wyndham, Kafka, Conrad, Sartre, Aldiss, Faulkener, Poe – I could go on."

We're getting towards that European influence cited by Brian Aldiss in Chapter Four, and he himself replied:

> To respond honestly, the list would be long, and include forgotten work. (Also writers compose lists of influences in order to reflect glory on themselves.) But I would have to say Zola, Thomas Hardy, Aldous Huxley, the speeches of Winston Churchill in the war, Shelley's poems, HG Wells, Lewis Mumford, AJ Cronin, Dostoyevsky, books on imprisonment, pornography, endless trash, and some sf, including, alas, Asimov, Van Vogt and Henry Kuttner. Oh, and many other things; Chinese poetry, for instance.

There's a similar international feel to the list supplied by Graham Dunstan

Martin:

> HG Wells, Aldous Huxley, George Orwell, Richard Garnett, David Lindsay, JL Borges, Hermann Hesse, Kurt Vonnegut, JRR Tolkien, Ursula Le Guin, Christopher Priest ... also folk tales, and Norse and Celtic myths. These are the influences that are easiest to discern; but, in a general kind of way, I do not believe that an sf writer should confine himself to reading sf. He needs to read the best mainstream fiction, and try to make his work as good as that.

If anything, among the writers who have come to the fore since the 60s, that instruction to "read the best ... fiction" seems to have been taken almost for granted, though I suspect that most of them would leave out the word "mainstream." Even new writers as determinedly science fictional as Eric Brown has shown himself to be have looked beyond the genre for their influences:

> All the writers I've ever enjoyed – though mainly, I must admit, the story-tellers, writers who have held me by their ability to spin yarns rather than dazzle with their intellect. I suppose I started writing because I wanted to entertain as much as I'd been entertained. (A few influences: Silverberg, Coney, Holdstock, Shaw, Peter de Polnay, Norman Levine, Jerzy Kosinski.)

(Though this shouldn't really come as too much of a surprise, after all, James White also gave, as an important influence:

> The Hornblower series of CS Forester, which to my mind was science fiction problem solving of the past. His stories left one feeling that one *knew* the problems of working and fighting a Napoleonic Wars frigate or ship of the line, and the hero had a very human and believable uncertainty about himself.)

Meanwhile Iain Banks, who first made his name outside sf, has a fairly determinedly science fictional list of influences:

> Everything. I always end up mentioning *Catch-22* and *Fear and Loathing in Las Vegas*, but in sf terms, I suppose all the obvious old names: Clarke, Heinlein, Asimov, then the New Wave in general, and Mike Harrison, JG Ballard, Barry Bayley, and John Sladek in particular, plus Sam Delany. After that I think my most formative years had passed, so I can't really mention all the people whose work I've admired since then. *Tiger! Tiger!* lies just about on the cusp here, as I came to the book pretty late. It's also worth mentioning that a hell of a lot of television has had an influence, as have films, though to a far lesser extent. ("Influences: Graham Greene, Saul Bellow and ... *Thunderbirds*?" Shit; there goes my Booker nomination.)

There's a strong suggestion running through most of the responses that the strongest influences come from childhood, that the books and writers with the most effect, the impetus behind someone becoming a writer and what sort of writer they become, can be traced back to the first books and writers encountered. So the younger writers, like Ian McDonald, are liable to have the more recent influences:

> Stylistically: Gene Wolfe, Ursula Le Guin, Joe Haldeman (*Forever War*), early Orson Scott Card stories have all at some time held places in my personal pantheon. Never was too keen on what James White (I think) calls the Bach quartet: Bradbury, Asimov, Clarke, Heinlein. Outside the genre; *Zen and the Art of Motorcycle Maintenance* has a close place in my heart, also Gabriel Garcia Marquez, Gunter Grass, Salman Rushdie (if the Ayatollah's death squads haven't got to him yet), CS Lewis, and Thomas Merton. Politically, I'm a wooly-minded liberal (small L), living in N Ireland you learn to mistrust politics and politicians at an early age. I despise the American right of science fiction writers: Jerry Pournelle should try living here for two years and then we'll see if he's so hot on the great gun fetish then. I could go on much longer in this vein, and with decreasing relevance.

In the main, the writers who responded took their literary influences from far and wide, often quite indiscriminately. David Redd, for instance, lists: "Paul Gallico, Arthur Ransome, Tove Jansson, Manning Coles, anything from Lionel Fanthorpe through Calvin M Knox to Henrik Ibsen"; and for John Brosnan it was: "Max Shulman, John Wyndham, Captain WE Johns, Jules Verne and John Varley." Though there was, occasionally, a resistance to the term "influence," one example of which was voiced by James Corley: "There was a time when I wanted to write like JG Ballard but I grew out of it. But he stayed an inspiration (as opposed to an influence) and so did William Burroughs and Borges and Nietzsche and Pete Townsend."

Sometimes there were quite close connections between influence and style of writing. Thus Robert Farago, a journalist, gives his major influences as: "the so-called New Journalism (subjective reporting using fictional techniques), Hemingway and Andre Malraux (French existentialist who wrote *Man's Fate*)." While Stephen Gallagher, whose work has shifted more and more towards horror, lists: "The short stories of HG Wells, most of the key figures in the early '70s horror boom, Nigel Kneale, and a dirt-cheap 1965 horror film called *Carnival of Souls*."

And sometimes the authors find it easier to recognise the influences on a portion of their output. Kim Newman, for example:

> I've seen a lot of movies and read a lot of books, but my fiction output is so slim that you'd have to talk about differing influences on each piece. My first published story, "Dreamers," was for instance an attempt to do a science fiction version of the sort of murder story Stanley Ellin or Cornell Wollrich used

> to write and which were dramatised on *Alfred Hitchcock Presents*. As a critic, however, I have definitely been influenced by David Thomson, David Prie, Doug Winter, Carlos Clarens, Andrew Sarris, Philip Strick, Cynthia Rose and many others.

Much the same applies to Simon Ounsley:

> The light fantasy I'm writing is influenced by Jack Vance, Fritz Leiber and, I suppose, Terry Pratchett! For the rest of my work, I like to think I'm starting from first principles. Of course this is wrong and there will be influences but if I think about them too much I'll just get worried.

In general, though, the response from most people was a long list of writers, about which we must bear in mind both Brian Aldiss' dictum that the author is probably romanticising the list to aggrandise himself, and the point that Neil Gaiman makes, that no list could be complete:

> I'm not sure that that question is answerable without either giving a ten page list of writers, artists, musicians, friends, situations, programmes, conventions, etc etc, or sounding terrifyingly pretentious by saying something stupid and true like "Life." One surrounds oneself with influences – they become the environment in which one moves. Different influences at different ages, filling different needs. A random sampling (off the top of my head) of people who have influenced what I've done, or how I've gone it, or the content thereof, would have to include RA Lafferty, Gene Wolfe, Clive Barker, Rudyard Kipling, ee cummings, Alan Moore, Stephen Sondheim, WS Gilbert, Samuel Delany, James Branch Cabell, Don Marquis, Eddie Campbell, Will Eisner, Lou Reed, Henry Mayhew, Robert Aickman, Harry Clarke, Saki, Ernest Bramah, Dave McKean ... and on, and on. I'm not sure a list like that would mean very much without some kind of explanation of exactly how I feel myself influenced by – or what I've learned from – each, and I find it impossible to convince myself that anyone would ever be interested in finding out.

Elizabeth Sourbut is also dubious of giving lists, but for slightly different reasons: "Whatever I was reading last week, they change with the phases of the moon. I don't know, they're probably obvious to everybody else, but not to me." While Kenneth Bulmer adds: "The input has been so wide and prolonged, cannot now say."

But these literary and artistic influences are only the start of the story, for many writers had to spread the net further to embrace a host of cultural influences. Briefly, Josephine Saxton names: "Religion, philosophy, science," Leigh Kennedy adds: "Other writers, society and politics," while Alasdair Grey broadens it to: "Experience and its artificial forms – books, art, films, etc."

In the end, however, most respondents went, in one form or another, for Neil Gaiman's "something stupid and true like 'Life'." David V Barrett is one: "Life; religion, anthropology, philosophy, psychology and sociology; mythic archetypes; history. Music, very much. The *feel* of places." Or, as Mary Gentle phrased it: "Thirty-two years of keeping my eyes and ears open."

To a degree, Lisa Tuttle echoes Neil Gaiman:

> Impossible for me to give a meaningful answer to this. Everything and everyone in my life, including lots of books. Chiefly, I suppose (like everyone) it is my early childhood, my relationship with my parents, my sister and my brother.

Or, as EC Tubb puts it: "Everyone is conditioned when young by what they see, hear, feel and read." Gwyneth Jones is another who harks back, among other things, to childhood:

> My life and times. Certain courses I did at university. Being married to a mathematician. Childhood holidays spent in the English Lake District. Camping holidays in mountain landscapes, various. Travel in general. Sympathy for the alien.

And this general range of influences was also echoed by Christopher Priest: "Travel, eavesdropping, looking at things, hanging around aimlessly"; and by David Redd: "People, places, news, maps, winter, summer, dreams, air, and stars."

Gwyneth Jones was not alone in referring to her education. Brian Stableford, for instance, offered as influences:

> The scientific world-view (as elaborated by writers extending from Francis Bacon to Karl Popper); an idiosyncratic moral philosophy (which might, if one wanted to be priggish about it, be fitted into a tradition extending from ancient Epicurian attitudes – especially the dictum "Nothing to Excess" – to contemporary soggy liberalism); the historical tradition of speculative fiction.

(There's that persistent term "speculative fiction" yet again. Is that shaping up to be one of the defining characteristics of British sf?)

While for David Langford it was: "A degree in physics, an amateur interest in mathematics, some work on military projects, and the Official Secrets Act."

Robert Irwin writes of: "A schoolboy infatuation with surrealism, my father's work as a psychiatrist, the '60s drug culture." Or, since Colin Greenland phrases it this way: "Sex and drugs and rock and roll."

Ian McDonald ties all these influences together and relates them to the work he does and the way he does it:

> I'm a psychologically oriented sf writer rather than an astronomical, or physical, or even cybernetic one – what interests me is not so mch what goes on out there, but what is going on in the heads of the characters. I'm interested more in the intimate sciences: psychology, biology, ecology, computers. A favourite motif (or cliché, depending on your point of view) is the change or expansion of consciousness of one of the characters in response to some technological breakthrough.
>
> When I'm working I like to try and find pieces of music which complement the work, a kind of musical notepad which summons up images, moods, ideas, incidents, the general feel and smell of the thing, a sort of mental pass-key into the interior world of the piece I'm working on. This sounds pretty damn pretentious, but it works for me.
>
> At the moment, I'm interested in the Third World and ecological issues – I hear you sighing, who isn't? but I have a deep contempt for the entire New Age thing, which is designer charlatanry.

It all ties together. As Alex Stewart puts it:

> Events in my life, or those of the people around me, my own fears and insecurities. Arguably secondary sources, like news items, other fictions, and so on, but these all have to be filtered through my world view before they can be used.

The society of science fiction writers, which we've noted before in relation to people starting out as sf writers, also serves as an influence. Christina Lake refers to: "Books I've read, news items, talking to other aspiring writers." While James Corley reports:

> One thing I did find when I lived in London was the evenings in the pub with other sf writers (even non-famous ones, and some indeed quite abstemious) was a great spur, a sense of common purpose? a sense of competition? I don't really know. I stopped writing sf when I moved to remotest Suffolk, maybe no coincidence.

And that's an influence that leaps the generations, because James White reports the same sort of thing:

> The most important early influence was undoubtedly the criticism, at times painful but always constructive, of fan friends (Walt) Willis and (Bob) Shaw. We knew and loved our science fiction and sub-standard workmanship was not allowed, especially from ourselves. The result was that in those early days the faults the editor would have found were corrected before final draft, rejections

were consequently few and, fortunately, the habits of self-criticism remained.

Closely related to that is the influence given by Eric Brown: "The strange 'need' to write – I suppose that's an influence." A feeling that is obviously shared by Jane Palmer: "I initially wrote only for my own amusement and will go on writing for publication as long as the opportunities exist."

While for others writing filled a more basic need, as Paul Barnett baldly stated it: "Money." EC Tubb explained:

> As regards a prime major influence that was simply cash. To write was to earn, not much, but a tempting sum in those times. To write more was to earn more – and when you're in a situation where you need money then the major influence is obvious.

Not that all influences are so straightforward. As one of the influences on her work Lee Montgomerie cites: "Jehovah's Witnesses (who knock at my door every time I sit down to type, tell me the world is coming to an end)." And there are those who do not like to talk about influences at all. Keith Roberts, for example: "I never talk about influences; because that implies imitation, or worse, comparison. And therein lies the trap. I suppose it might be safe to say Shakespeare; nobody ever succeeded in imitating him." While Paul J McAuley was emphatic: "I refuse to answer no the grounds that I don't want to incriminate myself."

# 2009

All the caveats raised by Paul Kincaid in his discussion of the 1989 survey about answers to this question – most importantly, the inevitable and even necessary partiality of any answer – apply here, too. (Including the one about money: Jon Courtenay Grimwood's response was simply, "Deadlines.") China Mieville's answer, for instance, is one of those where the link between the stated influences and the fiction we've read seems immediately apparent, but he attached entirely valid caveats:

> Obvious answers: The *New Worlds* writers, *Weird Tales* writers, *Doctor Who*, *Sapphire and Steel*, Dambudzo Marechera, Charlotte Bronte, Mary Shelley, Max Ernst and the Surrealists, *Dungeons & Dragons*, et many al. But I think the question of influence is generally not very usefully discussed, because you can be just as influenced by (say) the particular configuration of the high street on your way to school aged 11 (and I think I was), and of course there's all the influences that you're not aware of. So I'd say that asking a writer what their influences are is not by any means useless, but it's only very specifically and narrowly useful, and misses out at very least as much as it illuminates.

The "at very least," to me, suggests a need to be mindful against over-interpretation; a constant risk throughout this survey (we must never forget that, taking into account writers who this survey did not reach or who did not respond, it represents at very most only half the working sf and fantasy writers in the UK, and probably a smaller proportion than that), but one that never felt so apparent as during the analyses of the answers to this question. I'm going to talk a little bit about aggregate figures – since I think the survey is large enough for that exercise to be of some interest, and some help in identifying clusters of writers – but to put things in perspective from the start, the most commonly cited writers were mentioned by only about 1 in 8 of respondents. In all, over two hundred different writers were mentioned as influences; in a sense what's impressive is that there was any commonality at all.

At the same time, of course, the question of influence is central to discussion about sf and fantasy – the genres of the fantastic, and in particular science fiction, are routinely described by members of their community as a conversation, based on the idea that writers revisit and challenge earlier works. (That this is in fact part of the definition of a genre.) So it's not a surprise that for every writer for whom chasing after influences is a mug's game, for whom what is important about a work of literature is its *difference* to everything else, like M John Harrison –

> To whatever degree a book is made of other books, the mechanisms of assembly come from deep in the author's biography. Of my own experiences, the most emotionally productive and influential have not been reading or writing experiences; or indeed cultural-consumption experiences of any kind.
>
> Anyone who imagines that every novel can be understood by trainspotting generic templates, precursors or formalisms is not only being reductive: they're also depriving themselves of the main pleasure of reading. I suspect this is often a well-constructed defence against the human content or implications of a book. (Or perhaps against the recognition that in generically-assembled books there is no human content from which to defend yourself.)

– there is another writer more deliberately conscious of and careful about influences on their work. None more so, perhaps, than Adam Roberts:

> I might, if I had space, answer this question at some length, because influence is something I think about a good deal, and to which I try to respond explicitly in my fiction (which is to say: I consider all literature to be written in dialogue with the rest of literature, and more to the point I attempt to make this dialogue overt in what I write). It is not a boast, but is rather an observation about the requirements of the profession, to say that as a university academic in an English department I am very widely and well-read, in many spheres not limited to the canons of sf/f. All of this reading has of course fed into what I do, especially the traditions of the genre, the nineteenth- and twentieth-

> century literature (prose and poetry), theory and philosophy, the areas where I work: Tolkien, Browning, Le Guin, Nabokov, Dick, Dickens, Beckett, Asimov, Graves, Jack Vance. Those sorts of names. But perhaps a better way of coming at the question would be to contrast what I take to be the majority approach of contemporary sf writers – many of whom are of course just as well-read as I am, if not more so – with my approach: viz., most of the great writers of the genre start with science and technology backgrounds and interests, and integrate their literary interests into that. I come at genre the other way around. This may be a strength or a weakness, I'm not sure.

Between these two positions lies, well, just about everyone else who responded to the survey. Chaz Brenchley's response usefully highlights one of my working assumptions, namely that reaction against something is itself a form of influence:

> Oof. Tolkien made me a fantasy writer, but I try very hard not to write Tolkien-influenced fantasy; Asimov and Silverberg and Heinlein and Clarke defined sf for me, but Sturgeon and Ellison made me an sf writer, by showing me different ways to go. I try very hard not to write like them, too. It's all anti-influence, mostly. I love what Banks has done with space opera; I would love to write space opera, but I have to work out a way to do it not like Banks ...

Not surprisingly, Tolkien came up in this context more than once, as in Juliet McKenna's response:

> Tolkien, for first setting such an over-arching template for the fantasy genre, and now for setting modern writers the challenge of looking at the template and finding new angles and facets that reflect a contemporary sensibility. Modern crime fiction, for being plot and dialogue driven without sacrificing believable characterization, and for a realistic view on violence and its consequences.

McKenna was not the only writer to single out crime or noir writers as a particular influence, either; others who did so included Richard Morgan, Alastair Reynolds (who also echoed James White by citing CS Forester, Patrick O'Brien and Bernard Cornwell as writers he admires), and Paul Barnett. On the basis of this survey, the tradition of sf/crime hybrids, dating back to Asimov's *The Caves of Steel* and beyond, is alive and well.

A majority of respondents answered this question by providing a list of writers and other things they felt had influenced their work. Per the previous chapter, landscape cropped up quite often; and, as twenty years ago, a lot of writers offered some variation on "life, the universe and everything," either as the sum of their response (notably Chris Butler) or part of it. But many of the lists were interesting in themselves, and threw up unexpected (by me, at least) reference points at least as often as they seemed utterly distinctive to the writer who provided them. A small selection:

**Steve Aylett:** Old-time real satirists like Voltaire and Swift, thinking sf and fantasy like Greg Egan and Jack Vance, the desire to contrast with the drab sterility of most writing, and to write the kind of books I would like to read.

**Tony Ballantyne:** Diana Wynne Jones, for making me want to write, Chris Beckett, for his way of getting everything out of an idea, JL Carr for giving me an appreciation of how every word can count, Larry Niven, for his logical, structured approach, The Two Davids, Lodge and Nobbs, for showing that character is not enough, it is the interaction between characters that make a story, and Pat Mills for his breadth of influence.

**Chris Beckett:** Childhood/teenage influences: Ballard, Heinlein, Aldiss, CS Lewis and lots of '60s science fiction authors who I sort of collectively absorbed. Adult influences: Kurt Vonnegut (beautiful, spare, perfectly timed prose, wonderful ability to be serious and light at the same time), Kundera, Doris Lessing (seems to see beneath the skin of reality), Kazuo Ishiguro (especially *The Unconsoled*: a novel written using the narrative conventions of dreams), Le Guin, Philip Dick (interested in similar themes to myself, and I love his playful approach to sf conventions, and his clever literate prose).

**Alan Campbell:** My environment, and my favourite authors. I'm especially fond of Clark Ashton Smith, Mervyn Peake, M John Harrison, and Cormac McCarthy. Although I think the first two writers have influenced my work more than any others.

**Susanna Clarke:** GK Chesterton, JL Borges, Piranesi, *Star Trek*, *Buffy*, Neil Gaiman, Ursula Le Guin, CS Lewis, the English countryside, Jane Austen, Alan Garner, Ted Hughes, Conan Doyle, Dickens, the films of Miyazaki, American television, and many, many more.

**Paul Cornell:** RF Delderfield, AJ Cronin, Brian Aldiss, Christopher Priest, Dorothy L Sayers, Stephen Baxter, Arthur Clarke, John Scalzi, Geoff Ryman, Terrance Dicks, Steven Moffat, Ian Fleming.

**Jaine Fenn:** A few names that spring to mind right now: Iain Banks, Mary Gentle, William Gibson, CJ Cherryh.

**Nick Harkaway:** Douglas Adams, definitely. PG Wodehouse and Jerome K Jerome. Dumas and Conan Doyle. Then more recently, I'll own up to Mark Leyner, Neal Stephenson, and Don DeLillo.

**Frances Hardinge:** Susan Cooper, Leon Garfield, Alan Garner, Charles Dickens, Nicholas Fisk.

**Katherine Langrish:** The writings of Alan Garner, CS Lewis, Rosemary Sutcliff and Mary Renault. And the hill country of West Yorkshire where I grew up.

**Roger Levy:** Zelazny's *Lord of Light*, Chandler, Sladek, *Dungeons & Dragons*, *Forbidden Planet* (the film, not the shop), Moorcock, *Doctor Who*, Bogart, Kurosawa. Not in that or any order. And others I've forgotten for the moment. And newspapers.

**Toby Litt:** The world, what it has and what it lacks. Literary influences: Kafka, Poe, William Gibson, Henry James, Stanislaw Lem.

**Ken MacLeod:** In sf: Heinlein, Clarke, Asimov, the British New Wave (especially Harrison), Brunner's big books. In general: Marxism, libertarianism, the mid-1990s internet-before-it-was-famous, Dawkins on evolution, the extropians.

**Patrick Ness:** Peter Carey and Nicola Barker. Even though they're not sf, they are both ridiculously skilled at universe building and are completely unafraid of a strong voice. Right up my alley.

**Adrian Tchaikovsky:** Gene Wolfe, Peter S Beagle, David Gemmell, Jean-Henri Fabre, David Attenborough, Charles Darwin and human history.

The selection of influences is perhaps slightly more genre-directed than twenty years ago (another consequence of the British Boom? Most of the authors I've quoted above could be included in that generation; although only one respondent, Gary Gibson, namechecked *Interzone*, calling it "a lifeline for me in a dreary, rainy decade"), but is still, in the main, reassuringly wide-ranging.

As seen in many of the answers reported in chapter four, the question of influence has a bearing on the question of the Britishness of a writer's work. Michael Moorcock, in his answer to that question, stated that his work

> comes out of a mixture of Gothic influences from the late 18th century and early to mid-19th century, American pulp influences and a whole compendium of influences including Mervyn Peake and William Burroughs. I don't know if it's distinctively British. I suspect it isn't.

And in answer to this chapter's question, went on to say:

> Didn't we just do this? Influences range from PG Wodehouse to Raymond

> Chandler. Early science fantasy influences would have been ERB, Leigh Brackett, Ray Bradbury. But I don't read much sf/fantasy, and haven't since I stopped editing NW (you could argue that it was before ...)

Thus, as much as anything, demonstrating the partiality of any answer to this question. Interestingly, however, a number of those who had also participated in the 1989 survey remained quite consistent in their responses. OK, so Paul McAuley did incriminate himself this time around:

> Stories and novels I read when I was still extremely impressionable, from classic "Golden Age" sf to the *New Worlds* crew and beyond. A wide range of stuff beyond the sf genre – Ambler, Amis, Banville, Bellow, Burroughs, Calvino, Carter, Chandler, Dickens, DeLillo, Erdrich, Ellroy, Greene, Golding, Highsmith, Leonard, McBain, McCarthy, Marquez, Phillips, Roth, Updike, White. Etc. Although what I like and admire and what influences me is kind of hard to untangle, frankly.

And Paul Barnett thought less about money and more about, "Mark Helprin's novel *A Winter's Tale*. Writers like Chris Priest, Ian Watson, Keith Roberts, John Brunner – all in their very various ways – and more recently writers like Carlos Ruiz Zafon and Donna Tartt. Lots of pulp/noir writers, most especially Ed McBain. Dave Langford, for obvious reasons." And Stephen Gallagher offered only a general assessment: "Probably everything I was blown away by between the ages of 12 and 25. Thereafter I began to separate my sense of what was mine from what I'd read."

But Eric Brown listed Michael Coney, Robert Silverberg, Robert Charles Wilson, Rupert Croft-Cooke, and GK Chesterton as influences – the first two being holdovers from the earlier survey. David Langford was remarkably consistent, this time mentioning, "Physics, mathematics, detective stories, word and number games, love of computers, and too many years of reading far too much science fiction"; similarly, Iain Banks once again noted "Everything I ever read, I suppose," and highlighted the New Wave within sf. Lisa Tuttle, too, was consistent, even if consistently unable to answer: "My mind went blank. Uh. Probably my life, things that have happened to me, people I've met, the books I've read, landscape, artwork, music, movies, etc etc."

To get back to the matter of Britishness, John Meaney had one of the least British responses:

> In childhood: *Fireball XL5*, Robert Heinlein, Andre Norton, Clifford Simak, AE van Vogt. Later, Roger Zelazny (everything he wrote) and Frank Herbert (only *Dune*, but I loved it). In the decades since, it's non-sf writers whose writing resonates for me: John Irving, James Lee Burke, Robert B Parker and Stephen King are my heroes; and their books are my mentors.
>
> Oh, did you notice they're American?

> Of course, that's only the fiction. When it comes to other influences ... that's everything I've experienced and everything I've done. Me and every other writer.

Yet, despite what might be expected from some of the discussion in the preceding chapters, drawing up a tally reveals that the most-cited writers were British. As I already mentioned, no writer was cited all that often: but M John Harrison and JG Ballard received ten mentions each; Tolkien got nine (although some of those, as we have seen, were reactions against), Michael Moorcock and – the most-cited American – Ursula Le Guin eight; Charles Dickens, Arthur C Clarke and Alan Garner seven apiece; Isaac Asimov, Iain Banks, Gene Wolfe, and Raymond Chandler got six; and receiving five mentions apiece were Christopher Priest, Jack Vance, Robert Heinlein, Philip K Dick, Robert Silverberg, Graham Greene, Ray Bradbury, and John Wyndham. The limitations of these rankings are obvious – no accounting, for instance, is made of respondents who cited "New Wave writers," which could include several of the above – but it does seem striking that American writers don't feature until the lower tiers. On the other hand, in some ways what's striking is who *isn't* mentioned: HG Wells, for instance, received only two mentions, fewer than – say – Margaret Atwood.

And some of the most interesting (and longest) answers came from writers who seemed to be investigating their influences as they wrote. Nina Allan, for example, who also flew the flag for European-ness in this chapter:

> In terms of abstracts, I would say that my country of origin, the vital role that memory has always served in my life, and the huge love of the written word – understanding a thing or a feeling not just in physical or visual terms but in terms of written letters – have been my main influences. [...]
>
> Becoming acquainted with other European languages and literatures has been of incalculable value to me as a writer. Whereas you might argue that many English novelists have tended to become fascinated with manners, class and social mores, in European fiction the emphasis has always been on ideas. Discussions of philosophy, religion and politics have always been central to European literature, together with often more advanced notions of sexuality and the role of art. Sf and fantasy have always been welcomed into the European mainstream with open arms, whereas in England they have all too often been condemned as the black sheep of the family. It was a Russian writer – Vladimir Nabokov – who first made me want to be a writer, and a German novel – Thomas Mann's *Doktor Faustus* – that first revealed to me just how far the boundaries of speculative fiction could be stretched. All European writers are resistance fighters at heart, and do much to remind us that a little more intellectual anarchy in the UK would not go amiss.
>
> In terms of specific writers, I would prefer to say inspirations rather than influences because I am not a person or a writer who is easily influenced. The

> works of M John Harrison and Christopher Priest are a constant and ongoing inspiration. [...]
>
> I keep coming back to Ballard, his solitary doctor-antiheroes, his visionary landscapes, his cruel poetry, his sparse yet still scintillating use of language. For me, novels like *The Drought* and *The Crystal World* contain both everything that first drew me to sf and everything that keeps me reading and writing it. The single novel that has probably influenced me most in terms of its metaphors and symbols (and here I think I probably do mean influenced) is Arkady and Boris Strugatsky's *Roadside Picnic,* an influence extrapolated and enlarged upon in the radiant, visionary cinema of Andrei Tarkovsky.
>
> On my bedside table at the moment: Bruno Schulz, Thomas Ligotti, Paul Bowles. The list goes on.

Tim Lees reports facing up to an influence, and a perceived influence, and of writing for an audience that has learned how to read sf and fantasy:

> I've had a lot of comparisons made with Ray Bradbury, probably because I wrote a few stories with children as narrators. Ballard is much more of an influence (though if you read his very first stories, it's amazing how much they're influenced by Bradbury!). A great writer, much missed. It's difficult to keep the influence from being too overt, and I still write passages that read all too much like bad imitations of his work. One or two other writers have similarly infectious styles – Hemingway, Chandler, William Burroughs. Language is a virus, indeed.
>
> Other genre writers of importance to me include Lucius Shepard – I love the way he, like Ballard, combines good quality writing and sharp observations of the world, along with genre elements. And the way he keeps the weird stuff off-stage much of the time, hinting, rather than revealing all. Aldiss has a wonderful variety of work, everything from pulp sf to contemporary fiction, and Moorcock is a great hero, even if you have to be very careful how you recommend him to others ("No, don't read that, it's a pot-boiler..." Still, anyone who can produce a readable book in three days has to have something special going for them.)
>
> Really, though, I think childhood is the key thing. You're always trying to go back to that sense of seeing something for the first time. Personal experiences, of course, but also books, films, TV shows ... I think a lot of the time I'm taking things from that part of my life and re-writing them as "adult" fiction. I did a piece for one of the Elastic Press anthologies that was, essentially, a "grown-up" version of Edgar Rice Burroughs' Barsoom stories. Only barely recognizable as such. The huge back catalogue of f/sf can be mined the way earlier generations of writers mined classical mythology. The resonances are all there, if you just look for them.

For Justina Robson, on the other hand, the answer was straightforward, if, one suspects, somewhat tongue-in-cheek: "My own inner turmoil." Graham Joyce depends on "A recognition of the limitations of instrumental reason," while Andrew Crumey, along with Adrian Tchaikovsky and David Langford as already quoted, was one of the few who singled out scientific theory as an influence:

> Other than the usual ones (autobiography, chance), the most important is the many worlds interpretation of quantum mechanics, which I consider as significant an idea for our era as natural selection was for the nineteenth century. (I do not consider cultural importance equal to scientific truth; that's a separate question.) The most important literary influence is Goethe, who was of course a scientist as well as an artist. His novel *Elective Affinities* takes a particular scientific theory as framing metaphor for a drama of human relationships: a paradigm for many subsequent novels, particularly in recent times, among which some of my own might be included. The major ideological influence is the opposition between socialism and capitalism. The major creative influence is music: I am interested in finding ways of responding to EM Forster's question, what a novel would be like if it was like Beethoven's Fifth Symphony.

Tricia Sullivan is another whose main influences are, as she put it, "extra-literary":

> ... especially musical and media. Music has influenced me in that I think I think more like a musician, and I draw inspiration and ideas out of music. Media-wise, I simply mean things like watching *Star Trek* since I was six year old. I had sf in my head long before I started reading or writing it, and this had a way of sticking – at least for me.
>
> In terms of literary influences, it's impossible for me to identify them. I know what I've read and what I've loved and it's a long list, but to what extent that's visible in what I write is for the reader to decide. I know I owe one gigantic debt to Philip K Dick as a reader and as a writer – I'll say that quite safely. My work has been described as cyberpunk or post-cyberpunk but I never bonded with cyberpunk as a reader. I couldn't finish *Neuromancer* and I didn't come to Pat Cadigan's work until after I'd been "copying" her without knowing it. That was humbling because when I first read *Fools* I found out she was dealing with the same material as me, and making a better job of it, before I'd even got off the ground.

And in that last observation lies the great trap for readers and critics: can we really detect influence? Beyond the most transparent borrowings and homages, can we really unpick the relationship between what a writer writes, and what they have experienced and read? It is always so tempting to think that we can; and yet even the most obvious-seeming parallels can be dead ends.

More than in any of the other chapters, the responses here drive home the fact of the survey respondents as individuals. There are commonalities, yes, but to return to China Mieville's comment, only very specific and narrow ones in many cases. Even this small island, and this small field, it seems, contains great diversity in a great many combinations. So perhaps, like Mary Hoffman, we shouldn't think about it:

> I'm sorry; I simply don't think that way! I never think about influence, never use words like "inspiration." I can tell you what fantasy writers I like: I was brought up on Tolkien and loved LOTR as a child and teenager – still somewhat do in a nostalgic way and loved the films. But I can't enjoy the quality of the writing as a literate adult. I like Diana Wynne Jones and Margaret Mahy and Le Guin's *Wizard of Earthsea* (just the first three) and I adore Terry Pratchett. But I'm not really a fantasy reader, especially not High Fantasy. The major influences are Italy and wanting to write the sort of book I would have liked to read as a YA myself.

Except ... as Rhiannon Lassiter reveals, Hoffman has had her influence:

> Ursula Le Guin has influenced my mindset in science fiction and fantasy. Diana Wynne Jones and Margaret Mahy have influenced my young adult fiction in terms of genre, theme and approach. My mother, the children's author Mary Hoffman, is also a strong influence on me!

But that's a special case, perhaps.

# Chapter 7:
## *Do you detect a different response to your science fiction or fantasy between publishers in Britain and America (or elsewhere)?*

# 1989

There's always the chance, of course, that any characteristic of British science fiction is imposed from without. In other words that differences in publishing attitudes and practices may be reflected in the writing. This chapter, therefore, is an attempt to detect such differences as experienced by writers who've been published on both sides of the Atlantic. Of course that means many of my respondents have no contribution to make here. Samantha Lee is probably speaking for a large number when she says: "I should be so lucky to have an American publisher."

The ones who replied on the basis of the rejections they had received varied from David Redd, who found "No differences. Every one a rejection," to Alex Stewart who thought there was a difference: "I've never been published anywhere outside the UK; American editors tend to respond to my stuff with polite bafflement." But such responses probably don't help us a great deal.

Still, it is interesting to see if there are writers so distinctively British that they can't get published in America. Colin Greenland could be one:

> American publishers won't buy my work, but nor will any British publisher except Unwin Hyman. Cautious times (not that my visions are dangerous). A German and a Japanese publisher bought translation rights to my first novel, but declined my second and third. Gwyneth Jones observes that each of her books has been translated into one language or another, but no country has ever come back for more.

But that doesn't seem to say a great deal about national traits so much as about publishing idiosyncracies, as Brian Stableford says: "Publishers (by which one has to mean editors, they being the actual respondents) are so idiosyncratic that it's difficult to separate them into camps according to national boundaries."

On the other hand, David Langford's experience may indicate something of a different national taste:

> American publishers reject me rather more consistently, often with the memorable words, "This hilarious and side-splitting story/novel had us all rolling uncontrollably around the editorial floor in tears of hysterical laughter at the brilliance of the wit, but of course the humour is too British and the American public wouldn't understand."

And if it's not humour, it might be something else, as suggested by Langford's occasional collaborator Paul Barnett:

> Interestingly, quite a few years ago I tried to get off the ground a major book on CETI: this was rejected, synopsis unseen, by several US editors (including one JL DelRey) on the basis that only Americans had anything interesting to say on the subject. The idea that such a book might not take the Green Bank formula too seriously was apparently anathema to them, as was the idea that ETs might be really *very* different.

What this suggests is that American publishers are unwilling to let British writers wander onto what they consider their territory. Graham Dunstan Martin appears to have experienced something similar:

> I have hardly been published in America but have been told that US publishers refused *Time-Slip* because they regarded its Edinburgh setting as "outlandish and obscure." Apparently, if you're British, you're only allowed to set your books in London. Considering the transatlantic population of Edinburgh in summer, this seems a strange judgment to make. The true explanation must be American insularity – their reluctance to understand the rest of the world.

Insularity might also be behind Iain Banks' experience: "I do rather get the impression I'm talking a foreign language as far as most US publishers – and the majority of US sf readers – are concerned."

However, Lisa Tuttle suggests that what some see as insularity might have its basis in familiarity, or lack of it:

> I think there is much more interest in and enthusiasm for my work among British publishers than elsewhere, but then I live in London and know a lot of editors, and I only occasionally visit New York or Paris. (And I don't know *anything* about publishers outside Britain, France and the USA.) I am not exactly

> a best-seller ... it seems to be easier to publicise (and perhaps to sell?) a writer like me in this country than in the US ... London seems a smaller world than New York – but I do have a very one-sided view. Although I'm from America, I never lived in New York, and I'd moved to England by the time my first book was published. If I still lived in Texas, not only would I really have no idea what British publishers thought of my work, but I am quite certain that neither *A Spaceship Built of Stone* (The Women's Press, 1987) nor *A Nest of Nightmares* (Sphere, 1986) would exist as books. (In both cases, specific editors asked me if I had enough stories to publish as a collection ... my own and my agent's attempts to interest American publishers in this idea some years earlier had come to naught. Tor will be publishing *A Nest of Nightmares* in the US sometime in the near future.)

So, writers in this country tend to know editors in this country which helps – that makes sense. But there's also a suggestion that British publishers are more daring, which is rather borne out by Brian Aldiss:

> In a long career, I have had only three publishers over here (I speak of hardcover publishers, not sausage factories): Faber & Faber, Jonathan Cape, and Victor Gollancz, with Weidenfeld & Nicholson as a sort of side dish at one time. These three pleasant companies were happy to accept what I offered them; the only book they ever rejected was when Faber rejected *The Interpreter*, which showed their good judgment. They cared for quality more than subject matter, seeing it as their business to publish. In the States, publishers are far more quirky; one day, Random House will swear to take anything you write; next week, they reject something because it wasn't like your last one. Only Signet (pb) as it used to be and Atheneum as it was until yesterday have shown no great wish to control my writing.
>
> It must be added that I have had good relationships with almost all British paperback houses – very pleasant editors in the main. So are the editors in New York; but they are undoubtedly more driven and have less autonomy. So their favoured authors have less autonomy.

A number of other respondents expressed an unease about American publishing as opposed to the British equivalent. Garry Kilworth said:

> There is a different response from American editors (except Ellen Datlow, who seems to have a broader view than most) who tell me that my books are unsuitable for the American market. They seem to want material that explains everything in logical terms and leaves no mysteries.

That distinction between explanation and mystery might be a potent symbol of the difference between American and British science fiction. Another writer who sees a difference is Keith Roberts:

> As a lowly writer one never of course deals with publishers as such. A better comparison is with editors, and there's a sharp difference between Britain and the US. British editors will cut your throat with perfect politeness; that's the "gentlemanly" aspect. After which they usually do a pretty good job on the text. US editors work on the principle that they're Goddam more important than the guy who wrote the thing, and don't feel they've done their job until the text has been carved to fragments, with or without the writer's permission; though of course there are honourable exceptions to all generalisations. Something would certainly seem to have gone wrong, though, since the days of Herman Melville.

Paul J McAuley seems to feel much the same way, since he replied: "In Britain the notion that even an sf novel is something more than product has not completely withered away." And Josephine Saxton is also conscious of the "gentlemanly" aspect of British publishing: "The English are more polite – when rejecting especially." While Mary Gentle gives actual examples of the differences in editorial attitude:

> For the USA I had to take the swear words out of *A Hawk in Silver*. The American editor of *Witchbreed* tried to delete all reference to the characters being fat! (I have never worked this one out). The end of *Ancient Light* didn't seem to go down well with USA publishers. I suspect I do better in British and European markets, but can't quote figures. Japan just bought *Witchbreed* and *Ancient Light*, which is a bemusing thought.
>
> On the other hand, I've sold more short stories to America than anywhere else.

Christopher Priest says: "I find publisher response is very different in every country. I do worst in the USA, best in France. The UK is the median." But publishing response is a personal thing, and these differences may be as much down to the individuals involved as to anything distinctively British, or European, in his work. Certainly other writers report a very different attitude. Diana Wynne Jones, for instance, seems to contradict the experiences of David Langford:

> The response is not as different as anyone might expect. My American publishers tend to delight in anything humorous and obviously British whereas my British publisher goes for things which are more overtly strange. It seems to add up to much the same.

While Ian McDonald, whose work was published in America long before it came out in Britain, seems to feel his Britishness is an advantage over there:

> I think any success in America (and there was a lot of reaction to *Desolation Road*, both critical and from individual readers) was due to the fact that it was not an American sf novel, and that was what endeared it to Bantam, I think.

In fact there were as many British writers who preferred American publishers as there were who favoured their British counterparts. John Brunner has a strong reason for this: "British publishers prefer to buy US best sellers and reject even my books with UK settings. I have never made more than £3,500 in sterling in any given year." And James White backs him up:

> Usually stories are submitted first to the US, occasionally simultaneously to the US and UK, but often the UK publisher waits to see the US edition before making up his mind, and European, South American and Japanese publishers do the same. When a novel is published in the US, a new Sector General, for example, reprints of earlier books are reissued with it. The stories always clear the advance and there is a continuing trickle of reprint royalties fro the backlog, but the print runs have always been small and the sales effect minimal. This might be because the publisher considers me a competent, dependable and safe writer who always clears his advance and is good for a small profit, or to insufficiently forceful agenting over the years that did not secure the higher advances that would have ensured the book being pushed hard by the marketing people or, an idea that is, of course, totally unthinkable, that the stories themselves were at fault. Anyway, the end result has been that in the US and UK I am famous but not rich.

And there are others who feel much the same way. Barrington Bayley reports: "British publishers are even less keen than American ones," while EC Tubb says: "Publishers abroad seem more interested than those at home." Even Robert Irwin, whose literary fantasies might seem more at home on this side of the Atlantic, says: "The Americans seem to be a little keener on my fantasies, but I can't say that this has translated into much in the way of purchases; or advances. Still, the noises made are nicer."

Occasionally there is a reminder that publishing is a business with profit as much in mind as any other business. So even if, as Neil Gaiman says: "The Americans pay more. Mostly," they are in the main looking for the big seller, and it is success that generates success on either side of the Atlantic. As Stephen Gallagher says: "The response is about the same. Nobody really liked anything until *Valley of Lights* and now they like everything, including the stuff they didn't like before."

So the publishing response may vary from one writer to the next, or from one book to the next. It is a world of swings and roundabouts, as John Christopher says: "I used to sell better in the States; lately I think that's probably reversed itself." But whichever side is up, in the long run it amounts to the same thing. As Douglas Hill says:

> Nearly all my stuff has been published in the USA and here, and the Americans merely aim it at slightly older kids. But then publishers' responses, beyond "yes" and "no," tend usually to be so subjective, and so easily swayed by outside concerns, that they shouldn't be taken too seriously.

A final word on this subject comes from Gwyneth Jones, who brings us neatly back to our original starting point. If there is a difference between British and American sf it may not rest on the publishers so much as on the marketability:

> I feel that the people who would publish non-bestsellers (to put it politely) by obscure foreign writers are likely to have a lot in common whatever country they're operating in. If I was an American in the same category I believe I'd have less difficulty getting published over here, because "Americanness" is marketable in sf in a way that "Britishness" is not. For juveniles, the position's different. My juvenile sf/fantasy is perceived very differently in America by both publishers and public; briefly, more favourably and more seriously.

# 2009

A couple of years ago, Jo Fletcher, the Editorial Director of Gollancz, was a guest at the BSFA's monthly interview series in London. She had this to say about her imprint's editorial policy:

> I used to be able to read almost everything that was published in a year in Britain and America, but nowadays, Tor alone put out something like 30 books a month, or so it seems. No-one can keep up with that, and even choosing the best of what was available in America left no room for what was happening in Britain. So we made a decision a long time ago that we would look primarily to British authors. *Interzone* was doing a very good job of nurturing young writers, and there was a lot out there for us to pick from. [1]

The importance of publishers to the flourishing of British sf and fantasy over the past quarter-century is both obvious and stated less often than it might be. Without their confidence in British writers of science fiction and fantasy, there would be nothing we could try to label a Boom; and if Jo Fletcher's remarks are typical, that confidence has been waxing in the period between the Mexicon survey and this one.

Much of my interest in the responses to this chapter's question, therefore, resides in the question of whether there have been any detectable changes in editorial practice or writerly experience that might account for the changes in what has been published. So the obvious place to start (absent a survey of publishers!) is with those writers who responded to both surveys. Iain Banks dodged the question: "I probably would if I was capable of paying attention. These days I'm very easily distra – what was the question again?" But the others all offered some response. David Langford, for instance, finds that the US and UK have come closer:

> Not as much as in 1989. I used to whine that American editors tended to reject my "British humour," but either my Britishness has worn off, my lucky string of Hugos changed editors' minds, or I simply found the right editors. Most of my backlist is in print with Cosmos Books/Wildside Press in the USA.

In addition to Langford's offered explanations, it's worth noting that Cosmos/ Wildside is a datapoint in of one of the acknowledged changes in sf and fantasy publishing over the past decade or so: the rise of the small, or in some cases not-so-small-but-smaller-than-trade, press. As we'll see, these publishers have been important to quite a number of writers. In the meantime, here's another '89 alumn, Lisa Tuttle, who finds her fortunes have reversed:

> My last two novels were published in America but declined by British publishers, for reasons that remain obscure to me. Both are fantasy novels set in Britain. Prior to that, I wrote a couple of YA novels and a book for beginning readers, all commissioned by a British publisher, none sold in the US. ("Too British"? I can only speculate.)

While Stephen Gallagher's fortunes have declined only over here: "To UK publishers I'm a forgotten 90s horror writer. In the US I'm upmarket and literary." Eric Brown, on the other hand, reports no difference in response – "No. Their response is largely indifference" – a sentiment echoed by Brian Stableford: "Very little – there's absolutely no interest whatsoever in Britain and almost none in the USA and elsewhere." And nothing has changed for Christopher Priest: "Yes. I have always been published badly in the US." Paul McAuley has

> ... only just reacquired an American publisher, so there's a big difference right there. My current UK and US publishers share a touching faith in the possibility that one day my work will be more commercial than it currently is (I hope they're right). US publishers in general tend to be a little more hardheaded, but the market is tougher over there, so they have to be.

Is "hardheaded" a synonym for the phenomenon that Paul Barnett describes?

> US fantasy/sf publishers are at the moment, it seems to me, primarily interested in stuff that meets generic expectations. (There are, of course, some glorious exceptions among the editors.) This obviously lands me in some difficulties, because a lot of the time what I'm doing doesn't fit easily into those expectations.

Between them, these responses introduce the major themes of this chapter, most contested to at least some extent: the role, if any, of "Britishness" in success or failure; hospitability of the two markets to "stuff that meets generic expectations," and stuff that doesn't; and the more interventionist editorial process at American publishers.

Two sidebars before we get to those questions, however. The first is to say that the one thing that seems to not be in dispute is the truism that timing can be vital. Suzanne McLeod, for instance, says: "I write Urban Fantasy. It is currently more popular in the US and Germany, but becoming more so here" – suggesting at least part of the reason for the paucity of writers of urban fantasy (in the contemporary, Charlaine Harris/Jim Butcher sense) among the respondents to this survey. But those urban fantasy writers who did respond, such as Mike Carey, did not report any differences in experience between UK and US publishers. John Meaney said, "Yes, but some of that is timing. My recent Tristopolis books generated similar responses in Britain, America and Germany"; it's probably no coincidence that *Bone Song* and *Dark Blood* can be called urban fantasy if you squint a bit, and have been promoted as such in the US.

But timing can be a more individual factor, too, as Charles Stross' experience shows:

> A little. My agent is American, and I'm sold in the US first. My career trajectory is rising, but it's rising faster – by a couple of years – over there. The results are very visible in bookstores; I get about three times as much shelf-space in American shops as in equivalent British ones: I get sent on signing tours and see a fair amount of media promotion. My British publishers are somewhat more low-key.
>
> However, I think this is mostly a historical accident. My first British publisher – a small press – went bust; Orbit then picked up the pieces, but the result was a two year delay in my British publication track that resulted in me being handled like an imported American writer. They've mostly caught up now, and the gap is narrowing.

The second sidebar is to pick up on the mention of Germany above, and look at the role of elsewhere. Ian Watson put it front and centre:

> Elsewhere, such as Latvia or Hungary just off the cuff, publishers still seem quite interested in publishing me. I think Elsewhere is rather important, and must note an implicit anglophone bias in the question, whereas for instance

> in France SF writers are happily getting on doing their own thing. For which cause, among other reasons, I recently co-wrote what is probably the first (and maybe only, if you see what I mean) full-length genre book in collaboration with a writer whose mother tongue is different from mine. *The Beloved of my Beloved*, by me and Italian Roberto Quaglia. This leads to unique perspectives.

Other notable mentions of Elsewhere came from Mary Hoffman ("I have only been published by Bloomsbury in the UK and US, at least my fantasy sequence – plenty of other publishers. But there are 28 other language editions. I don't really understand the question"), Peadar O'Guilin ("Yes. My book was much more heavily promoted in Italy than in any of the English speaking markets, for example"), Jon Courtenay Grimwood ("Yes, massive ... I sold assorted East-European rights (Polish, Czech, Slovak, Hungarian and Russian, etc), as well as French, German, Italian and Turkish, etc, long before I sold US rights), and Stan Nicholls, who offered a run-down of his experiences in various countries:

> It rather depends on the particular publisher. And, indeed, the country. Without wanting to generalise, my experience with American publishers is that they tend to involve authors to a greater degree, and at more stages. They appear genuinely interested in what you think about proposed covers, engage you in promotions, that sort of thing. The US publishers I've been with run very slick operations, and seem better resourced, certainly going by the number of people who have specific roles in the process.
>
> My French publishers are a dream in these respects too (though tighter staffed); ditto the Germans of whom it's hard to avoid the cliché about them being very efficient, though they are. My Dutch publishers are excellent too. So by and large, outside the States, Europe's pretty good to deal with. Well, there are exceptions, but they tend to be countries with smaller publishing industries and more fledgling democracies. Some markets could be black holes for all you get out of them: you're paid an advance, the books are translated without reference to you, they appear (you might or might not be sent copies) and if you're lucky there'll be the odd royalty payment. One of the things I really like about my French, German and Dutch publishers is that I have a close relationship with the translators. If anything needs clarifying they just ask. I wish more foreign publishers would just do that; I'm sure it makes for better translations.

But in general, for most writers, the US/UK axis appears to still be where it's at, even if not all writers reported as pleasant an experience as Nicholls. This is not, perhaps, hugely surprising, given the historical interrelationship of the sf communities in the two countries, and that the American market is simply the largest English-language market; although it is probably also prompted by the phrasing of the question. I can't help feeling that if this survey happens to be repeated again, in another twenty years, it would be worth updating the wording to ask about differences between the UK and other countries, without further specification.

But for now, it is to the differences between the UK and US markets that we turn. As in 1989, not every writer who responded to the survey was able to fully answer this question. In all, 32 writers said yes, they did detect some kind of difference; 23 said no, they did not; 25 reported that they're not currently published in the US, or do not have sufficient experience to draw on to comment; and six said that they have more difficulty being published in the UK than the US. (These totals don't precisely match the total number of respondents because writers are tricksy beasts, and I coded some answers in multiple categories.) The role of Britishness – or Englishness – was commented on by a number of the writers who haven't sold to America yet, such as Tim Lees:

> I've seen my work in the States, but only in British magazines. I've never had a US publisher. I did once get a US agent to look at a mainstream novel I'd written, one very much concerned with social and political developments in Britain over the last couple of decades. "Too British," he said, though implied it might be published in the States if it found a UK publisher first. Which it did not. Ah well.

And James Lovegrove, who digs into what the term might mean:

> Yes. I'm "too British" for most American publishers, meaning, I suppose, I don't tailor my work for an overseas market and don't write about generalised settings that can't be appreciated without detailed background knowledge, and don't write the "outward-bound" kind of space opera that goes down well in the States.

It's certainly noticeable that the novels that allowed Paul McAuley to reacquire a US publisher (*The Quiet War* and *Gardens of the Sun*) are indeed a return to a kind of outward-bound space opera, if more low-key than most; and that Adam Roberts' only US-published novel (*Gradisil*) is also a novel of space exploration. But of course counter-examples are easy to come by.

It's interesting to compare these responses to that of Ramsey Campbell, for instance: "Really not at all that I can distinguish. My American publishers seem to like my stuff to stay as British as it is, and don't even copy-edit to tone that down." Maybe this is a horror thing, as Stephen Gallagher's response hinted earlier, since another writer from that area who's been more published in the US than the UK is Conrad Williams: "Publishers are still giving horror the cold shoulder in general over here. In the States I think there's more of a readiness to embrace it. The green shoots of recovery do seem to be around – novels such as Joe Hill's *Heart-Shaped Box* have made something of a splash, although it wasn't necessarily marketed as a horror novel."

Roger Levy reports interest in a science fiction novel for a different reason:

> I'm not published in the States, so that must say something. One small US publisher was interested in *Icarus*; I asked my editors, "Why, since it's anti-American," and he said, "That's exactly why." Which must also say something.

Again the small press crops up. As Vaughan Stanger put it, "A few US second tier pro/semi-pro editors clearly get what I do, but I reckon they take more risks than their Big Four counterparts." And, returning us to the issue raised by Paul Barnett, he concluded: "I do think that British editors are less conservative." Gareth Lyn Powell agrees, and somewhat echoes James Lovegrove's sentiment about what works in America: "British publishers seem happier to take risks on new talent and to engage with new technology, whereas certain American publishers seem stuck in the early Seventies, still churning out the same cheap and cheerful space operas." And Juliet McKenna says:

> British publishers seem somewhat more inclined to accept experimentation with the classic settings and tropes of the fantasy genre, moving away from the quasi-European-medieval template. American publishers seem rather keener on experimentation with the archetypal characters within those classic settings and tropes. As with all such generalizations, there are plenty of exceptions.

While Graham Joyce, published by Gollancz in the UK, says: "Very much. In the US they find it hard to see my work as genre at all"; although you imagine that other writers might find that situation more of a boon. Kit Whitfield's experience, interestingly, both supports this sense of a fluid, hospitable British market, and suggests that American genre publishers may be less hidebound than it so far appears:

> Oh yeah. In Britain I'm published by Jonathan Cape, a literary imprint; in America it's Del Rey, which is popular science fiction. I'd class that as pretty different! America, in my limited experience, is a bit more likely to classify something as science fiction because it has a science fictional component, whereas Britain can be a bit more flexible in its classifications. But I could be wrong about that; it might just be that I caught the eye of different editors who happened to work in different genre imprints.
>
> A lot of the difference is packaging rather than essentials. My editors in the different countries are all original, intelligent and sensitive people who've had insightful things to say about the books, and the different things they've spotted are probably as much a mark of their personalities as genres. Everyone's an individual.

Indeed, Ian MacLeod argues that the picture is the other way and that it's *America* that is the more open-minded: "I've often seemed to find particular obstacles to selling my kind of work in the UK. Even when they don't necessarily always buy my stuff, I've found that foreign editors are more attuned and sympathetic to the broader picture of what sf can do." Given that his most recent novel, *Song of Time*, has so far only appeared in a small-press limited edition in the UK, despite winning this year's Arthur C Clarke Award, he may have a point. On the other hand, so far, this particular novel hasn't been published in the US at all.

But his argument is echoed by others, including Kari Sperring: "Well, so far I haven't sold a novel in the UK! But I don't know, to be honest. UK publishers have been complementary, but said I'm perhaps not sufficiently commercial. DAW felt otherwise." Chaz Brenchley tells a similar tale: "At the moment I am published enthusiastically in America and barely at all in the UK (well, by the small presses but not the mainstream sf/f lines). Whether this is a response to my work or my sales figures is a judgement call; I know which way my judgement goes." And Mark Charan Newton disagreed with Gareth Powell's assessment of British publishers:

> I've only recently sold to Del Rey in the US, but I've not noticed any discernible difference. I think it's certainly tougher to get published in the UK – the number of publishers are few, and they are taking on only one or two new authors a year. Those aren't great odds for struggling writers.

There's the question of how books are marketed once they are purchased, too, as Graham Joyce suggested. China Mieville noted that, "The US publishers have, traditionally, done better covers, and have been rather more successful at crossing the genre border. Not to diss my admirable British publisher, of course." On the other hand, for Steve Aylett the question is not *where* but *who*: "It's more difficult everywhere to get interesting stuff published by major publishers, but smaller publishers are more into it (i.e. more likely to be interested in genuine originality) and there are more small/medium-sized publishers in the US than in Britain." Tanith Lee is similarly appreciative:

> In the beginning, apart from some childrens' work, British publishers wouldn't give me the time of day. But when I tried the States, DAW books, then under the command of Donald A Wollheim, responded instantly to my work (rejected until then – *The Birthgrave*, for example) and launched me on my true working life. Currently, while a lot of British publishers are again slamming doors in my face, the response from some of the best smaller presses in America has been, and is, soul-saving.

And as Andrew Crumey reminds us, the label attached to your books has no necessary correlation to their sales: "Publishers and bookshops don't market my work as science fiction in any country, as far as I can tell, though some reviewers call it science fiction. I do better in some countries than others; I put this down to statistical variance. Some places you get lucky, others you don't."

For some of the YA writers, any fussing about stretching the borders of genre is beside the point. Patrick Ness, for instance:

> Not really, but only because I write Young Adult books, so that concern becomes primary for both the US and UK. Everyone knows, though, that young adults are about the least snobby readers there are, so the difficulties others might bump into because of genre are really minimised in YA. Teenagers just want a ripping great story; if it's good enough, they don't care what genres it might use.

Similarly, Ben Jeapes said, "I have a YA publisher so it's hard to say; my editors don't base their actions on the science fiction content. Scholastic Inc. in the US had no difficulty with a novel about the Royal Space Fleet per se, but bafflingly renamed *His Majesty's Spaceship* as *The Ark*. However, this decision has also baffled other American YA editors I have spoken to, so it could just be a Scholastic thing." One issue that might have been expected to come up more often was only raised by NM Browne: "Yes. I think the US seems more worried by the violence and sensuality/sexuality in my books."

All of which perhaps underlines the importance of individual editors, a point singled out by Tony Ballantyne:

> Every time I think I've noted a different response, something comes along to change my mind. In my experience it is the individual editors' responses, regardless of their nationality, that are very different.

Justina Robson, Colin Davies and Peter Dickinson voiced the same sentiment. And there were British writers who just didn't have any significant differences to report – Mike Carey, for instance, or Alastair Reynolds: "I've never been asked to change anything, other than very trifling clarifications, and neither my British nor my American publisher has ever given me any pressure to shape my work in a particular direction (make it less gloomy, less noir or whatever)." Of course, Carey and Reynolds were two writers who identified most strongly with American sf, earlier in the survey. Richard Morgan was another, and reports a similar lack of interference:

> Not really – I've been lucky in both cases to get publishing houses and editors who are quite content to let me do my own thing and apply only the necessary minimum of professional oversight when the manuscript comes in. I keep hearing horror stories out of the US about massive editorial pressure to mutilate manuscripts so that they fit better into this template or demographic appeal, but I have to say from a personal point of view I've never suffered even

> the hint of that. Both Gollancz and Del Rey have always been behind me a hundred percent.
>
> There was of course the briefly (internet) famous *Black Man/Thirteen* controversy, but what got lost in the flurry there was the fact that – though I was, and remain, somewhat bemused about the *why* of it – I really wasn't bothered about changing the name; my books, after all, are often re-titled in European translation, and even the original UK name sometimes changes from the working title (*Altered Carbon* was originally called *Download Blues*, *Black Man* started life as *Normal Parameters*, and so forth ...) so bitching about the US change would have seemed a little hypocritical. *Thirteen* was my own idea as an alternative title, and the conversations I had with my New York editor about it were very much along the same lines as the ones I had with my London editor about dumping *Normal Parameters* in favour of *Black Man*. My only real concern when my books are published is that the content should remain unadulterated, and in that, I've detected no measurable difference in attitude anywhere I'm published.

But others, it seems, have. Nick Harkaway was not the only one to report that "the US is much more hands on. 'Can we change that? What would happen if ...? How about a new structure ...' The whole industry works differently there." And to return to Jon Courtenay Grimwood:

> When I did sell American rights, to a publisher I like and an editor I really respect, I had to go to New York to edit the books into a tighter third person point of view, and unpick the narrative.
>
> I'm not saying that's bad. My tendency – now ruthlessly suppressed. Well, slightly muted – to expect readers to work at it is not popular with all publishers, or all the public! And what seems obvious to me in my own work doesn't seem obvious to everyone else. At the high end, US critics seem to be more forgiving than UK ones, cutting an author slack for trying, albeit failing, to reach for something. At the low end, it seems the other way around.

The comments about critics there will be picked up in the next chapter. Meanwhile, M John Harrison has no such feelings of generosity towards American editorial suggestions: "My experience with US publishing was that the editor didn't trust the writer to be in charge of his own novel. It's easier for everyone if I'm originated over here."

The praise of both the UK and the US for open-ness to new or genre-stretching works came in roughly equal quantities, perhaps indicating that both markets, actually, are pretty healthy. Michael Moorcock could have it right when he says, "You're lucky when you get a smart editor," whichever side of the pond you're on; although nobody had stories of UK editorial intervention comparable to those mentioned or implied above about US editors, so that may be a real difference. But it may be worth ending this chapter by speculating how a survey of US writers would report on the UK market. Of course, the difference in size is vast, so Britain is not necessarily a high priority to "break into" in the way the the US can be for British writers; it's noticeable, however, that many of the most prominent and praised contemporary American sf writers – such as David Marusek, Peter Watts, Nalo Hopkinson, Hugo-winner Robert Charles Wilson, or double Hugo-winner Elizabeth Bear – are absent from British bookshop shelves. Perhaps the focus on best of British doesn't come without a cost.

**Endnote**

[1] Fletcher, Jo. "Best of British: Jo Fletcher interviewed by Graham Sleight"; interview at The Star Tavern in Belgravia, London, 22 November 2006, printed in *Vector* 253 (July/August 2007), p. 4.

# Chapter 8:
## *Do you detect a different response to your science fiction or fantasy between the public in Britain and America (or elsewhere)?*

## 1989

Publishing is a business where at least part of the criterion for success is being able to judge what will sell. So, having considered whether there is a difference in publishing attitudes between Britain and America, the logical next step is to find out whether any such difference reflects a difference in taste, interest and requirements between the reading publics in both countries. A few caveats must be borne in mind at this point, however. Only writers who have been published in both countries could possibly make such a comparison, so a large number of my respondents were unable to answer, either because they have not been published in America, or, in Ian McDonald's case, "Haven't had enough out in Britain to be able to compare." Furthermore, if the authors are to judge from direct reader response rather than from book reviews, they have to receive such response, and any reader who writes to an author is liable to do that mostly if they like the book, so adverse judgements aren't so much part of the picture. Some authors were ruled out because of lack of response; John Brosnan for instance reported: "The only response I've ever had was a letter from someone who liked *The Fungus*." Brian Stableford said: "The public hardly responds at all," and Josephine Saxton spoke of "Very little response from anywhere." While David Redd commented:

> The sample of responses was too small to be significant. British fan annoyed by symbolism, American puzzled by ambivalent psychological ending. Both sides of the Atlantic liked a panoramic sweep of ideas. (The vast majority of readers everywhere made no response, of course.)

Bearing all that in mind, however, the 19 authors who felt able to make the comparison were more uniform in their response than to any other question I asked. Barrington Bayley and EC Tubb summed it up most succinctly, they both simply replied: "No." Douglas Hill expands on that: "As far as detection is possible (i.e. through letters from young readers, contacts made on visits to US and UK schools, etc) no difference at all." While Alasdair Gray adds: "The critics are equally approving and disapproving in both places." Paul J McAuley has found: "In all cases, friendly but mild curiosity." And for Christopher Priest:

> It's difficult to judge response from the reading *public*, since I get so little of it. From the handful of letters received over the years I suspect that the average British reader is similar in taste to the average American, French, Italian, etc. Reader response is about the same everywhere: a few people like my stuff, while the majority either don't like it, don't know it or don't care.

Those who do express any kind of preference tend to favour the American audience. Possibly, as James White suggests, for purely practical reasons: "My work seems to be more popular in the US, but that might be due to there being more readers there." A point backed up by John Brunner, who remarked in the last chapter that more of his work is published in America than here:

> I seem to be equally warmly greeted at UK and US conventions, although I confess that at US cons more of the readers seem to have read more of my work. This may be due to the phenomenon referred to in answer to the previous question.

Though this may also be due to an innate American politeness that several people referred to. Colin Greenland, for example:

> The half-dozen Americans who have read books of mine have generally commented on them with more enthusiastic approval than my British readers, who tend to cavil. Perhaps Americans are just more polite (they are).

A point backed up by John Christopher, who comments: "Americans write more letters, but then that is their genial habit." Which may relate to the statement from Brian Aldiss:

> Obviously, one meets a bigger sample of one's readers in one's home country. This remark will be held against me, but I rather feel my writing is taken for granted in England at present. An instance is the *Helliconia* novels. They received a far warmer reception in the States than in England. Moreover, although the Americans suppose themselves, modestly, not to be a nation of letter-writers, I receive more fanmail from the States than from this country, though there's a

> faithful woman who writes from the Isle of Anglesey ... The Americans are much warmer in their responses than the British. Three books have been published on my writing; all of them in the States, none here – although the best one was by David Wingrove. Hands up any Brit who has read that book of David's.
>
> Let's face it, we have a history of being shits to our writers; the reception of the recent biography of JB Priestley is a case in point. Only Peter Ackroyd and Anthony Burgess, among reviewers, could afford the poor old chap – or his corpse – a few generous words; you'd think from the rest of the reviews that their writers had been personally assaulted by Priestly, rather than entertained.

Gwyneth Jones also seems happier with American critical response:

> I haven't had a great deal of experience of public response outside the UK but so far as I can tell from reviews alone response has been far more responsive. The US reviewing network seems far more extensive and communicative; of my juveniles I see reviews from children, teachers, librarians, which is very helpful. UK please copy. Generally, though this perhaps reflects a much larger and therefore more accomodating market, I find the US audience much more tolerant. Feminism seems to be accepted as part of life's rich tapestry over there, while over here it is seen as so extraordinary that often it's the first and only thing a reviewer sees in a book.

Garry Kilworth is another writer who has found a positive response from his American readers:

> Those American readers who have spoken to me about my books have said they enjoyed them, but perhaps those who hate or are indifferent to them have not bothered to voice their feelings. Editors are of course concerned more about a general response, than individual enthusiasm. They have no interest in a minority cult author, unless that author looks like gathering many more readers as a result of being thought cult-trendy.

Kilworth is not alone in tracing differences back to the publishers. Stephen Gallagher says:

> Over here, my publishers are taking a high profile. Over there I've been just another name on the list, but word-of-mouth and reader feedback has been prompting them to take another look at what they've acquired.

While David Langford echoes something Mary Gentle said in the last chapter about not understanding the ways of the Americans:

> One hard sf novel died rapidly in Britain but continues to sell in new US editions. A non-fiction book covering lots of the same material did well here but never made it into paperback over there despite a substantial hardback edition. That was the one about which an Ameriacn paperback editor said, "It's a bit negative about war." I don't pretend to understand this.

While Diana Wynne Jones just found:

> The public in Britain go for a slightly different range of books than those in America. For instance, *Witch Week* is far more popular in Britain whereas America is overboard for *Archer's Goon.* I have never been able to calculate beforehand what the response will be.

Neil Gaiman has his own perceptions of the differences between Britain and America:

> Well, the British are proprietorially proud of you (as long as they don't think you've "Sold Out"); the Americans are impressed by anything you do, think The British Are Weird and suspect it's Something In The Water.

After all that, however, Mary Gentle doesn't seem to find any difference between Britain and America, it's Australia for her: "The two adult sf books seem to strike home particularly in Australia." Oh well.

# 2009

The short version of this section is that little has changed, except that more of the writers surveyed were able to answer the question. Of the sixty or so writers who felt able to offer some sort of comment, two-thirds still said that no, they don't notice any difference in reader response between different countries. And, as several writers pointed out, given the relative ease with which authors can *find* reader response these days compared to twenty years ago (the "Summon Author" joke [1] exists for a reason), there's more reason to be confident in the absence of difference. Mark Charan Newton wrote that

> I can only really go by reviewers so far, but I think British and American sensibilities are more similar than we'd like to think, and the internet – review sites, blogs, etc – has shown this to be startlingly true. Current commentary suggests that any perception of the strengths and weaknesses of my writing isn't shaped by a reader's nationality.

Alastair Reynolds reported much the same: "I get a good cross-section of reader responses via my blog, my website, and of course I'm aware of things like Amazon reviews, and I've yet to detect any significant differences." And for Kit Whitfield, the joy of the internet "is that it's international, so I don't really meet my readers in national groups; they come from all over the place, and that makes for a nice, vibrant mix. Of course, this is self-selecting."

For some, the lack of a difference came as a surprise; Alan Campbell wrote, "I have always thought American readers were more optimistic, generally less morbid than us Brits. So I didn't expect dark anti-heroes to be as popular over in the US. I was wrong." Others, referring back to the last chapter, felt that reader-response will always be secondary; as Graham Joyce put it, "No, because the publishers want to drive and define the market, whereas some pockets of the public will always resist being driven by the market," while Juliet McKenna replied, "Not beyond the distinctions I've observed in publishers in the previous answer, and then only to a limited extent. Mostly reactions cover the same gamut the world over." And Roger Levy said, "Not really. People are people, I think. Publishers imagine they're not, sometimes, give them no credit. On the other hand, writers are naive. Maybe the publishers know what they're doing."

Andrew Crumey perhaps felt the problems caused by attempts to drive the market particularly keenly, and suggests that it's not always the fault of publishers:

> Members of the public are individuals and respond accordingly: I can't draw any useful generalisations. The response I've noted from sf critics in both Britain and America tends to be negative: when my work is viewed as science fiction it is often found not up to scratch. In that case I can only conclude that either I write bad science fiction, or else I don't write science fiction at all. When my work has been analysed according to standards of "Britishness" or "Scottishness," similar results have often been obtained. I once had my work reviewed as detective fiction, and again it was found wanting.

Many were more succint; among those who simply said, "no," or something similarly straightforward, were Joe Abercrombie, Chris Butler, Mike Carey ("No"), Mark Chadbourn ("None"), Paul Cornell ("Not at all"), Stephen Gallagher, Frances Hardinge ("Not noticeably"), Ben Jeapes, Rhiannon Lassiter, Paul McAuley ("Not that I can tell"), Adam Roberts, Al Robertson ("People that like it, like it; people that don't, don't"), Brian Stableford, and Lisa Tuttle. And among those who didn't feel they've received enough feedback to tell (either because they haven't been published in both countries, or because they simply don't receive many responses) were Will Ashon, Eric Brown, Elizabeth Counihan, Jaine Fenn, Stephen Gaskell, Gary Gibson ("Not as yet"), M John Harrison, Toby Litt, Deborah Miller, Justina Robson, and Adrian Tchaikovsky ("Ask again later..."). And Iain Banks dodged the question once more: "Right. As I was saying: yes and no."

Tim Lees offered a reminder that the data we're working with here may be skewed in many ways: "The only Americans I know who've read my work are Anglophiles, so I couldn't say." And Steve Aylett feels that things have changed for the worse: "Responses in the US used to be more independent than the UK because there were fewer reviews over there and less prompting as to what they were supposed to think. Now there are fewer reviews everywhere (less of a profile) so the responses are generally more honest everywhere, and more enthusiastic. There's not much difference between the UK and US." Although for some, similarity in response could be a matter of content; apropos his own work, Peadar O'Guilin cheerfully reported that, "Themes such as cannibalism have the same effect wherever you go – a mix of revulsion and fascination!"

Even many of those who thought they did detect a difference in reader response hedged their bets, such as Chris Beckett:

> Possibly I am more likely to be accused of being too gloomy by US readers than UK ones? UK readers are perhaps more likely to complain that my stuff isn't science-fictional enough. Not sure about this, though

His second suggestion was (tentatively) picked up by a number of respondents, offering another angle on the previous chapter's debate about how the two countries handle genre. Nick Harkaway's experience, however, leans in the other direction: "I think – possibly because of people like Pynchon or Michael Chabon – that there's less of an issue with it there. Here I get raised eyebrows occasionally – but then, I spend more time here, so I don't really know." And a similar response came from China Mieville: "Impossible for me to say. I think my stuff's slightly more read by less hardcore genre fans in the US, but as I don't live there, it's hard to be sure." Ian R MacLeod echoed his earlier thoughts about publishers: "I've never really detected any great patterns among people who like my stuff, apart from there being slightly less snobbery about sf in the broader public in most other countries other than the UK." Peter Dickinson put it in the strongest terms: "US readers take genre more seriously and ghetto-ise it less."

On the other hand, NM Browne's experience is that "USians are more likely to comment on my style too, which does not always fit their notions of 'good' writing," suggesting that on at least some axes American readers can be conservative in their own way. Kari Sperring noted that, "I've had a lot of good feedback from US readers, although I think my characterisation is more British, too – I've been told my characters play intellectual games and a number of US readers have said that the level of emotional exposition is lower than they like." And Paul Barnett finds that US reviewers, at least, can be the *strictest* about genre:

> A higher proportion of US reviewers become outraged if fantasies don't fit the templates; at the same time, there are those reviewers who really love it when fiction startles expectations rather than conforms to them, and those critics tend to treat my stuff possibly more kindly than it deserves. The same

> comments apply, I think, to US readers in general.
>
> I do believe, in parallel, that UK readers are far more tolerant of the fact that each of my books tends to be completely different from its predecessor – an attempt to resuscitate the Victorian fairy tale followed by a fantasticated satirical/political romp followed by an "if this goes on" mosaic novel in which deliberately each chapter uses a different style/"voice"/narrative technique from the last ... it seems extraordinarily hard for US reviewers to cotton on to the fact that a writer can choose to produce diversity rather than a continuity.

For Sarah Ash, "the most appreciative responses I've received have tended to come for America"; but Stan Nicholls finds that

> American readers are the toughest, the hardest to please. I get criticism from some of them about the tiniest details. E.g. Just recently I had a lengthy and quite affronted email from an American reader who protested that I'd used the word "swoop" four or five times in one of my (100,000 word) books. He thought it was too much, and why couldn't I come up with another word? Not that nitpicking's restricted to American readers, of course, and a lot of the feedback I get from the States is very positive. But some of it can be almost forensic.
>
> If you really want to draw criticism, wander into an area guarded by hardcore fans. It's happened to me with my series of *Orcs* books. Because there's a general perception that orcs "belong" to Tolkien, any use of them tends to enrage a portion of his fans, even if they have no idea what I'm trying to do with the subject. You should see some of the vitriol I get from that source. But other writers tell me *Star Wars* and *Doctor Who* fans can be worse, so that's something, I suppose.

There is a danger that the US readership gives the impression of being different simply due to its greater size. A correspondent such as the one Nicholls describes is going to stand out in a writer's mind, but if they're one in ten thousand, how many more of them (for writers who sell in both countries) are going to be American than British? This is not to say that, for instance, Americans are not more likely to respond, as Tony Ballantyne ("Americans are more vocal!") and John Meaney ("American readers are more likely to email me! Thanks, guys") report. Simply that this survey is not the way to tell if that is true, and that the majority of responses suggest that it probably does come down to individuals. James Lovegrove, for instance, finds:

> Americans who "get" my work seem to be those who don't read a great deal of sf/f as a rule, and therefore come to it armed with perhaps a better knowledge of British customs and references because they have read outside the genre as well as within. The French seem to appreciate what I do, in as much as they enjoy sf/f that doesn't always abide by the conventions and that is prepared to

state and discuss its ideas explicitly.

And there is of course the fact that books appear in different contexts in different countries – as Kit Whitfield points out, "Different packaging, different promotion, and inevitably this will have an effect on what people expect from the books." In Michael Moorcock's case, "The British public has a wider understanding of what I write. American public sees mostly only my sf/fantasy. French public has a different understanding, too. It all varies a little, but the public for sf/fantasy remains pretty much the same." And Chris Priest priest reports that

> My work was almost unknown in the USA until they filmed *The Prestige*. Now a lot of people in the USA have read that novel, but none of the others. (Nearly all of the other books are out of print ... US readers could look on Amazon, I suppose.) My stuff always seems to have done much better in translation than in English.

So it's not a surprise to find that there are writers such as Tricia Sullivan whose work has been consistently better-received in this country than any other; or to hear Mary Hoffman report, "Not really. I'm very popular in Germany and the Nordic countries"; or other variations in sales reported by writers such as Katherine Langrish ("Sales have been good in Japan, Spain and Italy. In America sales have been moderate"); or to find that writers writing particular types of fantastic literature experience differences in success. Conrad Williams, for instance, said that, "The American appetite for horror fiction seems to be healthier. There doesn't seem to be the stigma attached to it that exists in this country, where horror is the ugly relative nobody wants to talk to at the party." And Suzanne McLeod expanded on her comments about the new urban fantasy, and offered another take on the perception of genre lines:

> Same answer: I write Urban Fantasy. It is currently more popular in the US and Germany, but becoming more so here.
>
> I also think Urban Fantasy in particular is still seen as the flighty daughter of horror, fantasy and romance in the UK and as such isn't regarded as "serious," probably due to the crossover and blurring of the lines between UF and Paranormal Romance. (And yes, due to vampires having sex with leather-clad females instead of tearing out their throats [although sometimes they do that too!] – not that there's anything wrong with either scenario.) But when you think that romance readers are more likely to read outside their genre than any other reader, then it's always possible that PR/UF could be a way for more readers to discover the wider genre of sf/f, and not be put off by the unfamiliar worlds that sf/f can be set in.

Other responses were common to only one or two writers. Britishness was mentioned by Ramsey Campbell ("The occasional American reader does object that it's too British, though I haven't had that reaction elsewhere that I know of") and Paul Meloy ("I think that Brits like the use of language and place because they recognise something of themselves in them. I can't be sure, but I might put people off overseas because of this raw, uncompromising Britishness"). Ken MacLeod noted that "US readers more often focus on the politics, which seem to them extreme," an observation backed up by Jon Courtenay Grimwood:

> Readers in the US tend to talk about the politics, the strangeness of the characters, the exoticism of the locations. UK readers tend to take all that for granted and concentrate on whether I think my characters are insane, and whether their external/internal voices are real.
>
> Almost everything anyone can say about this is a generalisation. On balance, I think there is still a tendency for US markets to regard UK writers as depressing and UK markets to think of US writers as given to wish fulfillment. Even now, the idea that in a US novel, a happy ending means getting the girl, saving the dog, ruling the universe ... while in a UK novel, it means walking away with your life, just about holds, for publishers, at least. Although, no longer, I suspect, for US readers. It probably doesn't help that in my books the girl probably gets the girl, while the dog turns out to be the most intelligent character in the book and is dreaming the universe anyway. (I'm really trying not to do that now.)

Are those girls, in fact, a problem? Chaz Brenchley reported that "The only distinct difference I've noticed has been specific, over gay content: UK reviews uniformly failed to mention it, where US reviews uniformly felt obliged to highlight it, and there have been some poisonous responses on the net. But that says more about societal differences in general, I think, rather than responses to my work, per se."

So it seems that differences in readers' responses to a writer's work – if there are any – will, in part, inhere in differences in culture; but that differences in context, how the work is presented, and simply individual differences in readers are at least as, if not more, important. And that this is as it has been, more or less. Not an unexpected finding, really. But Richard Morgan sums it all up quite nicely:

> Well, yes and no. You do see some minor cultural hiccups sometimes when my work crosses the Atlantic – for instance, there were a number of comments criticising the amount of foul language used by the characters in my last novel, and these complaints were almost exclusively American in origin. The British (and Australians and Norwegians and French and Italians and just about everybody else) just took it in their stride. Ditto complaints about the explicit sex in my books, and bad reactions to the explicit political commentary in a couple of my nearer future scenarios. So it would certainly appear that, in general terms, there is within the US sf/f readership a group of people who

are far more uptight and tender in their expectations than any you'd find on this side of the Atlantic. Sort of *controversy virgins*, I guess you could call them, going to the literary marriage bed in the expectation that it's all going to be dewy-eyed candle-lit air-brushed cuddles.

That said, I think my books have found a readership in the US which is very much at ease with the kind of fiction I'm writing and relates to it every bit as enthusiastically as my British readers. And it has to be said that it was the Americans who started garlanding me with awards first. I picked up the Philip K Dick and John W Campbell Awards a long time before I got the Clarke. So clearly I was speaking at least as effectively to the American readership (or at least a portion thereof) as I was to anyone in the UK. And there is maybe a more whole-hearted, passionate enthusiasm in play across the Atlantic, which embraces new thins in a way the rather more conservative British literati take longer to do. Maybe.

Truth is, in the end I think it doesn't do to make too much of this cross-Atlantic cultural divide – there are, of course, substantial cultural differences between the UK and the US, and I think anyone who's been paying attention is probably aware of them; but within both populations, there is also quite sufficient variance of taste and mindset for a writer to find his or her audience and flourish in both countries.

**Endnote**

[1] Coined by Steve of the *My Elves Are Different* webcomic, here: <http://myelvesaredifferent.blogspot.com/2007/02/summon-author-is-good-term-for-common.html>.

# Chapter 9:
## *What effect should good science fiction or fantasy have upon the reader?*

## 1989

This was a trick question, I suppose. On the supposition that most writers would consider that what they are doing, or at least, what they are attempting to do, is good, this question is really asking, "What are you trying to do with science fiction?" From that, we might hope for an oblique look at more defining qualities of British sf, though in the end the answers are I think, probably inevitably, more revealing about individuals.

Some people, of course, avoided the question. John Brosnan replied: "There's no answer to that question," and Iain Banks said: "Leaving the easy questions till the end, eh? I honestly don't know."

While Paul Barnett reminds us that what the writer intends the fiction to do may have little or no relation to what the reader gets out of it:

> Whatever the reader wants to get from it – entertainment, profound ideas, you name it. I think, for most stories, what the writer wants the reader to get out of it is a secondary concern – although I'm not averse to popping in the occasional subliminal (or not so subliminal) political message.

There was the occasional response which suggested that science fiction should have nothing to do with such political messages, subliminal or not. Alex Stewart, for instance, replied: "Entertainment. That's it. If you want to change the world, go into politics."

But he was in a minority of one, since other respondents displayed a remarkable uniformity. Entertain, yes, but as John Brunner makes clear, it is the way he entertains that matters: "Entertain him/her by 'stretching the muscles of his/her imagination.' I quote myself, but I never found a better way of explaining it." Barrington Bayley makes the same point: "It should stimulate the higher cognitive function." In other words, the job of science fiction is to make the reader think.

Of course, it should do this through entertainment, as EC Tubb remarks:

> Any fiction, science fiction, fantasy or whatever, should entertain. If it does not do that then it cannot be called "good." I don't care how prestigious a book is, how strongly lauded by others, if it doesn't entertain me then, to me, it's so much wasted effort. I accept that to others the response could be different but I can only evaluate a work on my own terms. They are: does it entertain? Does it give grounds for speculation? Does it educate? Most important of all – when I've read the book, do I feel content? Have I enjoyed it? If I have it's a good book.

David Langford backs him up: "It should persuade readers to finish the book, and not leave them feeling hungry again half an hour later," and Jane Palmer adds:

> Personally, I believe the reader should feel they are getting value. Naturally individuals' tastes vary and the wider the scope of the market the better. I suppose the "effect" it should have on them is one of satisfaction at reading something which is of interest.

But still that idea of speculation and education is implicit. As Simon Ounsley says, "Good sf should make readers think about and reconsider the human condition, the world, and the way both might be heading. It should also entertain the reader enough so that he/she gets that far." Or, to give a selection of brief responses: "It should entertain, arouse, and make them think," Samantha Lee; "Pleasurable stimulus to thought and feeling," Alasdair Gray; "Stimulate the mind and the spirit. Positively," Josephine Saxton; "Make you think," Lee Montgomerie; and "To make you see," John Clute.

Such change is a great ambition for James Corley: "To be good it has to change the reader, however temporarily. At the very least a good book should dispel boredom. A few really great books have the ability to change the way you look at the world."

It is, to the majority of respondents, something in the nature of science fiction itself which necessitates this urge to stimulate thought. Paul J McAuley says:

> Stephen Hawking has pointed out that since philosophy devoted itself entirely to the study of language, there is an unfilled void between science and society. Good sf lives in that uneasy boundary. Like looking up at the starry sky after a couple of shots of whiskey, it should make the reader dizzy with the vast, subtle possibilities of the Universe. Olaf Stapledon apart, the whiskey is generally a better bet.

And Ian McDonald, having referred back to his quotation from Isaac Asimov in Chapter Two, makes the same point:

> As the literature of change, sf should be a denizen of the borderlands between ourselves and change. It's the boundary between humanity and technology, and as such has an important social role, especially in these Tofleresque days of miracle and wonder. Also, sf should hold up a distorting mirror to the society in which it is written (and I don't mean here just Thatcher's Britain, but the world society we are creating), it should give us a bizarre, distorted, but all the more revealing for that, perception of ourselves. I suppose then, at its heart, sf is an inherently radical, satirical and parabolic literature. Or it damn well should be. The general effect on the reader, therefore, should be reflection, and contemplation, and increased awareness. See, back to the psychological change of consciousness again. It should be the written equivalent of a mind-expanding drug. Only better.

There were others who picked up on the idea of the distorting mirror. Mary Gentle, for instance, felt sf should: "Unscrew their perception of reality. Bedazzle and amaze. Rearrange their analysis of human nature. Raise three loud cheers. Unsettle. Entertain, in all the best senses. Change people." Or, as Colin Greenland preferred to put it: "Surprise, delight, disorientation. 'Fun With Your New Head', Tom Disch called it." While Robert Irwin gave specific examples when he said: "I think that good sf should put extreme pressure on the mind, bending and twisting the mind like a glove – Piers Anthony's *Macroscope*, Priest's *Inverted World* and PK Dick passim are good examples of what I value."

There was a general impression that sf is able to stimulate new ideas because of its very nature. Christina Lake said: "Really good sf will change your perspective on something or enrich your imagination with possibilities that weren't there before." David Redd added: "Good sf should make the reader feel he is living in a different world, learning something new and strange, sharing an experience not possible anywhere else."

Brian Stableford was making much the same point when he said:

> It should elicit a particular delight associated with meeting ideas that one has not met before; it should make one think more deeply about the moral implications of future possibilities; it should make converts to the philosophy of progress; and it should add to the creative power of one's own imagination.

And again from Diana Wynne Jones: "The reader should enjoy it, enjoy it as something new and end up with a (sometimes unacknowledged) new insight into the way people live in the world." Or from David V Barrett: "It should make the reader stop in his tracks and see life and reality from a different angle. It should challenge the reader's assumptions and preconceptions – which is also what I mean by being subversive."

Gwyneth Jones is also aware of a political dimension: "a) To give pleasure: specifically the particularly refined pleasure of *understanding* something new. b) To instill relativism. One lesson of all good sf, satire intended or not, is 'it ain't necessarily so'."

James White looks at this from a very personal vantage:

> It should take him right out of himself, and make him/her use and stretch his/her mind, make him aware of viewpoints and characters he may never before have considered, and take him along with the ideas and events of the story to the extent, perhaps, that he gets more out of it than the writer was aware of putting in, and while doing these things the story should entertain, whether the entertainment takes the form of the direst prophecy or sheer escapism.

But Elizabeth Sourbut is careful to point out that sf, by its nature, has to reach out beyond the personal:

> Good sf should give people a new perspective on the world. They should come away from an sf novel seeing things a little differently, or aware of an aspect they hadn't thought of before. It's never just about people, people are a large part of it, but if that was all it wouldn't be sf – sf is about issues and larger trends, so it should make people think and wonder about what we're doing and where we're going and how we're going to get there.

Kenneth Bulmer backs her up:

> Succinctly – a book might cover this answer – it should make the reader aware that the world is an organism and part of a wider world and open his/her eyes to what has to be done now to make the future what we would wish. It has to be entertaining in the cant word otherwise people won't listen.

All of which is summed up by Graham Dunstan Martin in one very familiar phrase:

> A sense of wonder. A questioning of the nature of reality. It should promote social, political, scientific and metaphysical speculation. It should break down the assumption that the world is exactly as it seems to be. Fantasy (as opposed to sf) is at its best when it is (as in Le Guin or Robert Holdstock) psycho-myth. (This is, after all, the fundamental nature of folk tale.) In most of these respects, fantasy and sf have the potentiality to be more powerful than mainstream fiction. One day!

To be honest, I'm a little surprised that the phrase "sense of wonder" didn't come up more often, since it seems a perfect summing-up of this sort of position. However, Kim Newman would disagree, since he considered the effect of good sf should be:

> The same as all good fiction – entertainment, enlightenment, education, aesthetic pleasure, lots of other good things. I keep hearing people talk about sense of wonder and being forward looking, but I don't think these are necessarily the province exclusively of sf.

Quite a number of respondents felt that sf should achieve what any good fiction should achieve. Christopher Priest, for one: "It should have the same effect as any other fiction. Not necessarily in this order it should be moving, improving, entertaining ... and trying to add to the sum of human happiness and knowledge." Robert Farago felt that "like all good writing, [it] should conform to Dr Johnson's ideal: 'Utile et Dulce' (useful and sweet)." For Stephen Gallagher it's all about: "The illumination of character and the human spirit, the same as in any other form of fiction. While for John Christopher: "Like all good fiction it should entertain without degrading. If the writer is on the side of the moralities, so much the better, as long as it doesn't show through (if you're really good, like CS Lewis, this doesn't matter)." Eric Brown felt that:

> The same as good mainstream writing – it should enlighten the reader as to the human condition; should leave a reader emotionally moved and believing they have seen reality through eyes other than their own. Good fiction has the ability to show how others besides ourselves think and act, and as such should spread tolerance. (Or am I being too idealistic?) It should entertain as well, of course. I've heard it said that good sf should accustom us to the notion of change, which I suppose is true: it *should* – whether it does or not ...

But however much it is a part of the greater realm of fiction in general, there are regular reminders that sf does have something different, something extra about it. As Lisa Tuttle says:

> Like all good fiction, good science fiction should move the reader emotionally; in addition, it is important that it should be intellectually stimulating. I think good science fiction makes the reader look at the world in a different way – and, however briefly, question the status quo, and look with new eyes upon something previously ignored, taken for granted or unquestioned.

And that's a point of view shared by Leigh Kennedy:

> Good science fiction should excite the reader in the usual fictional way with interesting characters, intriguing plots, well-written prose, but should have the

extra edge of making them think about change, its possibilities and effects.

Garry Kilworth sounds what might be taken for a warning note, reminding us that different sf can have very different effects, and bringing it all round in the end to the quality of the fiction:

> It should have a variety of different effects, ranging from enjoyment to feeling disturbed, depending on what that particular piece of fiction seems to be aimed at. Ron Goulart wrote good sf, which I enjoyed for its sheer madness. Zamyatin wrote good sf, which being political, disturbed me. Sf should not be judged by a particular kind of effect on the reader, but by the quality of the storytelling.

But Brian Aldiss provides an example to show that sf actually can have an effect: "One reader – an American, of course – wrote to me that *Helliconia* had changed his view of the world. I knocked off work for the day and went for a pleasant walk in the woods."

We come back constantly, then, to the notion that sf should, in part at least, speak directly to the ideas and perspectives of the reader. As Douglas Hill puts it, comparing sf to cocaine:

> Sf should illuminate the mind, free the spirit, clear the sinuses, loosen the bowels, whatever. It should *stimulate*, in short, that range of thoughts and sensations and emotions and imaginings which otherwise would wither. And it should bring about an addiction to itself, or anyway a habituation. (I'm a schoolyard pusher ...)

In this common subversive attitude – to borrow David V Barrett's term – there may well be one of the most important distinguishing features of British sf. We draw on literary more than genre intentions, and the aim is to question, to undermine, to look from another perspective. This may lead to gloomy prognostications, to overtly political work, to an unsettling read, but such is seen as the purpose of sf. There is certainly no sense of the gung-ho optimism, the reinforcing of assumptions, that can be distinguished in the work of at least some American sf writers.

Of course, there's always one with somewhat inflated views of sf. Neil Gaiman, for instance:

> Well, I always feel that good sf ought to cure all his/her diseases, clear up his/her spots, stammers and embarrassing personal problems, provide all the vitamins and nutrients needed to sustain life, and leave the reader feeling like he or she has just been given the keys to a new car and a two week holiday in the luxury resort of his or her choice.
>
> That's *good* sf. *Incredibly* good sf ought to raise the dead.

# 2009

Michael Moorcock's answer put a finger on one of the problems with this question: "'Should'? We're getting into politics here, aren't we? A touch of the old fan messiahs?" Susanna Clarke felt similarly:

> I'm not sure what sort of answer you're expecting here. If it were possible to identify the right and proper effect of good science fiction or good fantasy, what do you propose to do with the books that have a different effect? Good science fiction and fantasy, like all art, can affect the reader in many, many, many ways – some of which you and I have not dreamt of yet and many of which depend as much on the reader as on the writer. The same book can affect us differently at different points in our lives, depending on what we need at the time; this is a good thing.
>
> One of the things I aim at is a strong atmosphere to my writing – an atmosphere which is reminiscent of other books but which tries to be unique. But I don't know if this is the primary effect a reader takes away from the novel or stories and I wouldn't prescribe it as something other writes ought to do.

Everything Clarke says in her first paragraph is true – and Ken MacLeod made the same point: "There are different kinds of good sf (can't say anything about fantasy) and different ways of having an effect: sensawunda, putting your brain through its paces (e.g. Egan), making you see the world differently, placing the everyday world within the context of a vast and ancient universe (or even wider than that)." Richard Morgan was wary of answering at all –

> That's a bit of a minefield question, to be honest. I'm extremely wary of making prescriptive templates for literature, cinema, drama, genre, what have you, not least because hard on the heels of prescriptive comes *proscriptive*, and after that we're all just down to tribal fucking squabbling and beating our sad little chests for attention in our particular corner. I have an instinctive dislike of the kind of person who can turn on a dime and give you a cut-and-dried answer to questions of this sort – science fiction should do X, good fantasy is Y, literature is Z, and so forth.

– although he did have some further thoughts, which we'll come to in a bit. My point right now is that despite these legitimate objections, I don't think the question is useless.

It is, to my mind, a question about emphasis. Accept that the potential elements of fiction remain constant from book to book, and genre to genre; then, to a large extent, what changes from case to case – what makes the effect of a given book different

– is the emphasis placed on those elements by a given writer. Which elements are foregrounded, and which are backgrounded: and, implicitly, which benchmarks a writer would prefer readers judge their work by. For some respondents, the effect of good sf and fantasy should be no more complicated than Deborah Miller made it: "To entertain, transport, and delight." For others, it seems, this is not enough.

So it's not surprising that many responses to this question offer variations on themes. The interest, I think, lies in which themes predominate now as opposed to twenty years ago; or among British writers of science fiction and fantasy as opposed to those in other countries; or among writers of science fiction and fantasy as opposed to other kinds of fiction. This survey can only approach an authoritative answer to the first of those three questions, because that's the only case where we have a control group, but it can perhaps suggest answers to the other two.

Most of the words, phrases and concepts that came up again and again will be familiar from twenty years ago. Ken MacLeod mentioned a few, and Stephen Gaskell sums up most of the rest:

> So many things! Firstly, it should make the reader sing the praises of this widely misunderstood branch of literature to all and sundry, leading to massive increases of sales for all purveyors of sf and f ... in fact, I am experimenting with a few concealed memes in my own work that should have precisely this effect ...
>
> More seriously, speculative fiction should make a reader more politically aware (and perhaps more active also), better prepare them about forthcoming societal change whatever the source (technological, ecological, economical), convey the majesty and diversity of the natural world, help them understand scientific concepts through dramatic means, thrill them, give them a mirror onto themselves, improve their personal relationships, lessen their prejudicial thinking, and, of course, open their eyes to alien procreation. Probably not all at once, mind!

The starkest comparison is probably with Will Ashon's response: "The same as any other good art. It's a means to an end, isn't it, rather than an end in itself?"; or, in more detail, Chaz Brenchley's response:

> Ach. (Have you noticed how most of my replies begin with some kind of exclamation? These is hard questions ...) I think good sf and fantasy should have the same general effects as good writing in other genres, any genres: we use stories to teach ourselves about the world and each other. The metaphors of speculative fiction are more spectacular, but sensawunda is a beast we ride to get where we are going, not an object in itself. (Sometimes, of course, where we are going is for-a-journey, rather than towards-a-destination. The sf-is-a-literature-of-ideas school might stand as exemplar: in an exploration of

> what-would-happen-if, the travelling is the purpose, the process is the point. But that's equally true in other forms of literature. Sf distinguishes itself by content, which is the least of it; it's not really about the rocketships.)

There was serious support for Ashon and Brenchley's position; over a third of respondents explicitly stated some variant of "The same as any other good art," and implicit in the responses of many more was sympathy with that position, perhaps representing a slight increase from 1989. And such responses came from a wide variety of the writers surveyed – including those who write primarily fantasy, such as Abercrombie and Alan Campbell, those who write primarily sf, such as Chris Beckett and Roger Levy, horror writers such as Ramsey Campbell, YA writers such as Mary Hoffman and Patrick Ness, and writers published as mainstream such as Ashon and Kit Whitfield. To return to Richard Morgan's response, for instance:

> That said, the project of creating fiction requires a skill set, like any other activity, and like any other activity, you can do it better or worse. So it's not unreasonable to lay out some broad guidelines for best practice, and I don't believe in special dispensations for genre here. A good sf or fantasy novel must be, first and foremost, a good novel full stop. That means engaging characterization, convincing sense of milieu, compelling story – in short, the salients of any good fiction. I have no sympathy for (or, really, understanding of) the mindset that says *sure, the writing style is for shit, the characters cardboard, the settings unconvincing, but hey it's a cool concept or a good fast moving story, so who cares?* To me that's like ordering a meal and saying you don't mind the fact the steak is burnt to a crisp, the sauce cold, and the salad unwashed, because, hey, the chips are good. I mean, come on, people.
>
> As to what all this adds up to in terms of effect upon the reader, I quite like Kafka's "a book must be the axe for the frozen seas within us." Good fiction moves you, I think, forces you to feel something when the storm of experience and day to day existence very often dulls that ability in us, especially as we grow older. And then there's Bradbury's argument for "telling detail," as specified in Faber's speech in *Fahrenheit 451*: "The good writers touch life often ... [books] show the pores in the face of life." Those two quotes balance out quite nicely, I think – you're looking for something that provokes emotional responses and engagement, but from a basis that's anchored enough in reality to convince. Without the latter, you're just not going to buy into the fiction enough to care, but without the former you're not going to care enough to buy in. So, as regards genre writing, I'd say that if your imagined future or fantasy landscape and the characters that inhabit it feel real and emotionally engaging enough to care about, then you've done your job well.

For these writers, sf is indeed a means to an end, rather than an end itself, although what that end is still varied somewhat. Ian R MacLeod, for instance, said:

> The same as any other kind of fiction, it should offer an intensification of the human experience, and tell us more about life in unusual or interesting ways. That, and keep us amused or horrified, enraptured or entertained.

While Mary Hoffman wrote:

> The same as any other good literature – expand their horizons and make them realise the world is full of other lives and other possibilities.

James Lovegrove:

> It should be a means for addressing the great issues of the age, and any age within the framework of a well-told story – much like any kind of fiction.

And for Kit Whitfield the goal is simply:

> The same effect that any good book should have. It should be an engaging read that touches the reader in some way.

These are not, of course, mutually incompatible responses. But they make me curious as to what a survey of writers who scrupulously avoid the fantastic might turn up; which, if any, of these "same as any other good literature" goals they might light on for their own work. (I suspect Whitfield is closest, if only because her goal is the broadest.) And whether, too, they would highlight any of the goals that sf and fantasy writers picked out as the "something extra" their genre reaches for.

China Mieville – after disclaiming, "I'm not the police! I can only say what *I'd* like it to do to *me*" – quoted more from Kafka, including the sentiment that "I think we ought to read only books that bite and sting us," and added, "I also think that sf/f/h is uniquely able, better than 'realism', to bite and sting, and that's why I love it. At its best." Toby Litt's "It should be realer than realism" seems to be reaching for a similar appreciation. And Lisa Tuttle wrote:

> The same as any good work of fiction, or even any work of art, although additionally I always hope that science fiction will make the reader *think*, and not just respond emotionally.

One imagines some non-sf writers might take exception to the implication that their work does not make readers think. And yet, thinking of one kind or another does seem to be important to sf for many of these writers. It's the "something extra" for Chris Beckett as well, for instance, though he was almost the only writer to specifically mention "ideas":

> All good writing should make the reader feel she's been given a treat. It should work on several levels not just one. It should provide escape into a world outside of the reader's experience. At the same time it should connect on as many levels as possible with the reader's experience, and provide the reader with a look at this world from a refreshingly unfamiliar angle. Good science fiction should be full of ideas, though not at the expense of humanity, so the reader comes away thinking about how the world works. It should move the reader, not just with "sensawunda" feelings (great though those are), but with pity, horror, excitement, hope. It should, if possible, make the reader laugh or at least sometimes smile. What is true of human beings is also true of the genre: we are easier to get along with if we don't take ourselves too seriously. It should make the reader feel like it is a genuine communication from the author, which is only possible if the writing has integrity and comes from somewhere at the author's core.

To pick just one thread from this answer: unsurprisingly, many writers, like Susanna Clarke, emphasised the importance of the created worlds of sf and fantasy. For Alan Campbell, this was (inevitably), "The same effect as good books in any other genre. It should quicken your heart, keep you awake at night, take you somewhere new." Others meant it more literally, even if – or *because* – such transport makes demands on the reader. On the sf side, Alastair Reynolds wrote:

> All my favourite sf novels were in some way threatening, difficult or strange to me when I first encountered them. I have never really enjoyed sf that was instantly familiar in its tropes, and I avoid anything that feels cosy or comforting or is in some way pandering to its readers' expectations. The best sf should unsettle the reader. It should leave them feeling that their world has become slightly unhinged, it should leave them with the ringing sense that nothing is going to be quite the same way again. I also feel that the most effective sf books appear to be artefacts from the future, in the sense that they carry a weird integrity, a sense of reportage rather than invention. *Schismatrix* achieves this brilliantly, in my mind, which is why it remains one of my favourites. But again I found it enormously unapproachable at first.

And on the fantasy side, Juliet McKenna wrote:

> It should enthrall, excite and entertain, taking the reader our of their everyday life to strange new worlds and realms of high adventure. By way of more subtle and lingering after-effects, to a greater or lesser extent depending on the age and inclination of the target audience, it should make the reader think;

> about their own society, their place within it, their rights and responsibilities to those closest to them and to the wider community. It should offer readers some insight into "the other," encouraging their growth as fully rounded human beings.

Katherine Roberts wrote that, "It should transport the reader to another world that is just as convincing as our own world," while for Elizabeth Wein, "You should be able to lose yourself in it; you should *believe* in it while you're reading it. And you should think about it afterward. In your head, it should *really exist*."

But the potential pitfalls of escapism were on the minds of several respondents who nevertheless held up sf and fantasy's ability to transport as a key characteristic. Frances Hardinge, for instance, wrote that, "It should allow the reader a moment to step clear of the ordinary clutter of the world, and see everything in an entirely new way. Even if it's escapism, it can be a holiday from which the reader returns with new insights as a souvenir" – a rather lovely way of putting it, I think. Tanith Lee also touched on the idea of a holiday, but felt it applied to all fiction: "The vacation will last ten minutes, an hour, or several days. It removes the reader from their own existence. But it is not escapist in any negative sense. Good fiction relates to our world, and our humanity, whether set in Ancient Rome, parallel Elizabethan London, or the farthest reaches of outer space ... It puts you not only on alien planets or inside alien historicity, but into other skins. Teachers of empathy, the best books are."

Among those less comfortable with sf and fantasy's efforts at world-creation was M John Harrison:

> I don't know. I try to write what I'd like to read. As a reader I like a mystery over a solution. I like a fantasy with something fantastic in it, not just a lot of people doing accurately-researched pre-modern politics and hitting one another over the head with accurately-researched swords.
>
> I want to feel as if I've been shown some part of human experience, or a gap in my experience of being human, or a deconstruction of what I think my experience is. I want to be able to recognise human beings in a text, not trait-paradigms.
>
> I want a story to enable me to access and acknowledge some part of my own humanity – so I want it to show me people doing acts, not puppeting about according to "believable motives" ascribed to them by the author.

But far more writers pointed to a role for sf, fantasy, and other fiction to entertain in what you could call the conventional ways: "A tale well told is what I'm always looking for as a reader," wrote Sarah Ash, "and certainly what I aim to write." Neil Williamson's view was similar: "I can only speak for what I look for from a book or story. I like a good genre story to be well told, entertaining and have at least a spark of uniqueness to its speculative element." For Stan Nicholls, story is important, but so is that old friend:

> This evokes yet another, far greater cliché, doesn't it? A sense of wonder. But, dammit, clichés become clichés because they're truisms, and no-one's expressed it better than in those four words.
>
> On a more mundane level, if I can put it that way, good sf/fantasy will present the reader with a well ordered, entertaining (not to mention logically consistent) plot; and if it makes people think, that's a bonus.

Compared to 1989, a greater proportion of respondents this time around mentioned wonder – about one in eight. And, aside from Chaz Brenchley above, those who did mention it, including Nick Harkaway, Mark Chadbourn, and Ian Whates, seemed to see it as a goal in itself, although usually not the only goal. Bob Lock was the only one to write that it "is the effect writers should be aiming at with their sf/fantasy. The reader should be left breathless and satisfied." For Ben Jeapes, it is linked to the sense of transport: "The sense of wonder! The reader should close the book with the feeling that they have been somewhere they could never have got on their own." For Elizabeth Counihan it is part of the package – "I'd put sense of wonder top, I think, though the reader should also care about the protagonists and the writing should be evocative with originality of concept or delivery, preferably both" – as it is for Justina Robson:

> I like sf/f to be a great escape, full of wonder (of any kind) with a strong storyline and fully realised characters. The best sf always strikes me as having a profound insight (not necessarily articulated as such) contained in it about the reality of the present (its present at time of writing) and humans in general. Like any fiction it should engage the reader sufficiently to keep them awake and make them feel their money wasn't wasted.

And Charles Stross was more specific about what wonder means:

> I think the job of sf/f is to make the reader look at the people and social artefacts around them slightly differently – to provide a different perspective on the human condition. Cognitive dissonance – but in a good way – is what we sometimes call "sense of wonder"; that mental whiplash that comes when we realize that the way things are is not the only way that things can be. ("It's the human condition, but not as we know it, Jim.")

Liz Jensen's response was a caution against uncomplicated enthusiasm:

> You should be stimulated, intrigued, entertained, and – yes – shocked and scared, too, by the power of science, and the ingenious ways in which it can be

> used and abused. Because gripping stories aren't about things going excitingly right: they're about things going excitingly wrong.

However, alongside these responses lie another cluster that seem determined to put the boom in British Boom; or, if you prefer, a sense of shock-and-awe, rather than wonder. Iain Banks leads the way here ("It should smack the gob and knock off the socks"), with support from Colin Harvey ("It should leave the reader stunned with wonderment"), Paul McAuley ("It should blow her mind"), Peadar O'Guilin ("It has to make the victim think differently"), Gareth Lyn Powell ("It should blow their socks off. It should take that whole cupboard of toys and use it to tell stories which just can't be told within the confines of 'mainstream' literature"), Al Robertson ("It should be like a bomb that goes off in their head, over a period of months, years; maybe even a whole lifetime. It should encode a variety of possible meanings, some of which they can assemble for themselves, in an entirely personal way, and some of which they can ignore"), and Tricia Sullivan ("Ideally it should blow up their head and make funky shapes with the pieces. Failing this, it should entertain in unpredictable ways"). Paul Cornell wrote that:

> I like the moment, and I think this defines sf, where, as the song goes, one feels that, "oh my God, I can't believe it, I've never been this far away from home." That moment of complete plunge into unknown stuff, where it's up to the reader to find the one or two carefully placed footholds that the writer has put there for them, while carefully denying them anything else. It's why I loved [Cory Doctorow and Benjamin Rosenbaum's] "True Names" so much recently: no footholds!

And John Meaney, providing perhaps the apotheosis of this approach to sf, linked its exuberance with sf's traditional curiosity about the world:

> There should be a massive BANG! Spattered on walls and ceiling, remnants of brain slurp and drip towards the floor ...
>
> How many people flick on a light switch without considering what happens to make it work? How many people think of TV as electrons dancing in magnetic synch across the nation like a subatomic Riverdance? Or look at tiny flecks on brickwork and think: Oh, fantastic, lifeforms are everywhere ...
>
> Everything's connected. Our 13.7 billion year old universe, like a giant sponge filled with dark matter filaments; our world existing for a third of that time; evolution and complexity turning stardust into living, thinking beings. How dare people – and mundane fiction – be so *ungrateful* as to ignore the wonder that surrounds and fills us?
>
> Sf should be adrenaline slamming straight to the heart, caffeine direct to the brain, injected with a hard, thrusting needle.

I think it's reasonable to suggest that the boldness evident in the last few responses is one characteristic of British sf over the last twenty years; and the evident emotion behind it may be one reason for British sf's successes in this period. This desire for emotional power can take different forms; Adam Roberts suggested that sf and fantasy "should do more than engage [readers] intellectually. It should do what the best poetry does, rather than doing what the best scientific articles do." But it's noticeable that what's missing compared to 1989 is, by and large, the suggestion that sf should in some straightforward way educate or inform.

On the other hand, the political edge that characterised the 1989 responses is still discernable, if perhaps in a smaller proportion of writers. The word "subvert" appeared only rarely in responses – Graham Joyce writing that "It should subvert at least as much as it should console," for instance. But the idea was implicit in responses such as Kari Sperring's:

> It should create a sense of otherness – of discovering a new society or time or place or space. It should raise questions – not always comfortable ones. It should question accepted norms or complicate or frustrate them. Good fantasy should be discomforting and ruthless, not fluffy and sweet. Same for sf. I don't generally think militarism and 'good' go together in sf though I feel strongly that it can and should be political. And sensawunda is always good!

And Jon Courtenay Grimwood's, which also echoes Al Robertson's comments: "It should get under our skin and stay there. The characters should enter our consciousness, and the ideas should seep into our minds and mesh with our own ideas." For Martin Sketchley, "Good sf or f should stimulate thought in the reader, increase awareness and propose alternatives to existing scenarios."

But by far the most common manifestation of the political impulse among the respondents to this survey (aside from the idea that sf should make you "think" which, as Ian Whates reflected, "seems a little too glib") was the idea that sf and fantasy can provide a distorted, revealing reflection of the world around us – as Conrad Williams put it, "a cracked mirror, giving us a look at something we recognise, but utterly new and slightly dangerous at the same time." Sarah Ash, for example, wrote that, "The best fantasy manages to find a new, slightly skewed way to look at life and the issues that intrigue and disturb us"; while Mike Carey suggested that, "Ursula Le Guin was right when she said that it's a mistake to see sci-fi as 'excursions outward' – many of the greatest sci-fi novels, movies and short stories are 'incursions inward': in other words, they're about us, our lives, the here and now, and not about the alien."

Keith Brooke argued that, among other things, "good sf/f should surprise and make the reader reassess – both reassess what they've just been reading up to that point, and reassess how they see the world in some way." And Rhiannon Lassiter replied that, "good science fiction should serve as an anagnorisis: opening the reader's eyes to a new awareness or possibility. Accomplished fantasy can also offer similar revelations and correlations to the world we know." Nina Allan, NM Browne, Ramsey Campbell and Jaine Fenn were among others who offered similar sentiments, in addition to those like Frances Hardinge and Justina Robson whose replies have already been quoted.

Of course, such revelations are not always explicitly political. Tony Ballantyne speaks to an equally important tradition of sf when he writes:

> Good sf should make the reader realise the world is a much weirder place than they first thought, that their life so far has been very narrow and provincial, and, most importantly, it should make them want to get out there and understand our place in the Universe and not to accept anything but the truth for an answer.

Gary Gibson wrote that good sf and fantasy should reveal "that there is so very much more to the world than what you perceive around you," while Ian Watson spoke of "The expansion of the imagination. Causing readers to think and feel what they haven't thunked nor felt before. To thunk boldly," and Adrian Tchaikovsky wanted sf and fantasy to "Expand the horizons, inspire big emotions, excite curiosity." Of course there is no doubt an element of the perspective shift in the shock-and-awe responses quoted above (you can see it in some of those writers' work); but relatively few respondents placed it as *central* to the work of sf and fantasy without tying it back in to reflection on our world, and our circumstances.

Finally, there is, for some writers, always an awareness that writing is a commercial activity. David Langford, for instance, wrote:

> A strange glazed look should afflict the reader, not unlike the symptoms of attack by the mind-blasting fractal basilisks of my best-known short stories. Compulsively, tragically, helpless to resist, the meme-infested reader is impelled to buy every Langford book available, and then acquire further sets for his or her family, friends, enemies, pets ... This, at any rate, is the ideal outcome. I don't think I've yet got it to work.

This is clearly somewhat tongue in cheek; but equally clearly, there is a serious point behind it. For Mark Charan Newton, the effect that good sf or fantasy should have is "Simply that readers are affected enough by your writing to want more of what you offer. There are no rules here, no good or bad – the writing is simply there – and tastes differ massively. The fact that a particular reader – whether they have a literary bent or seeking entertainment – wants to give more of their time to a writer's works is enough of a sign that said writer is doing something right." Roger Levy wrote that:

> Good writing, sf, fantasy or whatever, should question one's certainties and consolidate one's fears. It should leave you with a better idea of what to worry about, and why to worry, and a determination that until the world ends, you

> should spend your money on red wine and books.

While Andrew Crumey reported that, "As a writer I concern myself with stimulus more than response. I try to design the stimulus so that it will produce in the responder a free desire for repetition: something I would define as pleasure." Thus the eternal concern of science fiction as a commercial genre, which nobody summed up better than Christopher Priest:

> I always saw good science fiction as being in approximate 50/50 proportions. Roughly 50% of every novel or story should aim to be good, well-made entertainment fiction, intended to be read for pleasure and enjoyed on an uncomplicated level; the other 50% should challenge the reader with interesting or new ideas, with the use of good language, with real literary techniques, with complexity of structure, with overall seriousness of purpose. Trouble is, in my experience most people seem to want one or the other. Personally, I dislike brainless books as much as pretentious stuff. All the best novels find the middle ground somehow. Most of the books from a hundred years ago, or more, that we now think of as classics were originally written for a popular audience.

How much of the sf and fantasy written today will so survive, of course, is a question we cannot answer here.

# Chapter 10: *What do you consider the most significant weakness in science fiction and fantasy as genres?*

## 1989

This is the other side to the question I asked in chapter nine, and it received one of the biggest responses of any of the questions. In general, it seems that there is an awful lot wrong with the genre, which may explain one of the common themes that has emerged throughout this survey, a looking outside the genre to the mainstream and other inspirations and measures.

One line that was taken was that it is the nature of "genre" itself which is a handicap. Alasdair Gray, for instance, echoed his response to the last question: "Pleasurable stimulus to thoughtless prejudices. (This is the weakness of all artistic genres.)" While Paul J McAuley just said: "Willingness to stay in the ghetto." Keith Roberts replied:

> The question really answers itself by adding the rider "as a genre." Any popular medium must conform to the speed of the slowest ship; and as a result of progressive education some of today's readers don't make many knots. A writer of my acquaintance, faced with doing a TV spot, once made a crafty stipulation; that he would talk about his own work but nobody else's. Otherwise, he said, he sensed horrors looming; he said he could see himself only too easily being forced into the position of defending the literacy of EE Smith, or the politics of Robert Heinlein. What does irritate me occasionally is the attitude of a certain kind of fan, who rushes about trumpeting the originality and freedom of the medium. It is, as we all know, nothing of the sort; what the publishers want, and a large proportion of the public, is more of the same only longer. If I'd had any sense I'd have written *Son of Pavane* and *Pavane Rides Again*; heaven knows, I was asked often enough. I'd have lost any respect I may have won; but I'd have made more money. Kaeti was sculling about for the best part of three years before Kerosina came along; as a friend observed at the time, "It's all right

> being unconventional, as long as you're unconventional along conventional lines." Something that echoes Isaac Bashevis Singer's classic remark: "Of course I believe in free will. I've got no choice ..."

Much the same was said by Leigh Kennedy:

> That readers, writers and editors who claim that sf is an exciting, daring form of fiction actually defend conservative, trite, commercial hack work. There is some sf which is on a par with those authors who win Booker Prizes but we all know that much of it is as sophisticated as Mills and Boon. The greatest damage is to be defensive about the whole lot and pretend that *just because* it is sf or fantasy it is more intellectually advanced than romances or Zane Grey westerns. This defensiveness condemns the best works of sf to always being classified with the worst.

The problem would appear to be the ghetto mentality, as Ian McDonald suggested:

> There is a ghetto mentality in sf that I find distasteful, almost a kind of "come ye out from the midst of them" attitude as if somehow its purity might be tainted by contact with other forms of literature. Whoever it was said "Get sf out of the classroom and into the gutter where it belongs" is the worst kind of inverse elitist. By definition sf, as the literature of the possible, should be the literature that includes all others, a universal set of literary possibility, but rather it likes to withdraw itself to preserve some phoney ideology of purity. This of course only fuels the mainstream's antipathy towards sf, with the result that writers who do attempt to straddle the divide are sniped at by both sides. If sf is as good as we all think it is, then it won't be afraid to ride naked through the streets like Lady Godiva. But are we certain that it is?

This idea that the ghetto isolates sf was also remarked upon by Jane Palmer:

> Possibly the most isolating aspect about the sf and fantasy markets is the way they remain divorced from general fiction when many ideas in both fields overlap. The sf/fantasy genre should be the one that liberates and expands ideas, not fences it off with publishers' preconceived notions about what it should or should not contain. Promoting the feeling of being in a certain camp does not necessarily help encompass a potentially large readership who will tackle most forms of fiction as long as they are entertaining. The only rule I can think of that might enhance the sf/fantasy genre is that there should be no rules.

But of course the rules are part of the problem. David Langford picked up on the way writers are limited by genre expectations in his pet weakness:

> Science fiction writers who are too easily conned by the publishers' category labels into the belief that sf is a clearly bounded genre with an official list of acceptable forms and topics. (In fantasy the domination of form has gone further, with the continuing dogma that all stories must run to three volumes and include a mention of the Wild Hunt.)

This amounts to what Lisa Tuttle commented upon: "As a genre it has the weaknesses of *all* genres, limitations imposed from the outside. But I find it hard to think of a generalisation which would fit everything *I* consider to be sf."

Picking up on the idea raised by Keith Roberts and Leigh Kennedy that defenders of the genre end up having to defend the worst examples, Kim Newman felt that even as a genre sf isn't a match for some of its rivals:

> The weakness of all genre fiction is that the rules that make a work part of a genre also limit it. There is no rule that says sf should be reactionary, badly characterised, naive, stodgy or puerile, but a lot of it is. I don't read exclusively within science fiction and fantasy, but it does strike me that standards within the field are lower than within other categories. Isaac Asimov and Robert Heinlein, for instance, are hailed as Grand Masters, but they were writing genre fiction at precisely the same time as Raymond Chandler and Dashiell Hammett were writing hardboiled detective stories. The comparison does reveal, I think, that sf has always been a poor relation. Even today, I'd vote for Elmore Leonard over William Gibson as a major genre talent.

And this characteristic of the genre tends to have the effect of lowering standards, it becomes easier for the mediocre rather than the exceptional to get into print, because the mediocre more easily fits the genre demands. As Neil Gaiman points out:

> The most significant weakness is the same that any genre ghetto literature has – it's hard to get serious work taken seriously, and easier for bad or ill-considered fiction to get published if it fills the publishing need for an sf novel. (It can also get terrifyingly repetitious.)

Robert Irwin also feels that the clannishness of the ghetto is as much a handicap as a virtue:

> Its chief vice is also its chief virtue – its consoling tight-knit clannishness. It does give rise to herd-driven fads like the recent one for cyberpunk. And perhaps, perfunctory nods to exceptions like Ballard apart, it has unduly

distanced itself from mainstream fiction writing.

Which is part and parcel of Mary Gentle's complaint that there is too little awareness of what is going on beyond the genre walls: "Too much reliance on clichés, too great a lack of the past (i.e. writers' seeming unawareness of anything written pre-Tolkien/Heinlein, or outside the field); too much restrictive commercialism on behalf of publishers." All of which boils down to the concise comments from Colin Greenland: "Over-familiarity," Iain Banks: "Its past," and John Clute, referring to a current trend in American sf publishing: "A mania for sharecropping the already-seen."

The ghetto mentality which leads us to look back only upon the narrow straits of our own past were bemoaned by David V Barrett:

> The millstone of the Golden Age of sf still hangs around its neck. This has effects on three groups:
>
> 1. The public image of sf is 40 years out of date; this means there is always a prejudice, based on an artificial barrier, to be overcome.
>
> 2. The traditional tropes and conventions of sf can give readers preconceptions about the meaning of the content of a novel or story; they may read them on too shallow a level, missing the full meaning.
>
> 3. Writers can also be (consciously or subconsciously) straitjacketed by the conventions of the genre. This is more true of US sf. Writers can be afraid (or even constitutionally unable) to step outside these conventions and write truly challenging fiction. They can also, if they do write conceptually challenging or stylistically unusual work, or "fringe sf," find difficulty in persuading publishers to take their work.
>
> Also (and this too stems from Golden Age writing), the concentration on clever ideas rather than depth of characterisation, mood or place; and a willingness to accept poor quality writing if the idea is exciting (this is a fault in readers as much as writers, but writers give into to it too easily).
>
> Obviously there are writers who are bucking all this, and throwing off the millstone. Most of them, I think, are British.

So we come back to the idea that it is the ghetto itself which is the main problem with science fiction, and this can give rise to any number of subsidiary weaknesses, as Christopher Priest said:

> The single most important weakness is the fact that it *is* a genre. This encourages hackwork, imitation and feeblemindedness. Lesser weaknesses (which all derive from the main one) include:
>
> The assumed importance of writers whose only contribution is prolificacy.
>
> A concentration on "notions" at the expense of genuine ideas.
>
> *Locus*.

> SFWA and the Nebula Award. In general, too many awards and honours given to the wrong people for doing the wrong things.
>
> A fierce but defensive lobby of right-wing writers.
>
> A popular belief that good writing is something only poofters are interested in.
>
> A complete lack of critical standards.
>
> An absence of journalistic comment (see *Locus*).

David Redd offered a similar list of complaints:

> Every weakness in sf has been remedied by someone at some time, but not all the weaknesses all the time unless I have missed a major masterpiece. My impression of sf/fantasy is of a composite of different time periods due to reading old sf as well as new magazines etc. In general:
>
> Too many gimmicks and dull prose.
>
> No emotional range between blandness and narrative-hook drive.
>
> Over-reliance on conflict and violence.
>
> Clockwork plot mechanisms rather than exploring all the implications of a situation.
>
> Where are the *people*?
>
> Why isn't David Redd a world famous author? (Here the weakness is with me, and not with sf. I do miss me as an author, though.)

He didn't use the word, but it is clearly sf as a genre that hangs over most of these problems. But not everyone was so decidedly critical of the genre element, there was a counter view, expressed by Douglas Hill:

> Weakness? Obvious. It lies in the tendency of sf people to take themselves too seriously – thus becoming vulnerable to fashion-seekers, trend-mongers, academics looking for a flashy speciality, and the like. *Vide* this questionnaire. (When I hear the expression "sf's literary respectability, I reach for my ray-gun ...)

Kenneth Bulmer is presumably in this camp when he complains about: "A lack of love for science fiction as sf." Barrington Bayley certainly is when he declares: "Since it defines itself as a genre, it doesn't have weaknesses as a genre. What some outside see as deficiencies (i.e. cursory treatment of character) would weaken the genre if 'rectified'."

James White appears rather fatalistic about the breaking down of the ghetto walls:

> It seems to me that science fiction is no longer clearly defined, and is spreading

> into fantasy on one side and the mainstream on the other, with the result that nobody is sure where it is going or what it is supposed to be. For the reason mentioned earlier I cannot name names or stories, but it seems to me that it is a matter of literary entropy, a breaking down of the simple into the chaotic, and there is nothing anyone can do about it.

But EC Tubb mounted a vigorous defence of the values of science fiction, particularly against the depredations of film makers who use sf without being a part of it:

> Basically the apparent inability of those in authority to take the genre seriously. Science fiction, to them, is Bug Eyed Monsters. Their contempt for the intelligence of their readers, viewers, etc, is obvious as is their total lack of any scientific understanding or knowledge. They have no idea as to astronomical distances. A galaxy, to them, is the same as a star system, a dimension, a universe. The one thing none of them ever do is ask the advice of those who are expert in the field. The writers who, if nothing else, have learned the basic elements of their craft. None of them seem to be included among the script writers. None of them seem wanted.
>
> But even ordinary writers are not above blame. To them science fiction isn't really literature at all. So they play games with it, throw in fantasy, forget logic, don't bother to learn the elements of astronomy etc. Above all they fail to entertain. I don't know the cure. I know I've tried to introduce science fiction to ordinary readers without success. They just can't understand it and are not willing to take the trouble to learn. Thinking of many books, the late Heinlein's for example, I can't blame them.

John Brunner felt very much the same when he complained about:

> The falsified version of its potential due to the bad habits of those film producers who throw a million bucks at the special effects department and at the last moment may perhaps remember that a script writer is called for ... but fire him if he tries to make the plotline logical. Who could take *Star Wars* seriously after seeing the X-planes flying through nonexistent air? I suppose the answer has to be: millions of ignorant twits who also like to hear loud bangs in empty space.

Another respondent who would probably not be applauded by EC Tubb and John Brunner takes a somewhat different tack. For Stephen Gallagher the main problem is:

> The science. It's become far too esoteric and far too extreme. It's hard to give a toss about a tachyon, and you can't relate dramatically to a quark. The

> black hole was science's last decent contribution to sf, and even that has been qualified and devalued. Science has to try harder; we need our domed cities and humanoid robots back. My proposal is that anybody who's ever worked for NASA should be automatically barred from writing sf.

He might agree with Lee Montgomerie, who worried that sf: "Scares off the technophobes." This ties in with the general unease with the genre role. As Garry Kilworth put it:

> The most significant weakness in science fiction: the denial of access to readers unused to its jargon; its apparent need to explain things to the nth degree; the glorification of its most uninteresting aspects (space opera, robots, etc.); the confusion of conceits with ideas (i.e. an idea might be that all mankind is directly responsible for the death of Christ; the conceit is that the story uses time travel to achieve this.)

It was Samuel R Delany who proposed the idea that science fiction is a language, but like any language that means it suffers the liability of being incomprehensible to anyone not raised to it. Paul Barnett agreed with Garry Kilworth about the "denial of access":

> The fact that so much of the stuff currently published is quite incomprehensible to the newcomer. This is inescapable, I think (if one tried to re-explain every standard sf base-concept as it appeared, the effect on regular readers would be risible), but it *is* a serious liability. Another frequent failing is the lack of proper plotting (although perhaps I'm the last to talk!) and of genuine *purpose*: often I find myself reading an sf book and asking myself, "What was that *for*?" All too frequently, I don't know the answer.

And Gwyneth Jones made the same point when she talked abot:

> The problem of the "accepted set of futures" which makes true sf inaccessible to non-sf readers in a peculiarly recalcitrant way. If literature consists of references to literature, sf is a closed area within this larger universe. It is very difficult for any of its light to escape.

Part of this isolation may lie in the attitudes to the genre, as Diana Wynne Jones suggested:

> The main significant weakness is that people enjoy reading it! Therefore the po-faced majority regard science fiction as non-serious because they feel that anything that anyone enjoys is bad for them.

Though as we have already seen in the discussion of the genre, the ghetto is as responsible as anyone else for creating and sustaining the isolation. As Elizabeth Sourbut said:

> It is hopelessly dominated by the English-speaking world and by Western cultural values. Sf can be about everything, anything, but for the most part it remains mechanistic, technology-centred, and wedded to capitalism. I would like to see sf writers and readers opening their eyes and their minds to the rest of the world. If we can't manage that, we might as well forget about the rest of the Universe.

And part of that capitalism is the commercialism that Brian Aldiss complains of when he remarks:

> That on the one hand it is not read by more people and that on the other it is wracked by commercialism. Put these together and you see that perhaps authors do not have sufficient pride in their calling or care for their reputation. A recent sorry case is Silverberg's signing of a contract to rewrite three ancient Asimov stories into novels. Who wants such novels? Who wants to see Silverberg do this ill thing to himself? Beyond the sf field, such a move would be regarded as ... well, I can't see it happening. It's hackdom. And I believe we are all diminished by it.

Which takes us back to John Clute's comments on sharecropping, and Kenneth Bulmer's on the lack of love for sf, and indeed all the complaints about the genre ghetto. Josephine Saxton clearly shares these common views when she lists as weaknesses: "Big business, repetitiveness, loss of contact with real ideas, morbidity, swords, sexism, sadism, overkill." A similar point was made by James Corley:

> Well a lot of it's too long. I mentioned Voltaire's *Candide*, it's a very short work but it's one of the great ones. When I wander into a bookshop and see another thousand pages of Trott the Barbarian, vol. XX, or some other multi-kilogram mega-epic I can only conclude a lot of people are going to get both a physical and a mental hernia. But of course as the genre gets more mature it's increasingly difficult to say anything fresh so I suppose they're substituting repetition for revelation. Without a doubt the sf novel depends on novelty far more than most types of fiction and I don't know many (any?) current writers who've got anything new to say.

Much the same point of view lies behind Brian Stableford's response: "An insufficiency of critical scepticism and analytical fervour in its treatment of ideas." Which gets an oddly synchronous response from Simon Ounsley:

> Writers don't keep up enough with current social and scientific developments and go in for the kind of serious extrapolation that Brian Stableford is calling for. This is probably because their motivations are closer to mine than they are to his.

However, most of the weaknesses of science fiction were identified as stemming from its genre characteristics, and of these the one most singled out for comment was, in Robert Farago's words: "The quality of the characterisation." Samantha Lee, for instance, dislikes: "Pulp writing where what people are wearing is given precedence over characterisation and a decent story line." Alex Stewart worries about:

> An obsession with technology at the expense of human values; a noticeable lack of imagination in depicting alien or futuristic societies, which all seem to be reflections of contemporary America; an implicit endorsement of violence and authoritarianism. These are most noticeable in American work, which dominates the field, and the British writers who try to follow that model rather than explore themes of their own.

Eric Brown criticised: "Weak characterisation ... and the works of David Drake, Jerry Pournelle, John Norman ...," while Christina Lake objected to the: "Tendency to shallow characterisation; the quantity of rubbish that gets published and sells in vast numbers." And for Graham Dunstan Martin:

> Its greatest weakness is the tendency for its characters to be cardboard or cliché. There are others, e.g. the predictable nature of many of its themes and plots. (This is particularly true of those repetitive fantasy trilogies.) However, these are weaknesses that do not afflict the best writers.

Yet again, for John Christopher, the problem is:

> Primarily characterisation. This is inescapable: the work put into building up the (fantastic) background is work that cannot go into characterisation. (Lewis agreed, but thought it didn't matter; one was better for having "humours" rather than "characters." Fine in his own work, but you have to be a genius to justify it.) There is also the weakness that the sf/fantasy writer has to suspend disbelief, either by going along with clichéd conventions or creating his own universe. This last really sorts out the men from the boys (women from the girls). For me the first volume of Julian May's series worked well, the second not quite so well, while the third started to bore me. I never read the fourth, and have picked up the first of the new series only sadly to put it down. The wallpaper's too familiar, and I've lost confidence in the wall.

That last metaphor seems to sum up most of the responses to this question. Maybe British science fiction is trying to build a new wall rather than paper over an American edifice?

Still, the final word has got to go to John Brosnan. When asked what was the major weakness in sf he answered simply: "Me."

# 2009

There's no doubt that reading the responses to the Mexicon survey is at times a sobering experience. Occasionally, I've wondered how anyone could have thought or said *that*; more often, and particularly in the case of this chapter, I think, I've wondered at the consistency of certain opinions ghosting across the years, even if the frequency with which they're stated has shifted. To read, for example, James White talking about the breakdown of the science fiction category; or Paul Barnett talking about the incomprehensibility of then-contemporary sf to the lay-person; or Elizabeth Sourbut talking about the domination of sf by English-speaking writers and Western cultural values – in all three cases, it seems as though the comments could have been made yesterday, in precisely so many words, and that they would represent the same mix of truth and wishful thinking as they did then. Which is a long way of getting to the point and saying that, as twenty years ago, this question generated one of the most voluminous responses.

Justina Robson's short essay of a response, for example, seemed attuned to this sense that the more things change, the more they stay the same, and that the reason is, as ever, related to the existence of genre – although not necessarily by the same arguments put forward in 1989.

> Any genre has weaknesses because writing is linear and there is a limited space. A genre is defined by what it chooses to notice as most important, so I guess they are all weak where they are forced to "dump" portions of the potentially whole experience. Good writers can get around this because they learn to shorthand extremely well, so there are people for whom there is no significant weakness. Generalising pointlessly I'd say that sf most commonly dumps human relationships and social interaction and fantasy dumps the true complexity of human character, because it is the feature most likely to interfere with fantasy's compact with heroism. Both of these dumped items are the main fodder for literary fiction, hence the historic relation of the three to each other, perhaps.
>
> My main goal as a writer was always to restore both of these dump features to the said genres, but when I set out with this mission I didn't understand the reasons as to why they had been dumped in the first place. I assumed it

> was because the writers were lazy or dumb. Whereas the great fictions that inspired me to write actually possessed those features as well as being sf and f of quality in their own right. I think I was just disappointed in the midlist of my formative years, that's all.
>
> Also, there's an age thing going on. Old farts like me want to see our understanding of the world reflected in books that capture our feelings about life's troubles and compromises, often our own failure to be as clear and upstanding as the heroes we used to love in childhood's stories and by whom we can still be moved. Hence our ability to guilt-trip ourselves for reading purely escapist fantasy. Younger audiences aren't ready for the jaded stuff, so the exclusion of this kind of thing from the most popular fantasy and sf would seem to appeal to them much more and rightly so.
>
> It's strange because I remember the whole New Weird debate having a strand that ran along these lines where NW was supposed to be the sexy grownup version of the old stuff, full of hard knocks and revelations that would almost evangelically inspire people to cast off the shackles of genre archetype and myth in favour of a kind of hardcore pseudorealism. Fat chance, I think, rather sadly, as there is a place for New Weird and its messages, but I suspect in the current climate not a very large place.

There's an awful lot packed in there that could stand deeper analysis, I think. The suggestion that genres arise because all writing is a necessary compromise of some "potentially whole experience" is, in light of the Mexicon response (and some others to this survey), quite radical; we may not be *able* to have it all, in most cases, and if that's so, is the compromise inherently dishonourable or – as Robson seems to suggest – honourable to the extent that it is desired by, and useful to, readers? And, of course, the corollary suggestion that what's wrong with sf is not that it compromises per se, but that one model of compromise routinely wins out over others.

Others, as I've hinted, still took the harder line, such as M John Harrison ("That it's a genre"), Michael Moorcock ("It's a genre. It contains the weaknesses of all genres in that it inhibits and constrains the writer because it's based on reader expectations"), and Christopher Priest:

> That sort of question. The attitudes behind it. The assumptions contained in it. "Science fiction" is merely a label used by (although not invented by) the book trade, and taken up and accepted by readers and writers, and therefore given more weight than it should have. In my view, any writer who says "I am only a science fiction writer" is selling himself or herself short. There are only novels or stories. Each should be judged on its merit. Writers should always aim for the best they know, and not rely on what they perceive to be genre attitudes to excuse weaknesses or shortcuts or jargon. You should always shove at the edges of what you think you can do.

Yet these writers were outnumbered by others who seemed to ask, "What constraints? What expectations?" One in seven responded along the same lines as Joe Abercrombie: "The genre is so broad and varied, and encompasses such a range in terms of its content and commerciality, that it's very difficult to treat it as a homogenous whole." Nick Harkaway, for example, wrote that, "If we're talking about a systemic weakness in the genre, I can't think of one. There are bad books – weak dialogue, bad characterisation – but that's not unique to sf or particularly prevalent," while Nina Allan made the same point: "It doesn't have a weakness. Weaknesses may be present in particular works or the works of particular writers, but the genre itself must be just about the most exciting and inclusive and flexible on the planet." And Neil Williamson argued, "I don't think as a genre it necessarily has to have a weakness. A good sf or fantasy story should be able to incorporate any and all of the elements that make other types of fiction successful." Similar sentiments came from NM Browne and Colin Davies. For Frances Hardinge, "The genre is still a rather artificial catch-all category for a lot of books that don't fit anywhere else, and which are light years from the still-lingering public perception that 'fantasy' means dragons and 'science fiction' means spaceships." And, perhaps most tellingly, Mike Carey took a different route to Christopher Priest, yet ended up at the same point:

> Do genres have global strengths and global weaknesses? Do genres even exist, apart from their convenience as marketing tools? It comes down to texts.

For these writers, then, there is no *necessary* connection between the fact that fantasy and sf are genres, and any weaknesses that may be apparent in sf and fantasy works. In a sense, this is what we might have expected after chapter one: if you believe that sf and fantasy can do and be anything, then of course you're going to be happy to claim an identity as a writer of sf or fantasy. But as Deborah Miller's response shows, for some writers this attitude is linked to another, perhaps more familiar one; she said that the biggest weakness was: "Only the perception of it by non-readers. Not our problem really! The sf/f genres are really smart, powerful, and the most creative of all genres."

David Langford fell into this camp, picking up on Diana Wynne Jones' response to the Mexicon survey:

> I think someone gave roughly this answer in 1989: the fact that it's a *popular* genre is a weakness since it brings automatic marginalization. Sneers from ignorant outsiders and defensive drum-banging from within the ghetto both blur the vital distinction between good and bad genre writing. Then there are all the ad-hominems from journalists who – perhaps troubled by the enormous commercial success of media sf/fantasy – reflexively spew stuff about anoraks, geeks, nerds and lack of personal hygiene, with the general charm of a sea-slug defensively ejecting its intestines at some perceived threat.

> As you know, Bob, *Ansible* has a morbid habit of collecting relevant quotes (not to mention the writhings of authors attempting to place clear black void between their Future-Tech Scientific-Romance Utopian/Dystopian Alternate History and nasty old science fiction): see <http://news.ansible.co.uk/others.php>.

Similar sentiments came from, among others, Jaine Fenn ("Sf is still largely perceived as lightweight escapist entertainment by those who don't read it"), Stephen Gallagher ("It's not so much a weakness within the genre as around it – the attention given to mainstream writers who say they're 'using the form' while naively presenting common tropes"), Tim Lebbon ("The stigma attached to it") and Ian Whates:

> The general perception that the genre somehow represents an immature and inferior style of fiction, not to be taken seriously. I think media other than literature is at least partially to blame for this. Along with a few very good examples, there have been some embarrassingly poor sf/fantasy films and TV programmes made. I think sf has become synonymous in many people's minds with OTT melodrama, wooden dialogue, sub-standard plots, dodgy special effects, oh, and not forgetting the ubiquitous space ship. Fantasy likewise, but substitute a pointy-eared elf and maybe a dragon or two for the space ship.

... whose stance is surely in sympathy with that of John Meaney, who said: "Hollywood. Mind you, there are novelists who write about aliens with DNA or suchlike nonsense, on a par with sound effects in space ... but the psychological associations with film and TV repel as many readers as they tempt into our genre." But it may be worth noting that, aside from Langford, the only respondents to speak of the "ghetto" were Stephen Gaskell – who also cited *Ansible*'s "As Others See Us" segment, and wrote, "The moment an author such as Margaret Atwood or Audrey Niffenegger breaks out from the label is a bittersweet one – it's a reminder that a wider audience exists for speculative fiction, but at the same time it reinforces the ghettoisation of the genre" – and Kit Whitfield, who in any case focused on the flipside of that particular coin:

> Self-ghettoisation, to coin a horrible word. A lot of science fiction and fantasy readers get mocked for liking those books, and that's bad, but some of them react to this by declaring that every other genre is rubbish, which is just as bad – or, on a lesser scale, by starting to see sff as a political category rather than just one of a number of ways of describing a book. This can lead to the genre turning inwards. Sometimes sff can have a rather embattled attitude, and that's not a creative atmosphere, because there are beautiful, wonderful books in every genre and shutting oneself off from them is simply cutting off your nose to spite your face. Other genres are not our enemy. If you read them openly, they're not even very Other.

Or, as Stan Nicholls put it: "I wish we'd all stop being so damn defensive about what we do." For Paul Cornell, the problems of this attitude are even more pernicious:

> The way it looks in on itself. Only our crowd allowed, outsiders stay away, you're only allowed in if you say you write sf, rather than if you just do. That's what's led to an almost medieval worship of the coming apocalypse, because we've been bad people and deserve global warming. Which is kind of the opposite of what the initial sf project was. An invasion of young faces and their authors would help. But we're going to have to be the ones to open the gates, they're having enough fun for themselves over there in their camp. (And other strained metaphors.)
>
> This insularity means you still get the odd Stalinist review that regards a book as politically suspect. That is, literally, the reviewer didn't like it because they didn't agree with it. (It was Churchill who said something about loving Liberalism and hating Liberals, wasn't it? Instead of "Liberal," insert any description of anything I am. I'm vastly suspicious of any club that even sends me the forms.)

The argument about sf's tendency to look inward will be taken up again later by many respondents. (And you have to wonder how it might tie in with Tricia Sullivan's suggestion that "British sf/f is significantly understaffed by non-white writers and needs more of the global viewpoint that Ian McDonald's work exemplifies ... We need more chicks in sf, too. I think if we had those two things going on, then the gripes I have with a lot of genre content would take care of themselves. I could get some new gripes, then.") But for now, we'll turn to those respondents who focused on the unique *challenges* posed by sf and fantasy. Toby Litt, for instance, highlighted "A failure to create futuristic/entirely other psychologies (Ballard a notable exception)." For Alastair Reynolds, the immediate challenge is structural:

> For me, it's the tension between the literary exploration of a novel idea, and the need to have some sort of "plot," which in turn opens the door to melodrama. You begin with a real cool sfnal idea which you're going to examine in all its ramifications, but then the engine of plot dictates the introduction of some kind of adversary, and before you know it you've got car chases and big explosions. This is obviously endemic to Hollywood sf, but I'm acutely aware that much of my own work conforms to that shape.
>
> In the literary sense, even if you avoid the clichés of shoot-outs and explosions, stories can also become endlessly recomplicated with far too many characters and subplots. It's something I'm working against, but at the same time I enjoy the mechanics of a good, well-crafted thriller and I wouldn't want to lose that entirely. I suppose what I'd aspire to write is an sf novel that was a genuine, intelligent page-turner, but which also illuminated a big central idea, without

> drifting into melodrama. Clarke was good at this, because his novels were often constructed in such a way that the adversary was space itself, or the deep sea, or the limits of engineering ... there were no "bad guys" or sinister conspiracies, but at the same time the books were intensely readable and compelling.

Colin Harvey also spoke of, "The obsession with 'tight plotting' – life isn't like that. The best writers manage to make their plots seem organic, but even so there's an artificiality about tying up every plot thread that I occasionally find irritating." And for Tony Ballantyne, much media sf sets a bad example for a different reason:

> Not a weakness as such, but there are some sf stories that have to be told in a simple, straightforward style if the reader is to follow them. Stories told in such a prosaic way can be dismissed by those seeking a more literary style, but I feel they are missing the point. I feel we are failing as a genre for not successfully communicating our aims to the wider public. Worse, we fall into the trap of trying to include elements or styles in our work that don't need to be there.
>
> An example would be the recent series of *Doctor Who*. I heard episodes being praised for their treatment of character, relationships and romance. The science fictional element was mentioned rarely, if at all. Now, it could be argued that *Doctor Who* is family entertainment, not science fiction, and this is fair enough, but good science fiction has additional elements to character and style. You can remove the latter two and still have good science fiction. We should give more recognition to that fact and not slavishly try to emulate the mainstream.

This is taking Justina Robson's idea that genres are defined by their choice of focus to an extreme, I think.

The challenge that attracted most comment was raised by Deborah Miller: "I think it's possible that sf writers are struggling at the moment to find 'new possible futures' as tech catches up with them and their ideas." Jaine Fenn linked this problem to the challenge of communication that Tony Ballantyne spoke of: "I think the fact that the bright future earlier sf envisioned hasn't come true may have damaged the genre, making optimistic sf less credible, and making writers of near-future sf justifiably wary of predictions that could be disproved before their story even sees print." Rhiannon Lassiter turned the responsibility back on writers: "Science fiction has been slow to tackle the emerging politics of the end of the 20th and beginning of the 21st century."

For Gareth Lyn Powell there's a related practical challenge:

> Personally, I desperately hope the printed sf market continues to thrive and survive, but at the same time I also realise that if the next generation

> of prospective readers isn't coming to us, it's up to us to reach out to them. Without them, the genre will grow old and die. We have to set our stall where young and old alike can see and engage with it and if that means giving some of our work away on-line, then so be it. You only have to look at Google, Facebook, YouTube, Amazon and iTunes to realise the Internet's fundamentally changing the way we communicate, the way we shop and the way we share information and interact with one another. As science fiction writers, we should be at the forefront of that revolution and if the publishers want to survive, they're going to have to do something to attract that global audience.

Whereas for Charles Stross it is the imaginative work which is harder now:

> The besetting weakness right now, in sf (I wouldn't presume to comment on fantasy) is a consequence of the way the late 20th and early 21st century has turned out. We're living surrounded by the shrapnel of a technological and scientific explosion so vast that most of us can barely grasp what's happened. We're also working in a genre defined by key texts written in earlier, simpler times. It's easy for lazy writers to ignore the challenges of dealing with the reality around us and to simply write adventure yarns and escapist fantasies that rely on stock props from the sf toy chest, regardless of plausibility, believability, or consistency with the known laws of physics. Writing realistic near-future sf has become unbelievably difficult, to the point where writers have in many cases stopped trying.
>
> At the same time, the field has been colonized by backpackers from the literary faculty, who appropriate the contents of the toy chest and use them as, well, metaphors (rather than building blocks), sometimes with little understanding of their significance.
>
> But the biggest weakness is: as an art form, written sf in its current form is getting close to a century old. Most art forms do not survive the life expectancy of their founders, while retaining their initial vibrancy and openness; by the third generation, most of the active practitioners are "second artists," recycling standard clichéd tropes and running variations on the classics. Comforting, reassuring, classics – which are the trump of death to an art form based on cognitive dissonance and a sense of wonder.

Stross was far from the only writer to make that last point; indeed, concerns about sf's inwardness, or self-referentiality, or repetitiveness were mentioned by just under half of respondents, and outweighed the other major clump of concerns – those about style and character – by over two to one. "Poor character development," wrote Katherine Langrish, and "It can be written very badly and still get published," said Paul Meloy; others who agreed with one or other of these comments, and usually both, included Eric Brown, Elizabeth Counihan, Liz Jensen, Roger Levy (who also cited "swirly covers"), Ken MacLeod, Ricardo Pinto ("not enough craftsmanship"), and Elizabeth Wein, who suggested this as the downside of the rise of the small press: "Clunky writing – lack of style. I think there's nothing inherently wrong with the genre – quality will and does out. But possibly because there are more small publishers and niche markets available to sci-fi and fantasy writers, more claptrap gets published than is true in mainstream fiction. But I am very, very picky."

Still, given the numbers raising the issue, it's tempting to suggest that many now agree with Nick Harkaway that problems of characterisation are "not particularly prevalent"; or at least, with Vaughan Stanger that, "Characterisation remains a problem, though less so than, say, 30 years ago." Similarly, for some of those who highlighted style, the issue was not – as it has been in the past – a matter of basic competence, but as Adam Roberts (perhaps somewhat wistfully) put it, "I might wish writers in the genre be as adventurous and scrupulous when it comes to literary form and style as they are when it comes to content and ideas." China Mieville felt the same:

> There are plenty of exceptions to this, of course, so hedged around with a thousand caveats, but ... perhaps something of a disinclination for formal experimentation. Combined with a geek predilection (which I share, but think perhaps we should fight), for dotting all 'i's and crossing all 't's, the triumph of a spurious totality in the dialectic between totalising invention and mysterious/ numinous uncontainable within the fantastic: feeling the need to explain to much, or cover all the parts of a map. The tension's the strength, not a collapse to one or other center of gravity.

Susanna Clarke wrote eloquently on the same theme, and considered it as a particular challenge for fantasy:

> The problem I'm going to outline below is not so much a weakness in fantasy as a damaging misconception about fantasy. There's a common assumption that, when building imaginary worlds (Middle Earth, Narnia, etc.) the writer ought to strive to make them logical, consistent etc. – for example if there are trains then it ought to be clear that this is a world with an industrial revolution. Thus when Lewis allowed the beavers and fauns of Narnia to have printed books and sewing machines, then it is considered a fault in the writing. The more I think about it the less I'm sure that this is true. I think this idea comes about because quite proper assumptions from other genres have been transferred to fantasy. In other sorts of stories the demand for logic and consistency is reasonable – the unravelling of a murder in a detective novel cannot possibly be satisfying unless the crime was committed in a coherent and comprehensible world. The same is obviously true of certain kinds of science fiction. But a fantasy story is not like this.

> We think an imaginary world ought to be a coherent alternative to this world and so ought to match this world in having a set of logical rules that govern its existence and development. But an imaginary world is never an alternative to this world – it is a skewed representation of this world. Imaginary worlds are places where we meet and touch symbols and ideas in solid form – orcs, for example, are badness personified; dragons are solid symbols of wildness and flight. In *The Lion, the Witch and the Wardrobe* printed books and sewing machines are symbols of home, peace and security; Lewis needs to contrast the peace and goodness inside the beaver's dam with the dark and danger outside and so the books and sewing machines are a wholly reasonable element in the book.
>
> For historical reasons fantasy gets put with science fiction, but the fantasy genre, I suspect, is actually much more closely related to children's fiction and to poetry.
>
> An imagined world in fantasy literature needs to be emotionally compelling to the reader and believable enough to support the story.

It's also true to say that for some respondents, such as Tanith Lee, the technical limitations of sf and fantasy are intertwined with the sort of staleness identified by so many other respondents: "Bad writing, as in any genre. Specifically in the sf/fantasy field, it seems to involve a kind of sterility (I *don't* mean clean spare prose) or over-imitation." In Chris Beckett's answer, consideration of one seems to lead (inevitably?) to consideration of the other:

> Wooden characters. Characters who are just plot vehicles to whom spurious personality traits have been bolted on (I'm not fooled by humourless, nerveless, remorseless action heroes, to whom a bit of pathos is added in the hope of making them seem more interesting and human). A character, like a real person, should act in a way that comes from his personality, experience and circumstances. Nothing wrong with escapism per se, but both genres sometimes seem to cater for a need on the part of essentially quiet, timid people to escape into control fantasies of action, heroism and violence. I dislike that. By all means write about brave heroic action men and women if you really can imagine what it would be like to be such a person. Otherwise write about the kinds of people whose skin you can actually imagine being inside.
>
> I dislike the glorification of war and violence in both genres. Some years ago I was in a car crash in which I was unhurt but a stranger died. I remember thinking to myself at the time, "Later this scene will have a vivd, spurious glamour – the sense of being on the edge, the dream-like quality of it all, the adrenaline – but in fact now that I am actually in it, it has no glamour at all. It's just ugly. I must remember that." I suspect war is like that.
>
> I think both genres are very seriously in danger of being gobbled up by their own clichés. Tolkienesque hierarchies of sentient beings who use medieval

> technology combined with magic... FTL, gigantic starships, gigantic empires, gigantic everything...

There seemed, however, to be several aspects to this problem of familiarity. A couple of respondents, such as Colin Davies, suggested that, "It is too hard for many people. That's not to say that it's too clever, or superior, but that it requires a way of reading and understanding the world of the story that not everyone is willing or able to do"; a twist on the idea discussed in earlier chapters that sf writers see the world in a particular way. Katherine Roberts agreed:

> It can turn some readers off completely. Some people simply cannot stomach the strange names or the imaginary settings, and I've noticed that younger children in particular can have difficulty getting into a completely fantasy setting unless there is something familiar to guide them into the book (for example a school setting, even if it is a school for fairies or wizards!). Once they are into your fantasy world, however, children tend to enjoy the ride and believe in all types of magic, whereas adult readers need a lot more convincing that the magic is real.

But this was a definite minority response. More common was concern about what Al Robertson described as, "Spending too much time worrying about how the furniture's arranged, rather than just sitting down on it and talking all night about interesting things"; that is to say, in Gary Gibson's words, "Looking inward – stuff that's highly referential, particularly in the context of other sf stories. Pandering to an audience in the know, in other words. It's quite sad." Mark Charan Newton, like Paul Cornell earlier, sees damage in the attitudes that go with this:

> I can only see a minor weakness at the community level: I suspect that the in-fighting (online or otherwise) and perceived cliques can do a lot to prevent new readers from becoming involved in fandom, and certainly tires people out. I've known of a few authors to simply walk away from online activity for these reasons. But I don't think much can be done about this – putting together humans to discuss their passions will inevitably lead to problems.

Or as Peadar O'Guilin put it, the great weakness of sf and fantasy is that "it's far more likely than any other genre to disappear up its own asshole and to pull the ladder up after itself." Or Steve Aylett: "It tends to crawl further into itself, repeat itself or the ideas of others, set up boundaries to imagination and stop at them, while using as many words and wasting as much paper as possible."

This sort of repetition, identified by writers such as Joe Abercrombie, Ramsey Campbell ("Too much is innately, even routinely, conservative – I mean artistically as much as politically"), Mary Hoffman ("The great JRR can have had no idea just how much drivel he was opening the gates to"), Graham Joyce, Rhiannon Lassiter, James Lovegrove ("Authors relying too heavily on the existing corpus, using ideas and language that other authors have already established"), and Conrad Williams, is for some against the basic goals of the form. Paul McAuley wrote that, "It's too often a literature of comfort, patched out of old science fiction," while Adrian Tchaikovsky noted that, "A lot of fantasy/sf can be formulaic, which results in books that only interact with the reader in reinforcing their preconceptions and stereotypes, rather than actually taking them anywhere," and Alan Campbell mused, "It's all very nostalgic, which is fair enough, and yet the genre is ideal for exploring much darker, stranger places." For Juliet McKenna, unconsidered repetition is pernicious:

> Too much referring back to hypothetical Golden Ages and thus re-using stock narratives and stereotypical characters to comply with the perceived boundaries of the genre as defined in those periods. As well as promoting predictable stories this can perpetuate outdated attitudes to race, religion and gender.

It's here that we seem to get down to the heart of the matter: sf and fantasy as conservative. "This sounds ironic," wrote Tim Lees, "but it's true":

> I think the problem is two-fold. On the one hand, publishers, ever keen to maximise the profits, go where they see a guaranteed target audience. If it's worked before, it'll work again. (Let me say, I've nothing against profit, but there's a business culture these days that will not take on long-term projects with profits maybe three, four or more years down the line – which is exactly what happens in writing.) The writers, too, have to earn a living. So Moorcock trots out another couple of Elric novels, keeping himself and family alive. The difference with Moorcock, of course, is that he's probably also doing something rather wonderful at the same time with a completely different project.
>
> Secondly, there's a fan base – without which sf could not exist – who want to see the same thing over and over again. I'm not attacking sf fans for this – God forbid – and many are, indeed, widely read and open to new concepts, new ways of writing, etc. But it's the same with any fan base. Ian Rankin's fans all want another Rebus. And so on. I'm like that, as well. If I'm in the mood for a particular kind of book, that's what I want. If the author doesn't provide it, I may not go back to him.

Another way of putting this is, as Iain Banks said, "a bit too comfy sometimes – not ruthless enough (this is probably as much self-criticism as anything else)." Mark Chadbourn's response suggests this can indeed be seen as a systemic problem: "Too much is innately, even routinely, conservative – too much similarity, not enough diversity"; though it's difficult to say whether this is seen as a weakness inherent to genre, or a weakness of this genre, at the moment. Chaz Brenchley was concerned that, "Any genre is weakened as a form by the quantities of commercial pulp at the base of the pyramid ... The corollary of which is that so much classic sf is allowed out of print. Sf is maturing into an iceberg, with only a small percentage of it easily accessible." Will Ashon argues that this is always the case: "It's the same weakness we seem to have in anything that's sold for its existence. Too much crap competing for too little space."

But Kari Sperring's response suggests that it may be a right here, right now thing:

> Sentiment. No, seriously, we are drowning in gross nostalgia – for a caring, fluffy Middle Ages, for Perfect Heroes, for Bad-Ass Vampire Chicks, for Cool Marines with Big Guns and a lot of other (often very US-centric) clichés. It's a particularly cloying kind of denial, too: Hollywood never-never. A lot of it is deeply reactionary and deeply superficial and it bores me silly. We can do better than space (soap) opera and My Little Unicornery.

While Ian Watson's concern is:

> Perhaps too many people nowadays write principally in order to become published authors rather than having a special and unusual point of view to put over, which ought to be the reason for writing a story or a book. A story or book should be an act of discovery by the author, by which in turn readers discover new things. I sense a kind of consensus fiction, the making of the sort of stories that *F&SF* or *Asimov's* are likely to publish, for instance. Workshops tutored by celeb authors may lead to clone-fiction. Perhaps workshops should be tutored by the equivalents of Salvador Dali rather than by master wordsmiths.

There is a sense underlying some of these responses that sf and fantasy may be a victim of their own success; that what we have here is a warning. Paul Barnett detects:

> ... a certain complacent self-censorship within the field. I've been on editorial panels galore at conventions where the first answer from genre editors to the usual tedious question "What are y'all looking for?" is of the order: "You gotta grab us by the throat in the first paragraph. You don't do that, buster, you're trash."
>
> It seems to me no surprise, in light of this, that almost all the best skiffy/fantasy novels I've read in the past decade or so have been published on mainstream not genre lists, and that quite a few of them have been in translation. In a sense I've got nothing against instant hooks; yet the very fact that they seem to have become a *requirement* has made them a complete turn-off for me: if I pick up a novel with a wonderful grab-you-by-the-balls opening

> sentence I'm quite likely to put it back down again on the grounds that the novel itself is probably puerile.
>
> But the other important thing to change in this very personal little equation is *me*. As I've become ever boringer, older and, um, fartier I suppose, I find I have less and less patience with the easy-entertainment side of culture.

Which takes us right back to Justina Robson's argument about there not being – and perhaps needing to be – more space for more visions of what sf and fantasy can do and be than there currently are. Of course, as Keith Brooke reminds us: "You can't please everyone, and in sf/f that's even more the case"; but perhaps the answer to the problem is genre after all. Perhaps, as Lisa Tuttle suggests, "the weakness of any genre fiction is that it tends towards simply gratifying the reader's expectations, and repetition of formulas, rather than challenging the reader or breaking new ground." And perhaps, having had a period of quite ambitious ground-breaking, the danger of sliding into something more limiting is particularly acute.

It is a danger that everyone involving in producing and consuming sf contributes to. (Adam Roberts: "I might wish fans a little more demanding.") Jon Courtenay Grimwood, I think, sums this up nicely, when he says that the greatest weakness of sf and fantasy as genres is simply:

> Safety ... It's market imposed and publisher imposed and self imposed. Our inability to really push the boundaries is a weakness, although in the middle of a recession, with sales of custard going through the roof, and every market scrambling for its equivalents, that's not about to change soon. We need to reinvent, but we're trapped in a culture that wants not just, "the same, but different," it wants, "the same, done only slightly differently" ... *Twilight* is what you get when you follow those rules. *Let The Right One In* is what you get when you break them and reinvent.

I know which I prefer.

# Chapter 11: *What do you think have been the most significant developments in British science fiction and fantasy over the past twenty years?*

## 2009

One problem with accepting questions from twenty years ago is that they set the terms of the debate: they create a presumption that what were then pressing issues, or issues of interest, are going to still be pressing or of interest now. The response to the survey suggests that this is in fact the case, at least to an extent, but an index to what might have been missed would still be useful. Hence this chapter's question – intended as broadly as possible, in the spirit of the rest of the survey. Its secondary purpose is to act as a test of the rest of the chapters: are the trends that I've drawn out of writers' answers the ones that they themselves perceive as significant?

Of course, straight away the question has a problem, as Andrew Crumey spotted: "In literature, I would say the only measurable development is the passage of time." Or, as Kit Whitfield put it: "I like to take every book on its own merits rather than seeing them as developments." A better word, it now seems, would have been *changes*, which avoids the teleological connotations that can be taken from *development*. Admittedly, as Stan Nicholls points out, some changes may also be developments –

> I think it's indisputable that the general standard of writing, purely on the craft level, has improved markedly. As it happens I've recently been re-reading a raft of classic, or at least vintage, science fiction, and it's notable how poorly written so much of it now appears. Of course this is partly down to the fact that just about everything ages (while a small proportion of the very best work matures), but in my opinion it underlines the impression that sf in the past was much more concerned with ideas than literary elegance. It's nice to see this being redressed.

> As an unashamedly commercial writer, I consider the best development over the past couple of decades has been the increasing professionalism of our fields. It's now possible to make a full-time living out of writing science fiction and fantasy. I'm not saying it's easy, but the prospects are better than they have been historically.

– but most, surely, are just changes. At the same time, from some perspectives, the answer may simply be "not much": as Kari Sperring prefaced her response, "I'm a medievalist: twenty years is a bit short!" And given that the individuals being surveyed are working writers – rather than, say, busybody critics – for a fair few respondents, some variation on "I don't feel qualified to say" was an entirely reasonable answer.

Nevertheless, most respondents pointed to something, and several particularly common responses emerged, helpfully summarized by Richard Morgan:

> Hmm – tough one. Would depend a lot on your defining parameters. In purely demographic terms, of course, you're talking about the re-launch of *Doctor Who* and the advent of Harry Potter. Both of those have unquestionably sown the seeds for a massive influx of fresh, young readers and viewers into the genre, and we should all be very grateful for that. But taking a more quality-based and adult approach, I suppose I'd prefer to cite Iain M Banks' re-invention of space opera in his Culture novels and China Mieville's paradigm-shifting Bas-Lag fantasy trilogy – both those sequences have been a huge tonic for the genre in terms of imaginative power and reach; in many ways you could say that they were the base building blocks for the so-called British sf/f Renaissance.

Tricia Sullivan offered an overlapping list:

> I guess I'd have to say:
>
> 1) The resurgence of space opera – who knew?
>
> 2) The adoption of genre values and viewpoints by non-genre-ghetto writers. I'm not sure what this means for the genre but I think it's probably good.
>
> 3) China Mieville.
>
> 4) As an aside, it's interesting to me that the huge impact of urban fantasy and paranormal romance has only been dimly felt here in Britain. I can't say that's a bad thing; but it's an interesting non-development.

Not every respondent agreed. Gareth Lyn Powell spoke up for "the notion of the singularity ... with every writer being forced to decide whether to address it or ignore it, and then having to justify that decision," while Tanith Lee described the challenge of the problem that "we should by now be living *in* sf, or fantasy – as the 1800s, the 1940s and 50s predictively detailed ... so the mechanism of literary invention is remodelling itself (often exquisitely) into a hundred playful forms. As we all mark time, on the threshold of an sf adventure which, for us, *still* hasn't yet got beyond chapter 3."

A few respondents highlighted the importance of changes in the real world; Liz Jensen spoke of climate change as "the biggest issue of our times. Soon, one way or another, it will have eclipsed many other issues. So I'm very excited about the way writers are beginning to address it, and to imagine a post-apocalyptic world"; a viewpoint that chimes with Conrad Williams' argument that, "The stagnation of space exploration seems to have bent our thinking back towards the Earth. There has been a slew of eco-fantasy/sf which I think will continue. I think it's a good thing to have our writers of the fantastic turning their attention to the deterioration of our world. It might lead us to meet head-on the challenge of rescuing it, rather than deserting it for pastures new."

Others respondents, such as Ian Watson, focused on specific writers: "New Gothic space opera, as in Al Reynolds, John Meaney, especially the bone books, Richard Morgan. Liz Williams. Ken MacLeod. Versatile Paul McAuley. You know what they write. Steve Baxter has bootstrapped himself from his earliest books into a grand master; *Flood* haunts me. Up and coming, Chris Beckett. Apologies to those unmentioned due to amnesia."

But by and large it was the topics identified by Morgan and Sullivan that kept cropping up – often, as was the case for Ian Whates, with some pride:

> I believe we're experiencing a golden age of British sf right now (and I stress the *a* rather than *the*), with more good British writers producing more extremely good science fiction than I can ever remember. There have always been quality British sf and fantasy writers, but not in this number. I remember when I first started reading sf back at the dawn of the 70s, book shop shelves were full of American authors. There were Brits as well – Aldiss, Clarke, Moorcock – but they were few and far between. Much the same was true twenty years ago. It isn't now.
>
> Along the way, British sf (with the likes of Banks, Reynolds and MacLeod) has also helped bring a new credibility to space opera, while such authors as the late David Gemmell and Joe Abercrombie have brought a new grittiness to "high" fantasy. Thankfully, sf is developing the whole time, and British authors are right at the forefront.

Again, as so often in this survey, we see confidence: a belief explicit in just over a third of responses to this question, and implicit in many more, that the past two decades have seen a boom, or a renaissance, or a golden age, for British science fiction and fantasy. Keith Brooke wrote of "a real flourishing of British sf"; Ken MacLeod described "The turn away from New Wave introversion and post-New-Wave gloom"; and John Meaney said, "We grow confident, maybe even aggressive ... and good for us!" Only Chris Butler explicitly disagreed: "Was it like this in 1989? I don't think that was a boom time for British writers either." Although for the US-resident Paul Barnett, the boom is somewhat artefactual, being driven by US recognition: "I explain patiently to friends that there were good Brit writers there all along; it's just that the US chose to ignore them for far too many years." However, what this chapter bears out, among other things, is Andrew M Butler's contention that this is a confidence supported by multiple pillars.

For one thing, as Elizabeth Wein suggested, "people seem to take genre writing much more seriously than they used to" – she cited as evidence "The acceptance of Pullman and Rowilng as mainstream writers (*children's* fantasists, no less!) – and perhaps also the surge in appreciation for graphic novels." Sarah Ash confirmed that:

> Wearing my children's librarian's hat, I would have to say that the publication of the Harry Potter books has brought many more fantasy readers (of all ages) into the genre – and has inspired the publication of many more fantasy (and some science fiction) titles, especially for the YA range (I'm thinking here of writers like Charlie Fletcher, Philip Reeve, Patrick Ness etc ...).

Perhaps not surprisingly, given that this is the year that YA titles won the Nebula Award (*Powers* by Ursula K Le Guin), the Tiptree Award (*The Knife of Never Letting Go* by Patrick Ness, jointly with Nisi Shawl's short story collection *Filter House*) and the Hugo Award (*The Graveyard Book* by Neil Gaiman), the significance of YA science fiction and fantasy, what Frances Hardinge described, "the growth of the crossover market," was a common theme. For respondents such as Iain Banks, Alan Campbell, and Elizabeth Counihan, it is primarily, if not entirely, a *fantasy* surge, and one that, as Katherine Langrish pointed out, is driven by both critical and commercial achievement:

> I can only really speak of children's fantasy, where the most obvious phenomenon has been the success of the Harry Potter books, which forced the public and publishers to take fantasy writing "seriously" at least in a financial sense. In terms of quality of writing, Philip Pullman's *His Dark Materials* trilogy has forced the same people to recognise that at least some fantasy writing can be "literary" and deal with huge themes.

Mike Carey, like Richard Morgan, linked the rise of YA with a telefantasy renaissance:

> It's worth mentioning the Harry Potter phenomenon, and the knock-on effect it's had on sales for other UK fantasy books. This has its counterpart in the TV revolution begun by Joss Whedon and then triumphantly taken up by Russell Davies. Sci-fi and fantasy is more respected and less underestimated now than it was when I was growing up.

Morgan's response is the closest anyone came to having a bad word for YA (i.e. not very close); but when it came to TV telefantasy, opinions were more divided. Paul Cornell championed, "The return of *Doctor Who*. Seriously. There's no better influence on young sf minds," and Al Robertson described:

> The development of sophisticated long form sf/fantasy on TV (goes hand in hand with DVD box set growth, which has changed the way people watch TV and thus the way it's made). Exemplified by *Buffy*, *Babylon 5*, etc. This related to the success of the *Lord of the Rings* movies which – even if in some ways flawed – made widescreen, epic fantasy seriously sexy. These, I suspect, drove the re-commissioning of *Doctor Who* which led to smaller scale genre TV including the wonderful *Afterlife*, *Being Human*, etc.

But not everyone was so keen. Deborah Miller was sceptical, not of recent TV and films in themselves, but of the effect others argued they have had: "Probably that the film industry has co-opted the genres so that they are "mainstream" in cinema terms – it is a strange irony that the literature end of the spectrum is still considered by some to be "niche" or alternative. People who go to see sf/f movies all the time might never consider buying the books or graphic novels." Stephen Gaskell wrote, perhaps somewhat wearily, of "*Doctor Who*'s lionisation as 'sophisticated' sf"; and Ben Jeapes was equally sceptical:

> The explosion in TV sf has been a significant development but not a particularly good one. We don't have any TV executives who are particularly aware of what constitutes good sf. Therefore they scramble to imitate either Joss Whedon or Russell T Davies, not realising that Joss Whedon has a very wide-ranging understanding of sf/f (so trying to imitate *Buffy* kind of misses the point) and RTD doesn't (so trying to imitate *Doctor Who* will get you nowhere: the strengths of the series predate RTD by a long way).
>
> On the plus side, the crop of authors who came up through *Interzone* are flourishing, and more power to them. Twenty years ago would a very good but not particularly famous sf author have got a £1m, ten-book deal? I think not.

Jeapes' second point finds an echo in Eric Brown's praise for "The number of writers who are writing core sf with care and attention to characterisation"; and Jaine Fenn offers a reminder that it's not just core *sf* which has been refreshed, in her argument that: "I think the movement to make fantasy more realistic (I think the word that's always used is "gritty") has saved it from dying, and I believe (though I'm happy to be corrected) that this came largely from British writers."

Tim Lebbon also used the g-word: "I think both genres are taken more seriously now, by readers and to an extent by writers too. Fantasy has become more gritty and serious, taking on some of the concerns – political, social – that used to be the domain of science fiction." And Adrian Tchaikovsky agreed that this change was real, and attributed it to a change in readership: "The development of urban fantasy; a move from saga-based fantasy with relatively clean morality to character-based fantasy with more moral ambiguity; I suspect a broader demographic of readers results in the opportunity for greater variety within the genre." (As for urban fantasy/paranormal romance, it was also noted by Justina Robson, though she agreed with Tricia Sullivan that it "doesn't seem to have had the same expression here" as it has in the US, "although its features are more noticeable in sf and f coming out at the moment, at least from female writers.")

But it was space opera that was the subgenre to be mentioned again and again. Neil Williamson noted that "lots of good writers have done exciting things in that field," while Peadar O'Guilin went so far as to suggest that "the British have left the Americans in the shade." And Jaine Fenn wrote: "I think it's great that we've retained the huge multi-world storylines and the sense of adventure and excitement whilst ditching outdated elements of the original space opera, such as colonial expansion, xenophobia, and sexual stereotyping."

And what of Alastair Reynolds, the million dollar man himself?

> The fact that British sf is now on an equal footing with American sf, in terms of prestige and even sales. I would credit *Interzone* with some of that, by fostering a generation of British and Commonwealth sf writers who had the attitude and ambition to take on the big names at their own game – writers like Paul McAuley, Gwyneth Jones, Greg Egan, Steve Baxter ... I would also single out the emergence of Iain M Banks as an sf writer, whose books paved the way for the "big space opera" boom of the late nineties, early two thousands. Without Banks there might not have been a Hamilton, and without Hamilton I doubt that my books would have found a ready market.

Again the vigour of British sf; again space opera specifically; and again *Interzone* which, primarily for its pre-Third Alternative Press incarnation, received props from Stephen Gaskell, John Meaney ("And let's hear it once again for David Pringle. He did us proud"), Gary Gibson ("*Interzone* has been a breeding ground for new writers, and that continues even now, despite it being sadly a bit diminished compared to what it used to be"), and Charles Stross:

> Two things. a) *Interzone*. Simon Ounsley's manifesto calling for "radical, hard sf," and David Pringle's follow-through. This launched and entire generation of new writers in a then-tired field; I suppose I'm probably the tail-end of it (insofar as my first story was published in IZ the same year as Paul McAuley's, but it took me an extra fifteen years to get a novel into print). If you take a cross-section through the *Interzone* generation you get: Kim Newman, Eugene Byrne, Steve Baxter, Pete Hamilton, Paul McAuley, Al Reynolds, and a bunch

> of less obviously successful writers – but basically, everyone who is anyone in British sf (fantasy: not so much) seems to have been in *Interzone* in its glory days, from around 1984 through to 1994.

But not everyone was so enthusiastic about this strand of sf's success. Ian R MacLeod, for instance: "Sadly, I think I would have to say the resurgence of space opera. Okay, it's a bit darker and more ironic than the first time around, and it can be fun to read, but really ...? I mean, come on ...!" And Chris Beckett doesn't have a problem with space opera in itself, but questions its effect on the market:

> I am depressed by the message I receive from publishers that they really just want space opera now. If that is the case and continues to be so, our genre will die. Aldiss, Ballard, Dick would never have emerged under such constraints. The ida that sf is really just space opera is already the idea that exists among non-sf readers in my experience, and contributes to the ghettoisation of sf as something separate from "serious" writing, as opposed to the wonderful vehicle for serious writing which it can be, and I have found it to be myself. (Not that there is anything wrong with space opera per se.)

At the same time, a number of respondents praised the freedom of the contemporary genre. Juliet McKenna, for instance, spoke of: "The pushing of boundaries; in the range of sources that writers draw upon, in the subjects that have been tackled, in the exploration of the overlap between sf, fantasy and horror, and in the blending of the whole range of speculative fiction with elements from the crime, romance, humorous and historical genres"?

And McKenna's response is, in fact, only one of two separate but related issues in play here. As Graham Sleight has argued, there are two types of "blending" going on in contemporary sf/f: on the one hand, the mixing of tropes and approaches within the field of the fantastic, as described by McKenna; and on the other hand, the mixing of the fantastic and the mimetic, as typified by works poised between "genre" and "mainstream." We've had plenty of labels for both kinds of approach over the past two decades; perhaps most enduringly, "New Weird" for the former and "slipstream" for the latter, but think also of interstitial, steampunk, New Wave Fabulists, paranormal romance, and so forth. Sleight's suggestion is that for reasons of pragmatism and convenience, in contexts such as this survey we can replace the whole lot with two non-value-judgement-laden labels: Tom for mixing within the fantastic, and Jerry for mixing of the fantastic and mimetic.

So, Michael Moorcock, like Juliet McKenna, was a Tom advocate:

> Probably the writers involved in the New Weird, who perhaps see the likes of M John Harrison as pointing the way through to some fresh development. I think of this as being Science Fantasy, which remains my favourite form in this

> area. It has many of the romantic elements of the so-called New Wave, which was primarily towards romanticism and away from the pseudo-realism, the rationalised "hard" sf of its predecessors. That said, the best proponents of the New Weird seem just as capable of writing, like Harrison and Mieville, in a style deriving, say, from another kind of neo-romanticism familiar from the spy fiction influenced by Graham Greene. Perhaps the greatest drawback to this kind of fiction is that it remains male-focused, like "cyberpunk" and most other subgenres. Urban fantasy seems to attract an interesting sort of woman writer, which may be why I like it.

But for Tim Lees, "The real change is the way sf ideas and themes have moved outside the genre. In this, we're perhaps catching up with the rest of Europe, where there's always been a healthy tradition of literary fantasy." Graham Joyce made a similar point – "That these two genres have exported their interests to so many other media/genres (or have been raided by other genres and media: whichever way you look at it, that's a success)." And so did Paul McAuley, in a way that perhaps starts to address Chris Beckett's experience: "Although there are now fewer British publishers of genre science fiction than twenty years ago, there's more science fiction being published outside the genre category."

Nina Allan wrote forcefully on this topic, describing a very different landscape to that seen by Beckett:

> Without questioning the broadening of the genre. We have thrown away the rule book, thank goodness, and an sf novel can now just as easily be set in a mental asylum or a courthouse as on board a spaceship. You can begin your story twenty thousand years into the future, or right now. There are always going to be "sf purists" who will insist that Russell Hoban's *The Bat Tattoo* isn't really fantasy, just as there will always be mainstream bigots who believe that anything that trespasses on the quotidian is somehow a degradation of literary standards. But on the whole such limited insight is a thing of the past.
>
> On the whole I believe that the "incursion" of broadly mainstream writers such as Kazuo Ishiguro, Toby Litt and David Mitchell into the field of sf and fantasy has to be a good thing. Not only does it precipitate the blurring of genre boundaries – always a good thing, in my book – but it also promotes discussion and argument and brings some welcome public attention to the subject of sf. While mainstream writers may not be in the forefront of innovation when it comes to science fictional ideas, their presence in the field can help us avoid complacency, and so raise our game.

One factor driving the shift, suggested Paul Meloy, might be readers:

> Writers like Mike Marshall Smith, Tim Lebbon, Charlie Williams, Conrad

> Williams and their ilk pushing boundaries with language and form, being deliberately, flagrantly intelligent and daring. Also the phenomena of cross-genre writing, which I guess has been emerging for the last twenty or so years. Readers and writers have probably grown and matured significantly in their tastes and preferences over this period and demand more than a narrow taxonomy of genres.

China Mieville made a similar point:

> Lord, I don't know. Perhaps it's a meta-development – the growth of a demographic blip of writers and readers who don't come out of the fan scene and aren't "hardcore" readers of the genre(s), but who are not afflicted, either, with the despite so prevalent among earlier generations of literary editors: and a concomitant much more respectful pilfering from and regard to the genre from friendly civilians. Combined, both for good and ill, with sf/f becoming a default cultural vernacular.

And yet other writers offered perspectives much more in line with Beckett's. Rhiannon Lassiter, for instance, sees balkanization more than blending:

> Young adult fiction has become more influenced by the major selling trends and yet is increasingly unrelated to the related adult genres.
>
> Genres are also increasingly sub-divided, in that I might say I am not aware of any significant developments in fantasy because the more exploratory and original work in the genre is classified by afficianados as its own speculative fiction subgenre.
>
> Speculative fiction generally appears to be more influenced by the bottom line. The general quality or salability of titles has perhaps increased as the wild variance between work at the top of its field and at the bottom has decreased. But few authors, even at the top of their field, appear to achieve literary distinction. (Although this view may be too subjective and it's difficult to judge the literary merit of contemporary work since it's impossible to assess its "staying power.")

Brian Stableford suggested that rampant Jerrying may eventually lead to "The effective extinction of sf/f as pretended genres; the future marketing of such works will inevitably concentrate on the establishment of brand-name authors, represented as unique literary voices, and the genre labels will be junked as (at best) useless or (at worst) deleterious." Perhaps, then, we should be looking not so much at *what* is published as *where* it appears. After all, as Tony Ballantyne points out, there are new players on the scene; he pointed to:

> The growing professionalism of the small press, and the quality of the product they produce. The internet may change things in the future, but the physical press is still the goal of most writers, and the medium of choice for readers. Two major prizes have been won this year by books published by small presses (Arthur C Clarke Award – Ian R MacLeod for *Song of Time*; Edge Hill Short Story Prize – Chris Beckett for *The Turing Test*). I think we are going to see more of this in the future.

For Steve Aylett, the growth of the small press is "the only perhaps positive thing" in a landscape dominated by "the increase in huge commercial fantasy series with no real innovation in them," while Chaz Brenchley praised:

> The emergence of a viable and vigorous small press. With the retrenchment of the mainstream publishers, their abandonment of midlist and backlist together and their aversion to risk, the independent sector is already bidding fair to be the saviour of diverse and ambitious genre publishing. It won't ever feed hungry authors, but it gives access and it finds a readership, it keeps the conversation going. Books exist that wouldn't otherwise. Especially novellas and collections, the uncommercial forms which prime the pump of genre.

It's a very different landscape to that described by some of the respondents quoted earlier. Ramsey Campbell highlighted the extent to which the small press is preserving those areas of the fantastic that are less hot property right now: "I'm going to say small press publishing, certainly as far as horror is concerned. Just as in the fifties, many of the most significant books are being published outside the mass market. It's one of the natural states of the field. Back then Arkham House led the way – now I would say our own PS Publishing does." While Stephen Gallagher described "The corporatisation of mainstream publishing houses, leading to massive loss of editorial know-how and the elimination of the specialised lines and imprints that were sustained by that know-how ... It's great that the small and indie presses do so much to keep the flame alive, but it's not the same."

And we should be asking *who* is telling the stories we get to read, as Kari Sperring argues, picking up on Tricia Sullivan's point from the previous chapter, and perhaps suggesting why urban fantasy hasn't done so well over here:

> I'd say the genres have been re-masculising noticeably: there is ever more emphasis on Big Books by Big Male Writers in sf, while British fantasy is being more and more sidelined and over-written by imports of Extruded Fantasy Product from the US and the Antipodes. I'd like to see more opportunities for UK writers like Jessica Rydill rather than "Gollancz Romancz" (which is deeply patronising to women readers) and clone trilogies. This is down to the narrowing of publication options here, mostly – we have really little more than

> Macmillan, Gollancz and Orbit. There are some very interesting fantasy writers in the small press – I'd particularly single out Fiona McGavin and George Udenkwo – but they aren't breaking into the mainstream – indeed, we have established UK fantasists who are only published in the US (Chaz Brenchley, Jo Walton).
>
> For me, the two most significant recent sf writers in the UK are Justina Robson and Ken MacLeod. The former is possibly the best writer of inhuman humanity to date and a wonderful satirist (especially on the perceptions and traps of femininity); the latter brings a much needed return to serious political analysis.

For the sake of precision, it should be noted that Walton now holds Canadian citizenship, but Sperring's point is well made, and there are plenty of other writers you could substitute into that sentence – Karen Traviss, for instance, whose *Star Wars* novels appear over here, but whose original sf has to date been published only in the US.

Some respondents, however, felt that the diversity they see in the small press *is* attracting attention – in the online world. As Bob Lock put it, the internet means "a vast market for writers, i.e. the many ezines, the small press publishers, the home-made webpages and blogs that get undiscovered sf/f writers' work out there and showcased." Mark Chadbourn and Suzanne McLeod also pointed to the potential for, in Chadbourn's phrase, "a global genre community that is increasingly blind to national borders." Or, alternatively, as Roger Levy put it: "Not the writing, but the stuff around it, the stuff it feeds off, and that feeds it: the internet." Mark Charan Newton delved a bit deeper:

> Mainly how the genre has embraced the internet – which has had two significant impacts. The first is that it has connected fandom. We were a network of passionate readers even before the internet, and now those readers are enabled and connected online, and can debate genre books relentlessly. For those who used to feel alone in their fandom, it takes a quick internet search to find a forum in which they can debate and discover new authors.
>
> This has a secondary effect. There used to be a couple of main things that could really influence what is perceived as a good book: reviews in magazines/newspapers, and publishers spending lots of money on advertising and promotion. Quality and success could be influenced by very few people. Now there exists a middle class between the wider public and publishers, of powerful and erudite bloggers – with their own very large and active readerships. They are reviewing sff books on such a large scale that they are beginning to influence the success of certain novels, and especially in announcing what is a "good" book.
>
> I'm of the opinion that the future is very much in the hands of this crowd

> of active online personalities – and this is a positive thing. Influence over what is perceived as a quality book has been taken away from a few review venues and diluted amongst hundreds. Which is not to say that the genre is becoming a popularity contest – but that more people have a say in what they think defines a "good" book. The cynic in me, however, still suspects that a big marketing spend and a commercial cover still wins the general public over.

It will surely be fascinating to see if Newton is right about the future; he may be – after all, the New Weird started with a discussion at an online message board – but at the very least I think he is correct that, in the present, traditional marketing can still rule the day.

For David Langford, the interconnected world goes to issues at the heart of the Mexicon survey, namely the Britishness of British sf, and its reception:

> Perhaps a greater sense of transatlantic community? My early years as a writer and fan were permeated with the notion of a deep divide between British and American sf. The feeling was that the Americans packed the Hugo fiction voting and scoffed at the "British gloom" of our writers' efforts. Now we're talking to each other more, thanks to the net; British Hugo nominations in the fiction categories are no longer blue-moon marvels; our space-opera renaissance in particular has proved highly exportable; and, I think, as traditional print publishing undergoes successive convulsions, there's more awareness that sf people on both sides of the Atlantic are passengers or crew in the same storm-tossed boat.

Some respondents answered this question by suggesting that any divide between British and American sf is indeed vanishing – or, as Colin Davies put it, at least "becoming increasingly elusive." For others, however, such as Colin Harvey, although the focus has changed, the Britishness remains: "We've got over the loss of Empire, and found that life goes on – that there's a universe outside of Wessex and Melnibone. We've rediscovered what Gardner Dozois calls sensawunda, albeit with a typically British cynicism and dry humour."

The answers to this survey suggest a number of topics that additional or revised survey questions could have addressed, but none seems so central to me as the question of readers: who is reading sf and fantasy, and how do they find the books? Among other things, this is inevitably a matter of marketing. For Jon Courtenay Grimwood, "The rise of New Weird showed we could play the press at its own game, create a label and hang a series of media stories around it, getting into all the main broadsheets in the process. As a journalist that was a significant development to me." But it's also a question that can touch on all the material covered in this chapter – the success of YA, of New Weird, of core sf and fantasy, and of the small press. Indeed, as the second half of Charles Stross's response argues, it lies at the heart of the questions the survey was originally constructed to address, too.

b) This is a bubbling-under trend, but: globalisation. This is manifest in a couple of ways. In literary terms, writers tend to produce work which reflects their hopes and fears about the world they live in; in sf, this tends to influence their vision of the future. Post-war British sf was traditionally pessimistic about the future, inward-looking, fearful – stereotypically, writing about the end of empire and the collapse of old certainties. But since the end of the Thatcher years, we've moved on; I can't help but think there's much less overt pessimism in British sf in general – or at least, less of a ubiquitous conviction that the future's going to be grim.

The other way globalization is influencing British written sf is in the way books are sold and distributed. We're seeing the globalisation of the English Language Rights market – Orbit, for example, insist on buying world rights rather than portioning out North American rights and UK/Commonwealth rights separately. British sf writers are increasingly sold into a world (English language) market. On the other hand? Our accents are sexy and different, as far as the American consumer is concerned. These effects are long-term and subtle, but just as you can find more American sf on British bookshelves these days, so it is that American consumers will find it easier to read British sf – if they want to.

# Contributors

Authors are listed in alphabetical order; the dates of the survey(s) in which they participated are noted at the end of their entry.

**Joe Abercrombie** is the author of four fantasy novels often described as "gritty": the **First Law** trilogy, beginning with *The Blade Itself* (2006), and the related standalone novel *Best Served Cold* (2009). In 2008, he was shortlisted for the John W Campbell Award for Best New Writer. **(2009)**

**Brian Aldiss** is the Hugo- and Nebula Award-winning author of, among other books, *Non-Stop* (1958), *Hothouse* (1962), *Barefoot in the Head* (1969), and the **Helliconia Trilogy** (1982–1985), individual volumes of which won the BSFA and John W Campbell Awards. He has also written sf criticism, including (with David Wingrove) the Hugo Award-winning *Trillion Year Spree* (1986), other non-fiction, and non-sf fiction including the **Spire Quartet** (1980–1994). More recently, his sf novel *HARM* (2007) was shortlisted for the John W Campbell Award. **(1989)**

**Nina Allan**'s speculative short stories have been published in *Interzone* and *The Third Alternative*, and collected in *A Thread of Truth* (2007). Her story "Bird Songs at Eventide" was shortlisted for the BSFA Award in 2006. **(2009)**

**Sarah Ash**'s first novel was published in 1995, and her most recent is *Flight into Darkness* (2009), which concludes the *Alchymist's Legacy* duology. She is the author of six other fantasy novels, including the **Tears of Artamon** trilogy (2003–2005), and a number of short stories published in *Interzone* and other venues. **(2009)**

**Will Ashon** is the author of two "low-intensity dystopia" novels, *Clear Water* (2006) and *The Heritage* (2008), with a third, *Work*, forthcoming. He has worked in music journalism, for magazines such as *Muzik* and *Trace*, and in 1997 founded Big Dada, the hip-hop imprint of the record label Big Tune. **(2009)**

**Steve Aylett** is the author of over a dozen books, including *The Crime Studio* (1994), *Slaughtermatic* (1997, shortlisted for the Philip K Dick Award), the (probably) post-apocalypse Accomplice sequence beginning with *Only an Alligator* (2002), and the satiric fictional biography *Lint* (2005). **(2009)**

**Tony Ballantyne** is the author of four novels which explore ideas about machine and alien intelligence: *Recursion* (2004) *Capacity* (2005), *Divergence* (2007), and *Twisted Metal* (2009), with *Blood and Iron* forthcoming. His early short fiction, including the BSFA Award-nominated story "Gorillagram" (2000) appeared primarily in *Interzone*; more recent work has appeared in the anthologies *Constellations* (2005), *Fast Forward 1* (2007), and *Subterfuge* (2008). **(2009)**

**Iain Banks** is the author of 24 novels, one short fiction collection, and one non-fiction book about whisky. First novel *The Wasp Factory* was published in 1984, and quickly followed by *Walking on Glass* (1985), *The Bridge* (1986), and *Espedair Street* (1987), all published as mainstream fiction, although some contain fantastic elements. His first genre science fiction novel, as by Iain M Banks, was space opera *Consider Phlebas* (1987), inaugurating what has become the extremely successful **Culture** sequence, which includes the Arthur C Clarke Award-shortlisted *Use of Weapons* (1990) and the BSFA Award-winning *Excession* (1996); his other sf includes Hugo Award nominee *The Algebraist* (2004). His most recent novel is *Transition* (2009), published – just to confuse matters – as by Iain Banks in the UK but Iain M Banks in the US. **(1989 and 2009)**

**Paul Barnett** is author or editor of many books, mostly as John Grant. Novels include *The World* (1992), *The Far-Enough Window* (2002), *The Dragons of Manhattan* (2008) and *Leaving Fortusa* (2008); his first collection was *Take No Prisoners* (2004). From 1989 he wrote, with Joe Dever, 12 volumes of the fantasy series **The Legends of Lone Wolf**. For nonfiction he has won two Hugos, a World Fantasy Award, a Locus Award and others; recent nonfictions include *Discarded Science* (2006), *Corrupted Science* (2007) and *Bogus Science* (2009). For some years he edited the artbook imprint **Paper Tiger**, for this receiving a Chesley Award. Born in Scotland, he now lives in New Jersey. **(1989 and 2009)**

**David V Barrett** is a journalist, critic and author. He edited *Vector* between December 1985 (#129) and February 1988 (#142). Most recently he is the editor of the non-fiction books *The New Believers* (2001) and *A Brief History of Secret Societies* (2007). **(1989)**

**Barrington J. Bayley** was the author of many short stories and over a dozen novels, including *Star Virus* (1970), *Chronopolis* (1974), *The Zen Gun* (1982) and *The Forest of Peldain* (1985). He was associated with the New Wave movement in the 1960s, with short stories appearing regularly in *New Worlds*. He died in 2008. **(1989)**

**Chris Beckett**'s first short story, "A Matter of Survival", was published in *Interzone* in 1990. Many more followed, culminating in the collection *The Turing Test* (2008), which won the Edge Hill Short Story Prize. He is the author of two novels, *The Holy Machine* (2004, first UK edition due in 2010) and *Marcher* (2009), with a third, *Dark Eden*, forthcoming. **(2009)**

**Chaz Brenchley** is the author of two major fantasy series: **The Books of Outremer** (1998–2003) and **Selling Water By The River** (2006–2007); the first volume of the latter won the British Fantasy Award. He has also published nine thrillers, three books for children, and more than 500 short stories, including "Terminal" (2007), which won the BSFA Award for Best Short Fiction. **(2009)**

**Keith Brooke** has written sf novels for adults and (as Nick Gifford) for children; the former include *Genetopia* (2006) and *The Accord* (2009), while the latter include *Piggies* (2003) and *Erased* (2006). He founded the webzine *Infinity Plus* in 1997, and edited it for ten years. His short fiction has been collected in *Head Shots* (2001). **(2009)**

**John Brosnan** was born in Perth, Western Australia in 1947, but moved to London in 1970, where he lived until his death in 2005. He was the author of at least twenty novels, mainly sf and horror, often funny, including *Skyship* (1981), *Slimer* (1983), *Carnosaur* (1984), *Bedlam* (1992), *The Opoponax Invasion* (1993) and *Mothership* (2004), as well as several collections of short fiction, and a number of books on cinema (sf and otherwise). **(1989)**

**Eric Brown**'s story "The Time Lapsed Man" won the *Interzone* Readers' Poll in 1988. His first novel, *Meridian Days*, appeared in 1992, and has been followed by many more sf novels,including the **Virex** trilogy (2000-2004) and, most recently, the **Bengal Station** trilogy (2009-2010), as well as a number of books for children. He is the editor of *The Mammoth Book of New Jules Verne Adventures* (2005). **(1989 and 2009)**

**NM Browne** is the author of eight YA novels, including *Warriors of Alavna* (2000), *Basilisk* (2004), and *Shadow Web* (2008). She was born in Lancashire and lives in SW London. **(2009)**

**Kenneth Bulmer** wrote over 160 novels, many pseudonymous, primarily in the sf, Western and historical fiction genres; within the sf community he was also active as a fan (he was Britain's TAFF delegate in 1955, and as an editor, working on nine instalments of the *New Writings in SF* anthology series in the 1970s. His most widely read work, the **Dray Prescott** series, consists of eleven cycles of novels published between 1972 and 1998, although some were first published in German and have only appeared in English this decade. He died in 2005. **(1989)**

**Chris Butler** is the author of *Any Time Now* (2001), and a number of short stories. He has also reviewed sf and fantasy for the *Infinity Plus* website. **(2009)**

**Alan Campbell** is the author of the **Deepgate Codex**, comprising *Scar Night* (2006), *Iron Angel* (2008), and *God of Clocks* (2009). He lives in South Lanarkshire. **(2009)**

**Ramsey Campbell** is one of the UK's best known and most acclaimed authors of horror fiction, supernatural and non, and the author of over two dozen books. His first collection, *The Inhabitant of the Lake and Less Welcome Tenants* was published in 1964; his first novel, *The Doll Who Ate His Mother*, appeared in 1976. He has won two World Fantasy Awards, for his short story "Mackintosh Willy" (1980), and his collection, *Alone with the Horrors* (1994), and numerous British Fantasy Awards, most recently the Best Novel Award for *Grin of the Dark* (2008). He has also edited a number of anthologies. **(2009)**

**Mike Carey** is perhaps best-known for his comics writing, which includes a lengthy stint on *Hellblazer*, and the entire run of *Lucifer* (2000–2006), which was nominated for an Eisner Award. He is also the author of the **Felix Castor** urban fantasy novels, of which there have been five so far, the most recent being *The Naming of the Beasts* (2009). **(2009)**

**Mark Chadbourn**'s first story was published in 1990; since then he has published fifteen novels, six nominated for the British Fantasy Award for Best Novel. His most ambitious work is the trilogy of trilogies comprising **The Age of Misrule** (1999–2001), **The Dark Age** (2000–2005), and **Kingdom of the Serpent** (2006–2009), which mix elements of science fiction, fantasy and horror. His short fiction has twice won the British Fantasy Award. **(2009)**

**John Christopher** is a pseudonym of Sam Youd. He is perhaps best-known for the catastrophe novels *The Death of Grass* (1957) and *The World in Winter* (1962), and the YA **Tripods** trilogy (1967–1968), but has written many other novels, including the post-ecopocalypse **Sword of the Spirits** trilogy (1970–1972),and the alternate history **Fireball** trilogy (1981–1986). **(1989)**

**Susanna Clarke** is best known for her Hugo- and World Fantasy Award-winning (and Man Booker Prize longlisted) first novel, *Jonathan Strange & Mr Norrell* (2004), described by Neil Gaiman as "unquestionably the finest English novel of the fantastic written in the last seventy years." Her short fiction, set in the same magical alternate history, is collected in *The Ladies of Grace Adieu and Other Stories* (2006). **(2009)**

**John Clute** was born in Canada, but has lived in the UK since 1969. He has been reviewing sf and fantasy since the 1960s, and writing encyclopaedias about sf and fantasy since the 1970s. The second edition of *The Encyclopedia of Science Fiction* (edited with Peter Nicholls) was published in 1993, and the first edition of *The Encyclopedia of Fantasy* (edited with John Grant) was published in 1997. His reviews have been collected in four volumes: *Strokes* (1988), *Look at the Evidence* (1995), *Scores* (2003), and *Canary Fever* (2009). His sf novel *Appleseed* was published in 2001. **(1989)**

**James Corley** is best known for three sf novels: *Benedict's Planet* (1976), *Orsini Godbase* (1978), and *Sundrinker* (1980). **(1989)**

**Paul Cornell** is a writer of novels, comics and television episodes. He is best-known for his work on *Doctor Who*; his notable novels in that franchise include *Love and War* (1992), the first appearance of the companion Bernice Summerfield, and *Human Nature* (1995), and his TV episodes include "Father's Day" (2005) and a two-part adaptation of *Human Nature*, "Human Nature"/"The Family of Blood" (2007). He has also written for *Casualty*, *Robin Hood* and *Primeval*, and is currently the writer for the Marvel comic *Captain Britain and MI-13* (2008–present). His two original sf novels are *Something More* (2001) and *British Summertime* (2002). **(2009)**

**Elizabeth Counihan**'s short fiction has appeared in *Scheherazade*, *Interzone*, and *Realms of Fantasy*. **(2009)**

**Andrew Crumey** is a novelist, and former editor of the *Scotland on Sunday* newspaper. He holds a PhD in theoretical physics, which informs much of his fiction. The first of his five novels, *Music, in a Foreign Language*, was published in 1994; the most recent, *Sputnik Caledonia*, which includes a depiction of an alternate, communist Scotland, was published in 2008. **(2009)**

**Colin P. Davies**'s short fiction has appeared in, among other places, *Spectrum SF*, *Andromeda Spaceways Inflight Magazine*, and *Asimov's Science Fiction*, most recently in the latter with "The Certainty Principle" (February 2009). His collection *Tall Tales on the Iron Horse* was published in 2008. **(2009)**

**Peter Dickinson** has written almost fifty books, including a number of mysteries for adults (particularly the **James Pibble** series, 1968–1979), and many sf and fantasy tales for YA readers. The best-known of these include the ecologically-focused **Changes** trilogy (1968–1970), *The Blue Hawk* (1975, winner of the Guardian Award), *Eva* (1988), and *The Kin* (1998). He received an OBE in 2009. **(2009)**

**Robert Farago** published a number of sf and fantasy stories in the 1980s, and now works as a motoring journalist in America. **(1989)**

**Jaine Fenn**'s first novel, *Principles of Angels*, was published in 2008; a second in the same future history, *Consorts of Heaven*, appeared this year, with several more to follow. Her short fiction has appeared in *On Spec* and *Fortean Bureau*. **(2009)**

**Neil Gaiman** is one of the most prolific and widely respected of contemporary British fantasy writers. His first work to gain widespread attention, the graphic novel *The Sandman* (1989–1996), won multiple Eisner Awards, and issue #19, "A Midsummer Night's Dream", won the World Fantasy Award for Best Short Story in 1991. Following several journalistic works, including *Don't Panic: The Official Hitch-Hiker's Guide to the Galaxy Companion* (1988), his first prose novel *Good Omens* (co-written with Terry Pratchett) was published in 1990. Subsequent novels include *Stardust* (1999; filmed in 2007, one of a number of Gaiman works to be adapted for the screen), the Hugo Award-winning *American Gods* (2001), and *Anansi Boys* (2005). His YA novel *The Graveyard Book* won the Hugo Award (and many other awards) in 2009. **(1989)**

**Stephen Gallagher** is a novelist, screenwriter and director whose work explores suspense, fantasy and horror. He has written for *Doctor Who* (the serials "Warriro's Gate" in 1981, and "Terminus" in 1983), *Bugs*, and many other TV shows. First novel *The Last Rose of Summer* appeared in 1978; other notable works include *Oktober* (1988), *The Boat House*

(1991), and the short story collection *Out of His Mind* (2004), which won the British Fantasy Award. **(1989 and 2009)**

**Stephen Gaskell** is a graduate of the Clarion East writers' workshop, whose stories have appeared in *Writers of the Future vol XXIII* (2007), *Nature*, and *Futurismic*. He lives in Brighton. **(2009)**

**Mary Gentle** is the author of ten novels, including the science fiction **Orthe** duology, *Golden Witchbreed* (1984) and *Ancient Light* (1987), the genre-bending **White Crow** sequence, parodic fantasy *Grunts!* (1992), and the immense *Ash: A Secret History* (2000). The latter won the BSFA Award and the Sidewise Award for Alternate History, and was shortlisted for the Arthur C Clarke Award and the James Tiptree Jr Award. Her most recent novel is *Ilario: The Lion's Eye* (2007), which was shortlisted for the *Locus* Award for Best Fantasy Novel. **(1989)**

**Gary Gibson** is a Scottish science fiction writer whose first novel, *Angel Stations*, was published in 2004. His most recent book is the second volume of his space-opera **Shoal** trilogy, *Nova War* (2009). **(2009)**

**Alasdair Gray** is best-known for his 1981 novel *Lanark*, which like several of his other books mixes realism with science fiction and fantasy tropes. Other notable novels include *Poor Things* (1992) and *A History Maker* (1994); his most recent book is *Old Men in Love* (2007). Gray is also known for his painting, which can be found in several public buildings in Glasgow, and for designing the covers of his novels. **(1989)**

**Colin Greenland**'s first published book, *The Entropy Exhibition* (1983), was a critical exploration of the British New Wave, based on his PhD thesis. A number of sf and fantasy novels have followed, beginning with *Daybreak on a Different Mountain* (1984), and including the **Plenty** series (1990–1998), the first volume of which, *Take Back Plenty*, won both the BSFA Award and the Arthur C Clarke Award in 1991. His most recent novel is *Finding Helen* (2002). **(1989)**

**Jon Courtenay Grimwood** is twice winner of the BSFA Award for Best Novel, for *Felaheen* (2003) and for his most recent novel, *End of the World Blues* (2006), which was also shortlisted for the Arthur C Clarke Award. His work is notable for its dialogue with alternate history and cyberpunk conventions. **(2009)**

**Frances Hardinge**'s first novel, *Fly by Night* (2005), won the Branford Boase Award for outstanding first YA novel, and was shortlisted for the William L Crawford Award for first fantasy book. She has published two further YA fantasy novels, *Verdigris Deep* (2007) and *Gullstruck Island* (2009), as well as a number of short stories. **(2009)**

**Nick Harkaway** is working on his second novel; his first, *The Gone-Away World* (2008), was shortlisted for the BSFA Award. **(2009)**

**M John Harrison** has been described as the guilty conscience of science fiction and fantasy. His novels have won the Arthur C Clarke Award (*Nova Swing*, 2006), the James Tiptree Jr Award (*Light*, 2002), and the Boardman Tasker Prize (*Climbers*, 1989); his short fiction is collected in *Things That Never Happen* (2002), and his criticism in *Parietal Games* (2005). **(2009)**

**Colin Harvey** is the author of the novels *Lightning Days* (2006), *Blind Faith* (2008), and *Winter Song* (2009); he has also edited anthologies including *Killers* (2008) and *Future Bristol* (2009). His short fiction has appeared in *Interzone* and elsewhere. **(2009)**

**Douglas Hill** was born in Canada, and moved to London in 1959, at the age of 24. Over four decades, he wrote over 70 young adult and children's science fiction books, primarily in an action-adventure mould, including the *Last Legionary* series (1979–1982), beginning with *Galactic Warlord*, the **Huntsmen** series (1982–1984), and the **Cade** trilogy (1996–1997). He briefly (1967–1968) served as an assistant editor on *New Worlds*; he also championed sf in his position as literary editor of *Tribune* between 1974 and 1981, and as an advisor on sf titles for several publishers between the 1960s and 1980s. He died in 2007. **(1989)**

**Mary Hoffman**'s first novel, *White Magic*, was published in 1975. Since then she has written over 90 books, primarily YA, junior fiction, and picture books (including the best-selling **Grace** series, beginning with *Amazing Grace* (1991), but including some works for adults (both fiction and non-fiction). Her most recent YA series are the **Stravaganza** novels beginning with *City of Masks* (2002), set between Islington and an alternate Renaissance Italy; the most recent book in the series, *City of Secrets* (2008), was nominated for the Carnegie Medal. **(2009)**

**Robert Irwin** is a historian and novelist; his best-known work of fiction is *The Arabian Nightmare* (1983), a combination of travelogue and fable focused on an English spy, hired by the French to travel to Cairo in 1486. Other novels include *The Limits of Vision* (1986), *Exquisite Corpse* (1995), and *Satan Wants Me* (1999). **(1989)**

**Ben Jeapes** is the author of four sf novels – *His Majesty's Starship* (1998), *Winged Chariot* (2000), *The Xenocide Mission* (2002), and English Civil War alternate history *The New World Order* (2004) – and three novels in the **Vampire Plague** series as by Sebastien Rook (2004–2005). He ran the small press Big Engine until 2003. **(2009)**

**Liz Jensen** is the author of seven novels, three of which have been longlisted for the Orange Prize: *Egg Dancing* (1995), *Ark Baby* (1998), in which all British women have become infertile, and Blitz novel *War Crimes for the Home* (2003). Her most recent book is the apocalyptic *The Rapture* (2009), which has been optioned by Warner Brothers. She has lived in France, the UK, and Denmark. **(2009)**

**Diana Wynne Jones** is one of the most celebrated British writers of fantasy. Among her many books, the best-known may include the **Dalemark** quartet (1975–1993), the **Chrestomanci** series (1977–2006), *Archer's Goon* (1984), and *Howl's Moving Castle* (1986). She is twice winner of the Mythopoeic Award for fantasy, and received a World Fantasy Lifetime Achievement Award in 2007. **(1989)**

**Gwyneth Jones**' novels have won the James Tiptree Jr Award (for *White Queen*, 1991), Arthur C Clarke Award (for *Bold as Love*, 2001), and Philip K Dick Award (for *Life*, 2004), while her short fiction has won the BSFA Award and two World Fantasy Awards. Her criticism is collected in *Deconstructing the Starships* (1999) and *Imagination/Space* (20009). She is also the author of a further nineteen YA and children's titles as Ann Halam, including the *Inland* trilogy (1987–1990), *Dr Franklin's Island* (2001), and *Siberia* (2005). **(1989)**

**Graham Joyce**'s most recent novel, *Memoirs of a Master Forger* (2008), earned him his fourth British Fantasy Award; he is also the winner of the World Fantasy Award for *The Facts of Life* (2002), and the O Henry Short Story Prize for "An Ordinary Soldier of the Queen" (2008). **(2009)**

**Leigh Kennedy** is the author of two novels, *The Journal of Nicholas the American* (1986) and *Saint Hiroshima* (1990), and a collection of stories, *Faces* (1987), which includes her Nebula-nominated story "Her Furry Face" (1983). She was born in Denver, Colorado, but has lived in the UK since 1985. **(1989)**

**Garry Kilworth** has written 70 novels and over 100 short stories. Early novels, including *The Night of Kadar* (1978), *Gemini God* (1981) and *A Theatre of Timesmiths* (1984), are mostly science fiction; more recent work, starting with *Hunter's Moon* (1989), and including the **Welkin Weasels** sequence (1997–2003) has been primarily fantasy or historical fiction. His most recent short fiction collection is *Moby Jack and Other Tall Tales* (2005). Novella "The Ragthorn" (1991), co-written with Robrt Holdstock, won the World Fantasy Award and the BSFA Award for Short Fiction. **(1989)**

**Christina Lake** is a librarian, sf fan and writer. She is the recipient of two FAAn awards for her fan writing. **(1989)**

**David Langford** is an author, editor and critic. He has won 28 Hugo Awards: for fan writing, for the fanzine *Ansible* and for Best Short Story ("Different Kinds of Darkness", 2000). His short fiction is collected in *He Do the Time Police in Different Voices* (2003) and *Different Kinds of Darkness* (2004); novels include *The Space Eater* (1982) and *The Leaky Establishment*

(1984). He has also written futurology (*War in 2080* [1979]), worked on *The Encyclopedia of Science Fiction* and *The Encyclopedia of Fantasy*, and reviewed for publications as varied as *White Dwarf* and *Foundation*. **(1989 and 2009)**

**Katherine Langrish** was born in the Yorkshire Dales, and has lived in France and America. Her novels include the Troll trilogy (2004–2008), and standalone novel *Dark Angels* (2009); forthcoming is *The Shadow Hunt*. **(2009)**

**Rhiannon Lassiter** is the author of eleven novels, all published as YA. These include the *Hex* trilogy (1998–2000), set in a totalitarian future Europe, and standalone fantasies *Waking Dream* (2002) and *Bad Blood* (2007). **(2009)**

**Tim Lebbon** is the author of two dozen books of dark fantasy and horror. First novel, *Mesmer* (1997), was nominated for the British Fantasy Society award for Best Novel; *Dusk* (2006) won in the same category, and he has been nominated numerous times for his short fiction. In addition, novella "Exorcising Angels" (2003, with Simon Clark) was shortlisted for a World Fantasy Award. Other books include *Dawn* (2007) and, most recently, *The Island* (2009). **(2009)**

**Samantha Lee** is the author of the **Lightbringer** trilogy (1979–1980), as well as a number of standalone fantasy novels including *Childe Rolande* (1989), *Amy* (2000) and *The Belltower* (2002). **(1989)**

**Tanith Lee** has twice won World Fantasy Awards for her short fiction, with "The Gorgon" (1982) and "Elle Est Trois (La Mort") (1983); her fiction has been nominated many times for World Fantasy, Locus, Mythopaeic, BSFA, and British Fantasy Society Awards. After several well-received YA novels, her first major work is considered to be *The Birthgrave* (1975), inaugurating a trilogy of the same name (1975–1978). Other notable novels include *Drinking Sapphire Wine* (1997), the **Tales From the Flat Earth** sequence beginning with *Night's Master* (1978), the **Books of Paradys** beginning with *The Book of the Damned* (1988), and **The Claidi Journals** (1998–2003). Her work spans many genres. **(2009)**

**Tim Lees**'s stories have appeared in *Interzone*, *The Third Alternative*, *Crimewave* and other magazines; his first collection, *The Life to Come*, was published in 2005. **(2009)**

**Roger Levy** is the author of three science fiction novels: *Reckless Sleep* (2001), *Dark Heavens* (2004), and *Icarus* (2006); the latter was shortlisted for the BSFA Award. **(2009)**

**Toby Litt** is the author of ten books, which range across many genres and are named in alphabetical order: *Adventures in Capitalism* (1996), *Beatniks* (1997), *Corpsing* (2000), and so on. Particularly of note here are visionary fantasy *Hospital* (2007), and generation starship tale *Journey into Space* (2009). **(2009)**

**Bob Lock**'s stories and poetry have appeared in *Cold Cuts* (1993), *Cold Cuts 2* (1998), in *Interzone* and in other magazines. **(2009)**

**James Lovegrove**'s first novel, *The Hope*, was published in 1990; his second, *Days* (1997), was shortlisted for the Arthur C Clarke Award. Other notable works include *Untied Kingdom* (2003), shortlisted for the John W Campbell Memorial Award, linguistically playful alternate history *Provender Gleed* (2005), double-novella *Gig* (2004), and the YA **Clouded World** series (2006–2008, writing as Jay Amory). His current project is a trio of military fantasy/alternate histories, beginning with *The Age of Ra* (2009). **(2009)**

**Ian R MacLeod**'s *The Great Wheel* (1997) won the Locus Award for Best First Novel; his most recent, *Song of Time* (2009), won the Arthur C Clarke Award and the John W Campbell Memorial Award (jointly with Cory Doctorow's *Little Brother*). His other novels includes the magical alternate history duology *The Light Ages* (2003) and *The House of Storms* (2005), the Sidewise Award-winning *The Summer Isles* (2005), in which a fascist government develops in post World War I Britain rather than Germany. His short fiction has been nominated for the Locus, World Fantasy, Sturgeon, Nebula, Hugo, and BSFA Awards, and is collected in *Voyages by Starlight* (1996), *Breathmoss and Other Exhalations* (2004), and *Past Magic* (2006). **(2009)**

**Ken MacLeod**'s politically-aware sf novels include the near-future **Fall Revolution Quartet** (1995–1999), the space opera **Engines of Light** trilogy (2000–2002), and a number of standalone novels including *Learning the World* (2005) and *The Execution Channel* (2007). His books have been shortlisted for the Arthur C Clarke, Hugo, Tiptree, John W Campbell and Locus awards; *The Sky Road* (1999) and *The Night Sessions* (2008) won the BSFA Award, and he is a three-time winner of the Prometheus Award for Libertarian sf. **(2009)**

**Graham Dunstan Martin** is a Scottish writer who has published fantasy for children, notably *Giftwish* (1978) and *Catchfire* (1981; both as Graham Martin), and sf for adults, including *The Soul Master* (1984), post-holocaust tale *Time-Slip* (1986), and *Half a Glass of Moonshine* (1988). **(1989)**

**Paul McAuley** has won the Philip K Dick Award (for first novel *Four Hundred Billion Stars*, 1988), the Sidewise Award (for *Pasquale's Angel*, 1994), the Arthur C Clarke Award and the John W Campbell Memorial Award (both for the dense near-future tale *Fairyland*, 1995). Novels such as *White Devils* (2004), *Mind's Eye* (2005) and, perhaps most successfully, *Cowboy Angels* (2007), married sf and thriller forms; recent space-opera *The Quiet War* (2008) was shortlisted for the Arthur C Clarke Award. **(1989 and 2009)**

**Ian McDonald** is perhaps best known for his sf novels and stories set in non-Western settings, especially the African-set **Chaga** books (*Chaga*, 1995; *Kirinya*, 1998; *Tendeleo's Story*, 2000), the India of *River of Gods* (2004) and the associated stories collected in *Cyberabad*

*Days* (2009), and *Brasyl* (2007). Both *River of Gods* and *Brasyl* won the BSFA Award, and were Hugo Award nominees. Other novels include the magical-realist Mars dulogy *Desolation Road* (1988) and *Ares Express* (2001), and the Philip K Dick Award-winning *King of Morning, Queen of Day* (1991). His short fiction is also collected in *Empire Dreams* (1988) and *Speaking in Tongues* (1992). **(1989)**

**Juliet E McKenna** is the author of three major, related medieval fantasy sequences: **The Tales of Einarinn** (five volumes, 1999–2002), **The Aldabreshin Compass** (2003–2006), and **The Chronicles of the Lescari Revolution** (ongoing). She is a founding member of The Write Fantastic, which aims to promote fantasy writers and the fantasy genre. **(2009)**

**Suzanne McLeod** is the author of the **Spellcrackers** urban fantasy series, with two volumes published so far: *The Sweet Scent of Blood* (2008) and *The Cold Kiss of Death* (2009). **(2009)**

**John Meaney** is a science fiction writer and black belt martial artist. His first novel, *To Hold Infinity* (1998), was shortlisted for the BSFA Award. Subsequent work includes the three-volume space opera **Nulapeiron** sequence (2000–2005), the gothic **Tristopolis** duology *Bone Song* (2007) and *Dark Blood* (2008), and many short stories. Forthcoming is *Absolution*, the first volume in a space opera series influenced by Norse mythology. **(2009)**

**Paul Meloy**'s short fiction has primarily appeared in *The Third Alternative* – "Black Static" (2004), which leant its name to the rebranded *Third Alternative*, won the British Fantasy Award – and *Interzone*. Collection *Islington Crocodiles* appeared in 2008. **(2009)**

**China Mieville** is one of the most lauded young British writers of sf and fantasy – or just "weird fiction" – and known for his interest in urban environments. First novel *King Rat* (1998) was shortlisted for the Stoker, Locus and Crawford Awards; second novel *Perdido Street Station* (2002) was shortlisted for the Hugo, Nebula and Tiptree Awards, won the Arthur C Clarke and British Fantasy Society Awards, and introduced Mieville's best-known setting, the world of Bas-Lag. Subsequent novels – *The Scar* (2002), *Iron Council* (2004), YA *Un Lun Dun* (2007), and *The City & The City* (2009), have been equally lauded. His short fiction is collected in *Looking for Jake and Other Stories* (2005). **(2009)**

**Deborah J Miller** is the author of four novels: the **Last Clansman** trilogy (2001–2004, as Miller Lau), which links our world and a fantasy Otherworld, and full secondary-world fantasy *Swarmthief's Dance* (2005). **(2009)**

**Lee Montgomerie** was a member of the early *Interzone* editorial board, in which capacity he edited several anthologies of stories from that magazine. He has also published a number of sf short stories. **(1989)**

**Michael Moorcock** has been influential as an editor – he edited *New Worlds*, the focus of the British New Wave, between 1964 and 1971, and again from 1976 to 1996 – and as a writer. He was the winner of the SFWA Grand Master Award in 2008, and his fiction (primarily science fiction and fantasy, but writing across many genres) has won the Nebula Award, the World Fantasy Award, the John W Campbell Memorial Award, five British Fantasy Society Awards, and been shortlisted for the Booker Prize. His most important works include the ongoing **Elric** sequence, beginning with *The Stealer of Souls* (1963) and *Stormbringer* (1965), the **Jerry Cornelius** quartet (1969–1977), *Behold the Man* (1966), *Gloriana* (1978), *Mother London* (1988), and the **Colonel Pyat** novels (1981–2006). **(2009)**

**Richard Morgan** is the author of six novels: the cyberpunkish **Takeshi Kovacs** trilogy beginning with the Philip K Dick Award-winning *Altered Carbon* (2002); standalone near-future satire *Market Forces* (2004), which won the John W Campbell Memorial Award; *Black Man* (2007), which won the Arthur C Clarke Award, and fantasy *The Steel Remains* (2008). All are notable for their serious engagement with masculinity, and with forms of oppression; also for being violent, action-driven thrillers. He has also written two volumes of *Black Widow* for Marvel Comics. **(2009)**

**Patrick Ness** is the author of the **Chaos Walking** trilogy of YA sf novels – *The Knife of Never Letting Go* (2008, winner of the James Tiptree Jr Award), *The Ask & The Answer* (2009), and the forthcoming *Monsters of Men* (2010). He has held dual American-British citizenship since 2005, and lives in London. **(2009)**

**Kim Newman** is a journalist, film critic, and fiction writer with a particular interest in horror fiction. His work is often highly referential. First novel *The Night Mayor* was published in 1989; notable books include *Back in the USSA* (1997, with Eugene Byrne), the **Anno Dracula** series (1992–1998), the first volume of which won the International Horror Guild Award for Best Novel, and *The Man from the Diogenes Club* (2007). He has also written notable works for Games Workshop, as Jack Yeovil, including *Drachenfels* and *Genevieve Undead* in the *Warhammer* setting, and several novels in the *Dark Future* setting. **(1989)**

**Mark Charan Newton** is the author of two novels: *The Reef* (2008), and Dying Earth fantasy *Nights of Villjamur* (2009), to which a sequel is forthcoming. He works in sf publishing. **(2009)**

**Stan Nicholls** has written thirty books, mostly fantasy and science fiction. His best known work is the **Orcs: First Blood** trilogy (1999–2000), which has garnered acclaim in many countries around the world; other recent work includes the **Quicksilver** trilogy (2003–2006). A sequel Orcs trilogy, **Bad Blood**, is in progress, with the concluding volume due in 2010. In 2007, Nicholls was awarded the Le'Fantastique Lifetime Achievement Award for

Contributions to Literature at the Trolls and Legendes Festival in Mons, Belgium. **(2009)**

**Peadar O'Guilin**'s first novel, YA sf *The Inferior*, was published in 2007. He is currently working on the sequel. **(2009)**

**Simon Ounsley** was a fouding member of the *Interzone* collective, and co-edited several anthologies of stories reprinted from the magazine. **(1989)**

**Jane Palmer** is a writer and illustrator. Her first foray into sf was the comedy *The Planet Dweller* (1985) (later sequelled by *Moving Moosevan*, 1990); also of note are *The Kybion* (original title *The Watcher*, 1986), which features an eclectic mix of tropes, and *Nightingale* (2008), whose heroine is "a six-foot, purple septuagenarian with a bad attitude". **(1989)**

**Ricardo Pinto** was born in Portugal, but moved to the UK when he was six years old. He is the author of a fantasy trilogy, **The Stone Dance of the Chamelion**, consisting of *The Chosen* (1999), *The Standing Dead* (2002), and *The Third God* (2009). **(2009)**

**Gareth L Powell**'s short fiction has appeared in *Interzone*, *Aphelion* and a number of anthologies, and is collected in *The Last Reef and Other Stories* (2008). His first novel, *Silversands*, is forthcoming in 2010. **(2009)**

**Christopher Priest** is one of the most significant British writers of the fantastic of the last forty years. His early novels, including *Fugue for a Darkening Island* (1972) and *The Inverted World* (1974), essayed relatively conventional sf conceits, the latter winning the BSFA Award. Subsequent work, particularly from *The Affirmation* (1981), was more ambitious. Priest was selected as one of the twenty Granta Best of Young British Novelists in 1983. *The Prestige* (1995) won the World Fantasy World, and in 2006 was filmed by Christopher Nolan; *The Separation* (2002) won the Arthur C Clarke Award. **(1989 and 2009)**

**David Redd** has been publishing science fiction short stories for over forty years; his fiction has appeared in *New Worlds*, *F&SF*, *Interzone*, and *Asimov's SF*, among others. **(1989)**

**Alastair Reynolds** is the author of nine novels, the most recent of which is *Terminal World* (2010), and two short story collections, *Zima Blue and Other Stories* (2006) and *Galactic North* (2006); his work tends to be expansive and broad-scale even when not outright space opera. Second novel *Chasm City* (2001) won the BSFA Award; he has also been shortlisted for the Arthur C Clarke Award three times, for *Revelation Space* (2000), *Pushing Ice* (2005), and *House of Suns* (2008). **(2009)**

**Adam Roberts** is a prolific academic, critic and sf novelist whose work is typically elegant and highly engaged with the history of the sf genre. Since 2000, he has published ten sf novels, seven sf parody/comedies (under various pseudonyms), a short story collection (*Swiftly*,

2004), several standalone novellas, a brief introductory work on science fiction (*Science Fiction: the New Critical Idiom*, second edition 2005), a serious history of the genre (*The Palgrave History of Science Fiction*, 2006), as well as regular essays and reviews. *Salt* (2000) and *Gradisil* (2006) were shortlisted for the Arthur C Clarke Award, the latter also being shortlisted for the Philip K Dick Award. The *Palgrave History* was shortlisted for the BSFA Non-Fiction Award; and his novel *Swiftly* (2008, not to be confused with the short story collection) was shortlisted for the Sidewise Award. His most recent novel, *Yellow Blue Tibia*, has been shortlisted for the 2009 BSFA Award **(2009)**

**Katherine Roberts** is best-known for YA fantasy trilogy **The Echorium Sequence** (1999–2003), the first volume of which (*Song Quest*) won the Branford Boase Award for children. Her subsequent work includes the **Seven Fabulous Wonders** fantasied history sequence (2001–2006), and standalone *I Am the Great Horse* (2006). **(2009)**

**Keith Roberts** was the author of twenty-one books, mostly sf, published between 1966 and 1997. His short stories "Kitemaster" (1982) and "Kaeti and the Hangman" (1986), and his novel *Grainne* (1987), won BSFA Awards; other work was nominated for Locus, Nebula, and Hugo Awards. His best-known book is probably the alternate history *Pavane* (1968), in which the Spanish Armada was victorious; almost all his work is notable among other things for its depiction of British (English) landscape. He died in 2000. **(1989)**

**Al Robertson** is a writer, poet and musician. His stories have appeared in *Interzone*, *Postscripts*, and *Black Static.* **(2009)**

**Justina Robson** is the author of eight novels; the first two, *Silver Screen* (1999) and *Mappa Mundi* (2001),were shortlisted for the Arthur C Clarke Award, while *Silver Screen*, *Natural History* (2003) and *Living Next-Door to the God of Love* (2005) were shortlisted for the Philip K Dick Award. Her work is typically concerned with consciousness and perception; possibly the most successful exploration of these themes so far is *Living Next-Door to the God of Love*, in which one of the characters is literally defined by the perceptions of others. Her ongoing **Quantum Gravity** series (starting in 2006, due to conclude in 2010) is a more playful approach to the same material that grows in complexity as it progresses. **(2009)**

**Josephine Saxton**'s playful sf novels include *The Hieros Gamos of Sam and An Smith* (1969), *Group Feast* (1971), *The Travails of Jane Saint* (1980), and *Queen of the States* (1986). The latter, concerning a woman who may either be mad or the subject of an alien interrogation, was shortlisted for both the BSFA Award and the Arthur C Clarke Award. **(1989)**

**Martin Sketchley** is the author of three sf novels: *The Affinity Trap* (2004), *The Destiny Mask* (2005), and *The Liberty Gun* (2007), which together comprise the **Structure** trilogy. His most recent published work is the story "Deciduous Trees", which appeared in the BSFA's 50th Anniversary anthology *Celebration* (2008). **(2009)**

**Elizabeth Sourbut** published numerous stories in the 1980s, in *Interzone* and other venues. She reviews for *New Scientist*. **(1989)**

**Kari Sperring** is a historian and fiction writer. Her first novel is the secondary-world urban fantasy *Living with Ghosts* (2009). which was shortlisted for the William L Crawford Award for First Fantasy Book; she has also published a number of short stories. From 2007–2009 she was the reviews editor of *Vector*, the BSFA's critical journal; her own reviews appear most often in *Vector* and in the online magazine *Strange Horizons*. **(2009)**

**Brian Stableford** is an sf critic and writer; he has published more than fifty novels, and been nominated for or won the Sturgeon, Nebula, BSFA, Locus, Arthur C Clarke, and Bram Stoker Awards. Notable works include the far-future **Hooded Swan** series (1972–1975), vampire novel *The Empire of Fear* (1988), the **Genesys** trilogy (1995–1997), and the six-volume **Emortality** sequence (1998–2002). Much of his recent work is biologically-based sf, including the Arthur C Clarke Award-shortlisted *Streaking* (2007), which posited a genetic basis for luck. He is the recipient of the Pioneer Award and the Pilgrim Award for his criticism, and has translated numerous works of French sf and fantasy into English. **(1989 and 2009)**

**Vaughan Stanger**'s sf and fantasy stories have appeared in *Interzone*, *Scheherazade*, *Postscripts*, *Nature*, and other magazines. **(2009)**

**Alex Stewart** is the author, as Sandy Mitchell, of numerous novels set in Games Workshop's *Warhammer* (fantasy) and *Warhammer 40,000* (sf) universes. Most recently he has written the Caiphas Cain series, currently six volumes long, which follows the exploits of a Commissar of the Imperial Guard. **(1989)**

**Charles Stross**'s energetic, idea-dense science fiction has seen him receive more Hugo nominations this decade than any other British sf writer, and one win (for the novella "The Concrete Jungle", 2004). The *Accelerando* series of stories (fixed-up 2005) brought him to widespread notice, although two significant series – the **Laundry** series of Lovecraftian spy adventures, beginning with Stross's first novel *The Atrocity Archives* (serialised in *Spectrum SF*, 2001-2002); and the worldwalking **Merchant Princes** series (2004–2010) – have also attracted acclaim. *Accelerando* is infamously informed by Stross's experiences of working for a web start-up company during the first dot-com bubble, but most of his fiction is geared towards readers of a technical, computer-literate sensibility. **(2009)**

**Tricia Sullivan** was born in New Jersey, and has lived in the UK since 1995. She is best known for her often surreal science fiction, including the Arthur C Clarke Award-winning planetary colonization tale *Dreaming in Smoke* (1999), immunological allegory *Maul* (2004), and the **Cookie Starfish** duology *Double Vision* (2006) and *Sound Mind* (2007). However, she has also written three fantasy novels as Valery Leith (*The Company of Glass*, 1999; *The*

*Riddled Night,* 2000; and *The Way of the Rose*, 2001). Forthcoming is a new sf novel, *Lightbringer*. **(2009)**

**Adrian Tchaikovsky** is the author of the **Shadows of the Apt** sequence, which describes an industrialising epic fantasy world. Three volumes have been published so far, the first being *Empire in Black and Gold* (2008), with at least two more projected. **(2009)**

**EC Tubb** has written over 140 novels in the science fiction, fantasy and western genres, many under pseudonyms. His epic sf saga, **Dumarest of Terra**, comprising over 20 volumes from *The Winds of Gath* (1967) to *Child of Earth* (2008) is probably is best known work; also of note are the **Cap Kennedy** space opera novels beginning with *Galaxy of the Lost* (1973), and standalone works including *The Space-Born* (1956), a generation starship tale. **(1989)**

**Lisa Tuttle** was born in Texas, and has lived in the UK since 1980. She is the author of twelve novels, five collections, and an *Encyclopedia of Feminism* (1986). Her short fiction garnered her the John W Campbell Award for Best New Writer in 1974; subsequently, "The Storms of Windhaven" (1975) and "Bug House" (1980, both written with George RR Martin) were nominated for Hugo Awards, while "Stone Circle" was nominated for a Nebula, and many of her stories have been shortlisted for Locus Awards. Notable novels include *Lost Futures* (1992), an alternate-realities tale that was shortlisted for the Arthur C Clarke, James Tiptree Jr, and BSFA Awards, horror novel *The Pillow Friend*, also shortlisted for the Tiptree Award, and fantasy *The Silver Bough* (2006). **(1989 and 2009)**

**Ian Watson**'s first novel, *The Embedding* (1973), won the Prix Apollo Award for the best sf novel published in France. Among the many novels and collections of idiosyncratic, imaginative sf that have followed, notable books include *The Jonah Kit* (1975), *The Very Slow Time Machine* (1979), *Under Heaven's Bridge* (1982, with Michael Bishop), the **Black Current** series (1984–5), and *The Butterflies of Memory* (2006). He is also the author of an series of novels set in Games Workshop's *Warhammer 40,000* universe, the **Inquisition War** trilogy; the novels are infamous for their challenging take on the source material, and have been out of print for some years, but are due to be reprinted in 2010. **(2009)**

**Elizabeth Wein** is an American author resident in Scotland. Her short fiction has been published in anthologies edited by Ellen Datlow and Terri Windling, and Sharyn November her novels include the Arthurian sequence comprising *The Winter Prince* (1993), *A Coalition of Lions* (2003) and *The Sunbird* (2004), and the **Mark of Solomon** duology (2007–2008), set in a version of historical Ethiopia. **(2009)**

**Ian Whates** is a fan and sf writer. He is currently president of the British Science Fiction Assocation, and runs Newcon Press and the Newcon series of conventions. His short story collection *The Gift of Joy*, including the BSFA Award-nominated title story, appeared in 2009, and two novels are forthcoming in 2010: fantasy *The City of Dreams and Nightmare*, and space opera *The Noise Within*. **(2009)**

**James White** was an Irish fan and author of many sf novels, most famously the twelve-book **Sector General** sequence (1962–1999), set in a multi-species space station hospital, and lauded for its inventive aliens. He produced many fanzines, and was awarded Retro Hugo awards for his fan writing for 1950 and 1953. He died in 1999; since 2000, the James White Award has been presented for the best short story by a non-professional author. **(1989)**

**Kit Whitfield** is the author of two novels, both published as mainstream fiction in the UK and as genre in the US: *Bareback* (2006), set in a world in which only a small percentage of people are *not* werewolves; and *In Great Waters* (2009), an unsentimental alternate history in which mermaids are instrumental to the balance of power in medieval Europe. **(2009)**

**Conrad Williams** is the author of 80 short stories and five novels, most recently post-apocalyptic horror *One* and dark fantasy *Decay Inevitable* (both 2009). His intense, literate work has received two British Fantasy Society Awards (Best Novel for *The Unblemished*, 2006; and Best Novella for *The Scalding Rooms*, 2007), and been shortlisted for the International Horror Guild and Shirley Jackson Awards. **(2009)**

**Neil Williamson** is a writer and musician based in Glasgow, Scotland. With Andrew J Wilson he edited the *Nova Scotia* anthology of new Scottish Speculative Fiction (2005). His own fiction has been published in *The Third Alternative*, *Lady Churchill's Rosebud Wristlet*, *Interzone*, and other magazines. **(2009)**

# About the Editors

**Paul Kincaid**'s criticism has appeared in the *Times Literary Supplement*, *Science Fiction Studies*, *Interzone*, *The New York Review of Science Fiction*, *Foundation*, *New Scientist* and other venues. He is a former editor of *Vector*, the BSFA's critical journal, and was for many years the Chairman of the Arthur C Clarke Award. In 2006, he was awarded the Clareson Award for outstanding service in the field of science fiction, and in 2009 his collection of reviews and essays, *What It Is We Do When We Read Science Fiction*, was nominated for a Hugo Award. He is also the co-editor, with Andrew M. Butler, of *The Arthur C Clarke Award: A Critical Anthology* (2006). **(1989)**

**Niall Harrison** is the current editor of *Vector*, and the reviews editor for *Strange Horizons*. His own reviews have appeared in *Foundation*, *The New York Review of Science Fiction*, and *Interzone*. He would like to thank Mark Plummer for the original push to update this survey, and members of the Third Row and the BSFA for reading and commenting on draft chapters. He would also like to dedicate this book to Nic Clarke, for her awesomnosity. **(2009)**